"This book was born of an expressed need of newer religious for more contemporary work on religious life and the vows. It led them to ask the questions: 'If not us, who? If not now, when?' The voices of its thirteen authors pulse with new energy that both inspires and challenges readers. In their sharing of personal stories and scholarly insights, they offer new interpretations to this constantly evolving lifeform in our Church and world today."

— Ellen Dauwer, SC
Executive Director of the Religious Formation Conference

"What has been timeless and essential to religious life, passed on for generations, finds both honor and new expression as these newer members of religious life articulate their experience. This is an important read for all who are interested in the evolution of religious life and its continuing vitality into the future."

— Nancy Schreck, OSF
Sisters of St. Francis
Dubuque, Iowa

In Our Own WORDS

Religious Life in a Changing World

Edited by
Juliet Mousseau, RSCJ,
and
Sarah Kohles, OSF

LITURGICAL PRESS
Collegeville, Minnesota
www.litpress.org

Cover design by Monica Bokinskie. Photo by Annmarie Sanders, IHM. From left to right, standing: Mary Teresa Perez, OP; Deborah Warner, CND; Christa Parra, IBVM; Susan Rose Francois, CSJP; Juliet Mousseau, RSCJ; Virginia Herbers, ASCJ; Thuy Tran, CSJ; and Madeleine Miller, OSB. Seated: Desiré Findlay, CSSF; Sarah Kohles, OSF; Tracy Kemme, SC; Amanda Carrier, RSM; and Teresa Maya, CCVI.

6 7 8 9

Library of Congress Cataloging-in-Publication Data

Names: Mousseau, Juliet, editor.
Title: In our own words : religious life in a changing world. / edited by Juliet Mousseau, RSCJ, and Sarah Kohles, OSF.
Description: Collegeville, Minnesota : Liturgical Press, 2018. | Includes bibliographical references.
Identifiers: LCCN 2017030088 (print) | LCCN 2017047803 (ebook) | ISBN 9780814645208 | ISBN 9780814645444 (ebook)
Subjects: LCSH: Monastic and religious life of women. | Nuns. | Catholic Church.
Classification: LCC BX4210 .I54 2018 (print) | LCC BX4210 (ebook) | DDC 206/.57—dc23
LC record available at https://lccn.loc.gov/2017030088

Contents

Acknowledgments

As is the case with any collaborative undertaking, there are many people who contributed to the success of this project for whom we are grateful. We are particularly thankful for Giving Voice and all its leaders who dreamt of, created, and maintained the space for younger women religious to experience peers and share their experiences of religious life with one another. This book grew out of connections and conversations that could only happen in a peer space of younger women religious.

Thank you to the Conrad N. Hilton Foundation, who gifted us with a grant that supported our collaborative process for writing this book. Because of the Hilton Foundation, we were able to meet in person for our writing retreat without worrying about how we would afford travel, housing, food, etc. This grant allowed us to be free to focus on the project itself rather than the incidental costs that might otherwise have been prohibitive to constructing such a collaborative effort.

Thank you also to the Sisters of St. Francis of Dubuque, who agreed to receive the grant money for this project on behalf of Juliet Mousseau, RSCJ, and Sarah Kohles, OSF.

Many thanks are also due to Annmarie Sanders, IHM, who joined us for the retreat week. Annmarie assisted us by framing the day with prayer and lending her writing expertise in one-on-one meetings with the writers. Thank you to the Leadership Conference of Women Religious for sharing Annmarie with us that week. It would not have been possible to find someone better suited for this task.

Thank you to Tracy Kemme, SC, and Tracey Horan, SP—affectionately called "Team Trac(e)y"—for their willingness to join Juliet and Sarah in person for a few intense editing days. Your assistance in polishing these chapters was tremendous, and we are truly grateful.

Finally, thank you to the many sisters who live religious life faithfully and serve as models to us and to the world. We hold you and your example in our hearts, and we know you hold us as well. Thank you to all those who have written about religious life up to this point. Your wisdom has shaped our thinking and touched us deeply. Thank you to all the sisters who have expressed delight and interest in our project and offered prayer and support. Every step of this book process was filled with grace and blessing—no doubt because of your care. Thank you to the many women who are continuing to say "yes" to religious life. We are grateful for your courage and your "yes," and we look forward to hearing your voices.

Introduction

This book is the fulfillment of a dream Juliet had three years ago. As she prepared for final profession, she was exploring her understanding of the vows even as she lived them. The books and articles she found available were usually published at least fifteen years before and were often written by women and men who had been in religious life for many years. Juliet gained a lot of wisdom from reading those works, but sometimes the realities they spoke of did not seem to fit the world she was entering so many years later. The demographics of the Church and of religious life changed rather dramatically between the 1990s and 2012.[1] Additionally, nearly all of those writings defined religious life by what it was not; those authors who lived through the changes of the Second Vatican Council invariably spoke of how religious life had changed. Juliet found herself longing to hear someone talk about religious life as it is lived today rather than in contrast to what it was over fifty years ago.

Sarah recalls a couple of conversations at the Giving Voice 20s and 30s retreat in which two women in formation asked

[1] Several sources speak to the shifting demographics of Catholic sisters today. The most comprehensive of these is Mary Johnson, Patricia Wittberg, and Mary L. Gautier, *New Generations of Catholic Sisters: The Challenge of Diversity* (New York: Oxford University Press, 2014). Another source for continuing research is the Center for Applied Research in the Apostolate (CARA), http://cara.georgetown.edu/.

the group what we were reading about the vows. They, like Juliet, were looking for something more current that would help them wrestle with how to live the vows they were preparing to profess in today's world. We went around the circle and discovered there actually was not much else to read besides what they had already discovered. After a similar conversation occurred again at the 20s and 30s retreat the following year, we realized that these materials did not exist yet because we have not written them. Juliet then called Sarah after Christmas in 2016 saying she was convinced now was the time to respond to the call we were hearing to write and to encourage others to join us.

When we first began planning this book, it was once again among a group of young religious who were under age forty. We were sitting around discussing the great scholars and writers who had shaped us or were shaping us in our formation. As we talked, we thought about how those greats were aging and that it seemed no one was taking their place. Sarah and Juliet remember realizing and looking at each other in that moment before saying aloud to the group that no one person could take their places, we need to hear all our voices, in their diversity, united around the topics that are most significant to us and central to our lives. And so our journey toward writing this book began.

From the beginning of Juliet's initiation of the project, our priorities were diversity and collaboration. These were our touchstones as we discerned who to invite to participate and how we would structure the process. We did not want a number of sisters to merely write and submit their chapters. We wanted to create a group that would engage in a collaborative process to shape this project. Therefore, participating sisters were asked to commit to monthly calls that helped us discern our chapters together and were followed by a weeklong writing retreat.

We discussed who should be invited to this project with a view not to who were the best writers, but to whose voices we wanted to put together. While the voices of male religious are important as well, we decided to limit our contributors to women. We wanted a cross section of the current Catholic Church and the women who are answering the call to religious life. That meant ethnic diversity, age diversity (though under 50), and diverse charisms and visions of religious life. We wanted to represent membership in LCWR as well as membership in CMSWR. We wanted sisters who considered themselves primarily apostolic, sisters who prefer to call themselves "evangelical," and missionary sisters. We deliberately limited our group to members of congregations that are not contemplative. We wanted members of communities who traditionally serve people who are poor, who are known for their hospitals, and who teach children and adults. We wanted orders who wore habits and those who did not. We wanted sisters who were in ministries of leadership, formation, and vocations, as well as sisters who had made temporary vows but were still in initial formation. While there are so many more who could have been included, we are happy with the variety of perspectives represented by the thirteen women featured in this book. However, we recognize that our voices are but a snapshot of religious life today in North America.

Just as our choice of participants was important, so also was our collaborative way of working together. We began by communicating over social media, using a private Facebook page. In August 2016 we started more intentional communications that led to four monthly video conferences. At each monthly conference, we checked in with one another and began formally discussing our desires for the project and what we thought it needed. In our first meeting, we asked ourselves, "What do you want to see included in this book, even if you are not the person to write it?" We then followed up with sharing what each one felt called to write. As we moved through the months and continued to pray together and individually, these topics shifted slightly, though they largely remained very similar to those initial inclinations.

For three of our video conferences, we read or watched talks given by significant figures in the study of religious life and used their words as a basis for in-depth conversation. For example, we read the talk by Márian Ambrosio, IDP, to the gathering of the International Union of Superiors General in Rome from May 2016 and found ourselves discussing the significance of who we are as women religious, articulated by how we do what we do, rather than the ministries in which we are involved.[2] We watched "Religious Life: Called to Undertake a Journey of Transformation," a talk given by Sr. Patricia Murray, IBVM, at an event sponsored by Catholic Theological Union's Center for the Study of Consecrated Life,[3] in which she challenged listeners to embrace a prophetic transformation in our lives that leads us into the unknown. Finally, we had a video conference call with Ted Dunn to discuss the results of his survey of younger women religious.

In all these conversations, we developed our friendship and trust among a group of women who did not all know one another. Even Juliet and Sarah did not personally know everyone who was invited to participate in the project. Prior to this project one sister was only known to the group via her participation in the closed Giving Voice Facebook group. When we met in person for a weeklong writing retreat in Houston in January 2017, we began a more intense time of work, prayer, play, and intimate conversations about what is most central to our lives. Because of the amount of work we had already done together through conference calls, sharing documents, and Facebook messages, we could begin from a place of familiarity, which allowed us to move more quickly into the deeper shar-

[2] Márian Ambrosio, "Weaving Solidarity for Life—Living and Witnessing as Women Religious of Apostolic Life," International Union of Superiors General Plenary 2016, May 2016, Rome, Italy, accessed May 8, 2017, http://www.internationalunionsuperiorsgeneral.org/wp-content/uploads/2016/04/Pl-2016_Marian-Ambrosio_ENG.pdf.

[3] Patricia Murray, "Religious Life: Called to Undertake a Journey of Transformation," Keynote address, Global Call of Religious Life Conference. Catholic Theological Union, Chicago, Illinois, November 3, 2015, accessed May 8, 2017, http://learn.ctu.edu/category/tags/patricia-murray.

ing that is characteristic of longer-established relationships. During the writing retreat, we formed a routine: morning check-in and prayer together, the bulk of the day for writing and quiet work by ourselves, followed by a return to small groups in order to spend time reading each other's writings and asking questions. In the evenings, we played cards, drank wine, colored, and laughed until our sides ached. The flexibility of the schedule allowed early mornings and late nights for those who needed other times to work.

One of the great delights of the week was to watch women who were anxious about putting their thoughts on paper courageously embrace the identity of fledgling writers. We witnessed the energy shift from initial anxiety to genuine enthusiasm to read and talk about what others were writing. Our afternoon critique sessions began with five minutes of silent prayer together and concluded with an opportunity to name insights or articulate what was emerging. We held each writer and her work gently. These were the most sacred of our times together. We found in one another's words our own voice spoken aloud across our differences. As one of us said on the closing day, "Your voice is my voice, is our voice." Our hearts are united with this precious common gift of religious life.

After our week together, most people had solid rough drafts of their chapters. Each sister continued to write and polish her chapter over the next couple of months, and the editing team of four sisters met for three days in Berkeley, California, for collaborative editing. This, too, was a sacred process, as we read and discussed each essay together.

In This Book—In Our Own Words

This book is made up of thirteen different voices of sisters spanning three decades from those in their late 20s to late 40s (at the time they were invited to write). Every sister in this book has at least professed her first vows, though approximately half of the group is still in initial formation. One sister has celebrated her 25th Jubilee. Six of the thirteen sisters (or 46 percent) are women of color. The writers represent thirteen communities and twelve charisms. While we made an effort to reach out to CMSWR communities, there are far more sisters from LCWR communities represented in this book. Three of the writers have served formally in congregational leadership, vocation, or formation ministries. Only about half of the sisters considered themselves writers, and a number of them needed encouragement to be persuaded into saying "yes" to this project. As a result of the diversity of writers, readers will find a wide range of writing styles in this book. Most of the writers engage theology, Scripture, spirituality, theory and/or current data on religious life as they relate their own insights in living religious life today.

The original impetus for this book was the lack of current materials on living religious life today in general, and the vows in particular. Therefore, the primary intended audience is those who are new to religious life and in formation. However, we believe that the wider audience of religious life will find much here to appreciate and discuss as well. Every chapter demonstrates the author's reflection on religious life "in (her) own words." This freed us up from the pressure of needing to say something brand new about religious life on every page. However, this book is valuable in providing examples of experiences of younger women religious today who are living in a world that is in constant flux. It also demonstrates how younger sisters understand and name their experiences through various theological frameworks. Even though living the vows was the original conceptual focus, this book covers a range of topics relevant to religious life today. The topics the writers explored cluster around three general areas: vows, identity, and leadership into the future.

The first four chapters of this volume focus on the biblical, theological, and experiential elements of living community and the evangelical counsels. Chapter 1 by Virginia Herbers, ASCJ, calls us to embrace community in the light of the communion to which Jesus invites us in the Eucharist. The second chapter, by Sarah Kohles, OSF, addresses what it means to take a vow from the perspective of the Old Testament story of Hannah. Third, Juliet Mousseau, RSCJ, explores the meaning of the vows of poverty, chastity, and obedience in the light of God's creation and vision of the human person. Fourth, Tracy Kemme, SC, claims the power of the vows as radical expressions of the love of Jesus in today's world.

The next chapters loosely encircle questions of identity as individuals and religious. Mary Perez, OP, articulates the relationship between the charisms of individual congregations and the global charism of religious life, opening the door for deep growth into identity. Desiré Findlay, CSSF, then speaks to her experience of growth in personal identity and sense of vocation through her congregation, using the images of the growth of a flower. Thuy Tran, CSJ, explores her identity as a Vietnamese-American woman, Catholic, and Sister of St. Joseph, through the lens of the paschal mystery.

Thuy's chapter segues into a third theme, that of interaction among diverse identities and groups of people. Madeleine Miller, OSB, speaks of the blessings, gifts, and challenges of living in communities that cross boundaries of ethnicity and age groups. Christa Parra, IBVM, uses her story as a Latina sister in a predominantly Irish community to illustrate her identity as a border crosser. Amanda Carrier, RSM, speaks to the unique ways women religious answer the world's need for compassion today.

A final area of interest among the authors is that of leadership that looks toward the future, beginning with suggestions for preparing younger members for leadership by Teresa Maya, CCVI. Next, Susan Francois, CSJP, speaks of her experience as a younger leader at a time when the direction religious life is taking is "foggy." The book concludes with Deborah Warner, CND, whose reflections echo many of the themes of previous essays, envisioning the future of religious life.

Though these four themes seemed to dominate the chapters, we also discovered a number of threads woven into multiple chapters. The world is constantly changing and so how we live as women religious is changing, too. These chapters reflect an honest struggle to name our experiences—the beautiful, the challenging, and the sometimes difficult aspects of religious life. Throughout these chapters, love for our sisters shines through consistently and strongly. An underlying hint of grief for frequent losses accompanies this love—sometimes it remains under the surface and sometimes it receives greater attention. The exploration of religious life as a countercultural experience shows up through a number of essays, though the concept of what is countercultural takes different forms in the hands of different writers. Finally, while certain chapters focus particularly on the vows and their theological and biblical underpinnings, numerous chapters explore the connection of the vows to other aspects of religious life.

Within the background of the larger conversation on religious life, it is meaningful to reflect on what is not contained in this book. As this book grew out of the questions of young women religious within the space created by Giving Voice, it was a natural choice to focus on the perspectives of women religious within this book. While the insights of our brothers in religious life are missing from these pages, we look forward to joining with them as conversation partners.

Our common discernment process allowed any significant area of conversation to emerge, and so no topics were deliberately avoided. It is interesting to note that none of the thirteen authors engage new cosmology. A few chapters lightly touch on environmental concerns, but they are not the primary focus of any of the chapters. Also, while a number of chapters acknowledge a relationship with the Catholic Church, none of the chapters explicitly explores the relationship between religious life and the Church or the hierarchy. Passing over these topics does not indicate that they are unimportant, unworthy of inclusion, or that younger sisters are not interested in them. However, we acknowledge that they were not the focus our sister-authors felt called to explore in this book.

This book is only the beginning of our larger project. Our collaboration together began with conversations: let us continue to talk about what it means to be religious women and how we must engage with our changing world. We need to embrace the diversity of religious life today, to hear the voices of all our sisters and brothers who seek to follow Jesus in this life. All along the path, our efforts have been validated by the simplicity with which the project moved forward. We trust that the Spirit of Wisdom has been guiding this work, and we eagerly place it into the hands of our readers in order to continue the sharing.

Juliet and Sarah

Communities in Communion: Shifting into New Life

Virginia Herbers, ASCJ

"It's not about winning." That's what winners usually say to losers to make them feel better, right? I sat around a table last night with a group of religious sisters playing Uno, and we all agreed that it wasn't about winning; but I venture to say that we likewise knew at the end of the night who walked away as winners and who didn't. So, if it's not about winning, what is it about? What happened around that Uno table was both personal and prophetic. It really wasn't about winning. We played five rounds, and each round held commentary, intrigue, meaningful interaction, distraction, occasional virtue, and plentiful laughter. That's what it was really all about, and that is what we call life in community.

I have been asked by students, family, even strangers, "What's the most rewarding part of religious life?" More often than not, as I ponder the question, the answer comes back swiftly, "community living." Being surrounded by women who have given their entire lives as a gift to the service of God's people, returning home each evening to a praying community, waking up each new day to launch into a mission founded on a common charism: these are all gifts beyond measure; and the accumulation of those gifts over the years is nothing short of true grace.

Then, the next question from those same students, family, and strangers usually follows in short order: "What's the hardest part?" With a wry smile, my answer is always the same: "community living." Put two or more women in the same house, and prepare yourself for the ramifications. How sheets are folded, when dinner is served, who holds the remote, where the car gets parked: these all become negotiations. Even in a religious house, it's not always pretty. Negotiations sometimes devolve into winning and losing.

Paradigm Shift

For quite a few years now, multiple authors have been writing about the sense that religious life is in the midst of a paradigm shift.[1] What does that mean exactly? "Paradigm shift" describes a general change in the consciousness, vision, or communal perception of reality in the current moment, and it can apply to any given social reality. These shifts occur when the prevailing worldview (the way things are and "have always been") no longer works well or fits the needs of the moment. Barbara Fiand writes, "Ours is a time when cultural paradigms are collapsing and the dualistic worldview which served so well for centuries in bringing us not only progress and prosperity, but also the spirituality to support them, has reached the limits of its own possibilities and is beckoning us from within its own demise to move beyond it and look for deeper, more authentic ways of seeing."[2] Does this apply to

[1] Sources in support of the "paradigm shift" in religious life include: Anneliese Sinnot, "Shifting Paradigms: A New Reality," in *Journey in Faith and Fidelity: Women Shaping Religious Life for a Renewed Church*, ed. Nadine Foley (New York: Continuum, 1999), 95–123; Sean D. Sammon, *Religious Life in America* (New York: Alba House, 2002); Diarmuid O'Murchu, *Consecrated Religious Life: The Changing Paradigms* (Maryknoll, NY: Orbis, 2005); and Amy Hereford, *Religious Life at the Crossroads* (Maryknoll, NY: Orbis, 2013).

[2] Barbara Fiand, *Refocusing the Vision: Religious Life into the Future* (New York: Crossroads, 2001), 12–13.

religious life today? A resounding "Yes!" is how most women religious would respond. Even so, I venture to say that there exists a substantial variety of contexts out of which the response so eagerly comes.

More than three decades ago, and consistently ever since, men and women religious have been charged with becoming "experts in communion."[3] This implies study, practice, and a commitment to the continual perfecting of the art that is communion. So what exactly does communion mean in this context? Communion has eucharistic, spiritual, communitarian, ministerial, and even social elements. If we in religious life are called to become experts in communion, then we would do well at least to consider how communion happens, because it emerges neither automatically nor naturally. I propose that communion is the result of our values, our choices in living, and our interactions in community. In religious life, I believe communion is expressed through our vowed commitment to God manifested in discipleship, community, and service.

Communion Paradigm

Our world and our society are divided in many ways today. Externally this is evidenced in politics, economics, and social inequalities, to name a few. Internally, the divisions are equally clear, as seen in the rise of depression and psychological distress. Division is the antithesis of communion. Such division, however, is often how we categorize reality, believing it to be both necessary for good order and generally harmless: Are you a morning or a night person? Do you exercise? Are you on Twitter? Aisle or window? Mountains or ocean? Windows or Mac? With each categorization, we have drawn separations, boundaries, and definitions of who you are and who I am, how

[3] The phrase was first used by the Sacred Congregation for Religious and Secular Institutes, *Religious and Human Promotion* (Boston: Daughters of St. Paul, 1980), 24.

those are not the same, and, if we're honest, usually which choice is considered better. This is not always bad, but it could be more insidious than we might expect. When you and I are different, there is usually a divide between us. You like chocolate, and I like vanilla; so, we cannot share ice cream. You are Republican, and I am Democrat; so, we cannot speak about politics in polite company. You are shy, and I am outgoing; so, we find each other intimidating. Difference implies division.

Yet that is not Gospel truth. Gospel truth promises that difference implies diversity, and diversity calls us to unity. Diversity and unity are thus mutually constitutive, not mutually exclusive. Diversity without unity is division, and unity without diversity is uniformity. In a Gospel perspective, what distinguishes or diversifies us enriches the whole, and what unites or unifies us is the variety of our giftedness.[4]

In her book *The Holy Thursday Revolution*, Beatrice Bruteau writes about the "communion paradigm." She describes it as "a symmetrical, reciprocal relation of enhancement of being: that beings may be, may become all that they can be, may act in maximum freedom and be valued for their incomparable preciousness. Here I am I by virtue of being in-you/with-you/for-you, not outside and not against—not even separate. Consequently, helping one another is always helping oneself, for the 'selfhood' itself has expanded in a complex, systemic way."[5] Since the first time I read this, I have been captivated by the possibility that there is another way of being, a fresh way of thinking, a new way to live in this world that is so characterized by division and separation. That way is *communion*. Bruteau's sense that the current paradigm shift can be characterized as a shift to a communion paradigm is a bold and beautiful call. But is it trustworthy? Is it possible? Is it even appropriate?

[4] Cf. 1 Cor 12:12-31.

[5] Beatrice Bruteau, *The Holy Thursday Revolution* (Maryknoll, NY: Orbis, 2005), 70.

Trinitarian Communion

As Christians, we profess a trinitarian God: one God, three Persons. "The doctrine of the Trinity affirms that the essence of God is relational, other-ward, that God exists as diverse Persons united in a communion of freedom, love, and knowledge."[6] This God is distinction without division, unity in diversity, diversity comprising perfect unity. Jesus Christ, the Second Person of that trinitarian union, is the very incarnation of our God. As a consecrated religious woman, I profess my vows to this God, and I commit to the vocation of *sequela Christi* (following the example of Jesus, the incarnate Word of God) in every facet of my living. Jesus is God-with-us in human flesh and bone. His very person is quite literally the embodiment of what communion in God looks like. Because our vocation is *sequela Christi*, we are committed in baptism, vowed in community, and consecrated in the Spirit to follow where Christ leads, live according to his example, and give public witness to all God's people. Beyond being appropriate, possible, and trustworthy, these combined elements of religious vows make the communion paradigm essential to the consecrated life.

Consider the sacramental reception of communion. We receive Christ's body in the Eucharist, allowing it to form us as a whole, with all our diversities, into the one Body of Christ, the People of God. We, in the physical consumption of the Eucharist, quite literally become what we receive[7] and are so transformed that, as Teresa of Ávila understood, we become the hands and feet, the body and blood of Christ himself. This is more than pious posturing—it speaks a vital truth to our world today. In a society trapped in the "obsession with

[6] Catherine Mowry LaCugna, *God for Us: The Trinity and Christian Life* (New York: HarperCollins, 1991), 273.

[7] Cf. Augustine of Hippo, Sermon 272, quoted in John E. Rotelle, ed., WSA, Sermons, Part 3, Vol. 7, trans. Edmund Hill (Hyde Park: New City, 1993), 300–1.

consumption,"[8] where advertising and media encourage an insatiable appetite to have more, to be more, to do more, we recognize the inexhaustible appetite we have for God. This craving for more, both in the hunger for the daily bread (Matt 6:11) that sustains us, and also in the hunger and thirst for righteousness (Matt 5:6), finds its satisfaction only in the commitment to make God's kingdom come, here and now. Inscribed on the altar in the provincialate chapel of my community is the Latin saying attributed to St. Bernard, "Jesu, qui te gustant esuriunt." (Jesus, whoever tastes of you hungers all the more.) This reminds us, over and against our culture of conspicuous consumption, that the more we come to know and receive Christ—in Eucharist and in encountering him in the members of his Body that we meet each day—the more we recognize that God is the source and object of our inexhaustible hunger. Rather than leading us into greater selfishness and greed, this hunger thrusts us outward on mission as a community of believers. We profess this in our beliefs, but in living it, we incarnate those beliefs, true to the vocation of *sequela Christi*, shifting gently but wholly into a new way of living and being: the communion paradigm.

Why Communion?

Of all the various paradigms that religious life could be shifting into at this moment in history, why the insistence that it must be to the communion paradigm? Because the alternative to communion is division, and what the future of women's religious life can absolutely not afford any longer is division: division of the old sisters from the young sisters, the conservative orders from the liberal orders, the new cosmology from

[8] Francis, *Laudato Sí* (Encyclical On Care for Our Common Home), Vatican Website, May 24, 2015, sec. 222, accessed February 16, 2017, http://w2.vatican.va/content/francesco/en/encyclicals/documents/papa-francesco_20150524_enciclica-laudato-si.html.

eucharistic adoration, LCWR from CMSWR, the faithful from the unfaithful, the relevant from the out-of-touch, the vibrant from the dying. Enough already—*enough*. If we in religious life are not one, then you are you and I am I, and "ne'er the 'twain shall meet." Do not misunderstand: I am not naïvely envisioning one single reality where all differences are subsumed into perfect unanimity. This is not about gathering around a campfire, holding hands, and singing "kumbaya" as we rejoice that our differences are irrelevant. Differences matter. Differences matter a lot, but they do not need to be divisive. They need to be recognized, acknowledged, wrestled with, validated, and integrated into the whole. And ideally, they need to be celebrated. Diversity yes, division no.

The communion paradigm does not have homogeneity as its goal; the hope of the communion paradigm is unity with vibrant, stunning diversity. It is about living together in harmony, knowing that some are singing alto and some are playing trombone, but we're all about the same song. It is about living in intercultural, intergenerational, and intercongregational communities, maintaining the integrity of our own identity while simultaneously needing others to maintain the integrity of theirs. It is about eliminating "us versus them" language—in our communities, in our conferences, and in our own belief systems. It is about moving away from comments like, "When we were your age, we used to . . ." "They can't understand our generation," "We support ecclesial authority," "They aren't serving the poor," "Why don't they let us lead?" and "We suffered so much to finally get rid of what they are now asking for!" The dichotomies of duality and division created by such language, and the belief system out of which that language comes, are in complete contradiction to the communion Jesus came to establish among his followers as an example of how to be fully human, how to live our lives as incarnations of the very love of God. The communion paradigm utterly obliterates such false dichotomies. It is not "us" and "them"—it never has been. Jesus did not establish his identity and values over and against anyone else—Father, Spirit, disciple, or sinner. The identity and values of God were literally embodied in his person, in his living and interacting, and he freely, indiscriminately, gave of himself to every single "other" he encountered. Moreover, he didn't just give; he entered into mutual relationship. He desired to receive the "other" as well. When the Pharisees labeled a sinner, Jesus invited himself to that sinner's house for supper (Luke 7:36). When the apostles called out "traitor!" Jesus bent to wash the feet of the one he called "friend" (John 13:5). When propriety and religious protocol stood in the way of relationship, Jesus unhesitatingly blurred the boundary and asked for a drink of water (John 4:7). Lines of distinction did not become lines of division.

Until they did. "When the Son of Man will come in his glory . . . all the nations will be assembled before him. And he will separate them one from another, as a shepherd separates the sheep from goats" (Matt 25:32).[9] So, what happens here and in a variety of other places in the gospels? Why does Jesus support separation of the nations? Why is Jesus not only encouraging but exercising division? I am not a biblical theologian, so this is not a challenge to the greater scholarship that more deeply probes this particular passage and its theological meaning. But looking at Jesus' selective separation in this case, how might we understand it from the context of the communion paradigm? What actually created this division, this lack of communion? Was it Jesus himself or was it something else? Ironically, it seems that what created the division between the sheep and the goats was their choice to treat "the other" as Christ, or not. Those who could not see Christ in the hungry, the thirsty, the naked, the stranger, the ill, or the imprisoned, those who could only see "the other": they are the goats who

[9] *The New American Bible Revised Edition (NABRE)* (Oxford: Oxford University Press, 2010). Quotations from the Bible will be from the *NABRE* unless otherwise noted.

are separate and separated. Those who saw no distinction between Christ and "the other" were brought into perfect unity with each other and with Jesus. How ironic. Perhaps the separation of sheep and goats is not an external punitive decision of the divine judge; maybe it is the natural consequence of a chosen worldview.

Diversity is a given; unity is a choice. What Jesus began, we are called to continue. As difficult a mission as it might be, nothing is more vital to—and, arguably, nothing more absent from—our world today. From the first decades of the missionary church, this truth has been heralded: we are no longer Jews or Greeks, slaves or free persons, male or female, but we are one. *We are one.* Did St. Paul eliminate religious, social, and economic distinctions? It doesn't seem so. Jews remained Jews, slaves remained slaves, and males remained males. The distinctions were not eradicated; they were identified as essential parts to a greater whole. "For in one Spirit we were all baptized into one body" (1 Cor 12:13). Without the uniqueness of each of the individual parts, the beauty and completeness of the whole is compromised. Likewise, without the cohesiveness of the whole, the individual parts lose vitality and become isolated.

The Communion Paradigm and Religious Life

So what might a commitment to the communion paradigm look like in women's religious life right now? We can only provide a sketch here. As noted above, the communion paradigm has its foundation in the reality of the Trinity, but its praxis is best apprehended through the lens of the Holy Thursday event, as suggested by Bruteau. In the Upper Room, Jesus gathered his closest friends together as a community, taught them that the true exercise of their authority was service, and affirmed their relationship to him and to each other as that of brothers and sisters. The sharing of communion was not only in the giving and receiving of his body and blood. Communion around the table was also expressed through discipleship, through community, and through service.

Discipleship

The vocation to the religious life begins with the sense of being called by Jesus to follow in a unique, personal, and entire way. No two vocation stories are identical because no two relationships with Christ are identical. Each of us has her own invitation story and her own story of response. Being a disciple of Jesus is personal, and thus the relationship of love between Christ and the beloved is always unique. Jesus values my giftedness, and he also values my limitations. He values my strengths as well as my weaknesses, recognizing that both are gifts from God and both have the potential to lead me either closer to God or further away. When beautification products encourage me to hide my blemishes (from myself and from others), and diet and self-help programs remind me that I am not quite who I should be, the Christ of the Upper Room says, "Come as you are. You have been chosen. You belong here—there is a place for you." The first step of discipleship in the communion paradigm is saying "yes" to Christ's invitation to come to the table. As if that weren't difficult enough, however, the second step is accepting the brothers and sisters sitting next to us. As I turn to my left and to my right, I see an unlikely set of characters that I am asked to call community. I notice one who stinks of fish, one who is so young he has to claim his stake at the head of the table, one who has a sordid history of being a liar and a cheat that really can't be forgotten, one who insists on holding the strings to the purse and dictating how its contents are spent, one whose mother is always kind of hanging around asking for special privileges for her children, one who fades into the background so easily I can't even remember his name, one whose temper flares often enough to gain herself a not-so-flattering nickname. This is a merry band of followers, to be sure. Accepting the invitation to discipleship is about more than just me. It's also about accepting everyone else's rightful place at the table. Thus insists the communion paradigm.

From a stance of communion, I claim that you are inherently valuable and lovable, regardless of your history, your attitude, or your sin. You are my brother; you are my sister. As family, we are one. The paradigm of division would have us be ranked: the good kid, the misfit, the rebel, the pride of the family. The paradigm of division has a value scale upon which our place is determined by external codes and norms. In the communion paradigm, I am called to the table by Jesus who values me simply because he does, simply because I am. Looking to my left and to my right, I see that he values you simply because you are. The true call of communion is to be able to say to you with my own voice, "I love you; sit next to me," "I am trying to love you; sit next to me," or "You don't seem to love me; sit next to me." Can we be one big, happy family? Maybe we cannot, but what we can do is strive to be. The communion paradigm is not about perfection, remember; it's about unity. Even if unity is not attainable this side of eternity (not even Jesus could accomplish it), it is not thereby rendered worthless. We must never let the perfect be the enemy of the good.[10]

How does this apply specifically to religious life? The vow of chastity expresses our belief in our inherent value: that we are the beloved of God, and we claim God as our one, true love. We also insist that the same is true for you . . . and you . . . and you. The vow of chastity is first and foremost about love, but it is also about an expanded view of what it means to be lovable. In my profession of exclusive, complete love of God, I find that I am committed to loving God in and through each "you" I meet. You are the beloved as well. You and I are one in Christ. We are different, and we are one. Together, we

[10] English variant of an aphorism attributed to Voltaire.

form a community of disciples—unlikely characters all, possibly, but a community nonetheless.

Community

Jesus gathered the disciples in the Upper Room around one table, and Paul tells us that the community of believers who formed the early church shared all things in common. Privilege and prestige had no place in the coming kingdom of God. The one community was made up of various individuals, various traditions, and various stations in life. In giving of Christ's body and blood, no one received more and no one received the "better part" (Luke 10:42). All received of the same bread, the same cup (1 Cor 11:25). The elders didn't get first pick; the youngest didn't get the scraps. The religious elite didn't get to choose at which end of the table to recline, and the lower class didn't have to wait to be served. In communion, Jesus gave all of himself to each person—without distinction, without comparison, and without evaluation. Our society parses out who gets what, when, and why. The global refugee crisis, the growing discrepancy between rich and poor in our own nation, inadequate access to health care, food or shelter: these all demonstrate lines of privilege drawn between one group and another and drawn by one group for another.

We in religious life are not immune from drawing these lines. How many of our own religious congregations know about separate dining rooms for the professed and those in formation, accountability structures that differ depending on your level of authority, or submission in letting the loudest voices prevail over and over again? These are lines of division, not of communion. If we think, choose, speak, and act out of a communion paradigm, we will resemble the community gathered at Christ's table more closely than we will resemble the help-yourself, youngest-last buffet line that so often characterizes our convents and monasteries. At Christ's table, each received the same bread and cup passed on from Christ through their brothers and sisters. The table is not the point, however. What is truly at issue here is how we receive one another and how we give to one another. What we have to offer has been given from Christ, and what we have to receive from each other is the very person of Christ. Can I turn to each person gathered at the table and share with you, as my brother or my sister, everything that has been given to me, the entirety of my treasure, that it might become for you life and hope and joy and peace? Can I expect the same from you? This is communion. This is true wealth: the giving and the receiving of all that is you, of all that is me, and of all we are together in Christ.

Our true wealth, our true treasure, is in and for Jesus Christ. When we profess a vow of poverty, this is our claim: that God is enough. There is no more need for hoarding or protection of comfort zones, no more need to focus on scarcity or lack. God-with-us is enough. So if I am missing something of necessity, I can turn to you, my sister, with my need, believing that you can and will provide what I am lacking. If we are both lacking, we will turn outward even further to discover where we might be filled. This turn outward is the quest for God, and as we orient ourselves together in this search, we expect that God will be found. God exists in our encounter with every "other," and so we go forth to meet God, to encounter Jesus, in the wider community. This is the stuff of mission, of our call to serve.

Service

The paradigm of communion is in essence a contemporary commitment to live according to the Holy Thursday events, where Jesus gave clear instructions for his followers to do two things: to do for one another what he did for us when he washed our feet, and to break the bread in remembrance of him. We have been speaking thus far of the latter commandment in reference to the communion paradigm. Now we turn to Jesus' question to the Twelve in the Gospel of John after he finished washing their feet: "Do you realize what I have done for you? You call me 'teacher' and 'master,' and rightly so, for indeed I am. If I, therefore, the master and teacher, have washed your feet, you ought to wash one another's feet. I have given you a model to follow, so that as I have done for you, you should also do" (John 13:12b-15). With perfect clarity, Jesus told his disciples—and through them, tells us now—that there is a new way of being when it comes to authority and leadership: the way of servanthood. Not in Jesus' kingdom nor in communion living will a title or a position define your importance. Never again will your academic degrees or your family name provide you with greater influence. No more will your past experience or lack thereof be of any consequence. "Do you want to know how to follow me more faithfully?" Jesus asks. "Watch and learn, friend; watch and learn. I remove the outer garment, revealing that I am just like you—we are no different. No clothing, no title, no accretion or external trappings distinguish us; we are one. I take up the basin of water and a simple towel, normal stuff really, but with incredible power to cleanse and heal and soothe. I sense what you feel; I see what you need. And so I stoop to wash your feet—your dirty, swollen, blistered feet. I don't ask how you got so dirty; it is irrelevant to me. I know only that it is time for communion, and I am here to serve you, that we might come to the table together" (cf. John 13).

Pope Francis, in his apostolic visit to the United States in 2015, visited the Curran-Fromhold Correctional Facility in Philadelphia, the city's largest prison. He used the story of Jesus' washing of the apostles' feet to frame his remarks to the prisoners, most of whom were serving life sentences:

> That is why we see Jesus washing feet, our feet, the feet of his disciples, then and now. We all know that life is a journey, along different roads, different paths, which leave their mark on us. We also know in faith that Jesus seeks us out. He wants to heal our wounds, to soothe our feet which hurt from travelling alone, to wash each of us clean of the dust from

> our journey. He doesn't ask us where we have been, he doesn't question us about what we have done. Rather, he tells us: "Unless I wash your feet, you have no share with me" (John 13:8). Unless I wash your feet, I will not be able to give you the life which the Father always dreamed of, the life for which he created you. . . .
>
> The Lord tells us this clearly with a sign: he washes our feet so we can come back to the table. The table from which he wishes no one to be excluded. The table which is spread for all and to which all of us are invited.[11]

The vehicle for communion is service to one another, and this is the only justifiable use of power in the communion paradigm. Authority based on any other principle may be expedient, it may even be effective, but it is not Gospel.

So, we in religious life profess a vow of obedience. This obedience claims authority resides in servant leadership, and power must be used for the common good in order to bring about ever more authentic communion among the people of God. Does that mean no one is in charge, that everyone is equal? Jesus was neither an authoritarian nor an anarchist. The communion paradigm does not render the vow of obedience impotent with a generalized sense of authority equally distributed among members; in fact, it is just the opposite. The communion paradigm insists that true authority must be exercised by the one to whom it has been entrusted, and it must be exercised in the same fashion Jesus exercised it in the Upper Room through the washing of the feet. First, remove the separations between you and me—the outer garments. Then, find the means through which all parties can come to the table readied. Most likely this will have something to do with genuine dialogue, honesty, reconciliation, and humility from

[11] Francis, "Address of the Holy Father," Vatican Website, September 27, 2015, accessed February 16, 2017, http://w2.vatican.va/content/francesco/en/speeches/2015/september/documents/papa-francesco_20150927_usa-detenuti.html.

all parties. Finally, understand that the role of servant to the common good is shared among us, and just as the "master and teacher" has done for us, so I must be willing to do for each person in the community. Obedience, from the perspective of the communion paradigm, allows for each vowed religious to recognize that she is a single and necessary part of a much greater whole. The uniqueness of her singularity demands full, generous, and mature investment in the larger community just as surely as the common good, the common "project" of the community, requires authentic attention to the needs and particularities of each individual. There it is again: diversity forming unity, unity comprised of diversity.

We're Getting There

This may all seem relatively "pie in the sky." After all, it's virtually impossible to reconcile the diversity within myself ("I really want to eat healthier, but there's cheesecake tonight"), much less broaden it out to my religious community ("I'm pretty good at tolerating quirkiness—well, everyone's except *hers*"); and the thought of universalizing this for humanity is a nice thought, but . . . come on. So, is it even worth the attempt? The short answer is "Yes." The longer answer acknowledges that if we abandoned all things unattainable simply because of that characteristic, there would be no reason to be Christian at all, much less a consecrated religious. The practice of virtue, the practice of vow, the practice of religion itself: these are all practices. It is not about attaining perfection; it is about perfecting the practice in ways that lead us and anyone who crosses our path closer to God. It is about becoming one in Christ Jesus.

Religious life is in the midst of a paradigm shift. We in religious life must choose the direction of that shift, and communion is the most compelling, necessary, and authentic choice. Just as the Uno game last night wasn't about winning, neither is the human endeavor. Weirdly, I think that card game had something to say about the truth of this moment, namely: It said, "Show up as yourself, engage fully with everything you've got, expect conflict, intrigue, occasional virtue, and plentiful laughter, and know that in the end we will walk away—winners and losers both—as sisters in Christ."

Something Old, Something New: Hannah's Vow (1 Sam 1–2) Touches the Lives of Women Religious Today

Sarah Kohles, OSF

The words we say matter. The words we say can build up or destroy. My extroverted self has choked on my own foot too many times to count. The words that define our lives deserve attention. In the months leading up to my final vows in 2011, I recited the vows I would profess to myself every night as part of my evening prayer and throughout the day as I pondered the gravity of these words for my life: "I, Sister Sarah Kohles, in the presence of Sister Nancy Schreck, this Franciscan congregation, and the Christian community, vow to God forever to live poverty, chastity, and obedience according to the Rule and Constitutions of the Sisters of St. Francis of the Holy Family." My journal entries from that time lead me to recall the significance of proclaiming these vows *forever*. I felt all the squirminess that comes with declaring these words would guide my life always. Vows fascinate me because they bind me together with my own sisters, as well as women religious everywhere, though the precise words we say might differ. Vows connect us and create a common story between us, an underlying relationship across communities that is deeper than our separate community charisms. Vows are also not new, but stretch back into the Scriptures—both Old and New Testaments. The sacred words of Scripture bind us together with biblical figures through a common story. Reading both the vows in the Scriptures and the lived experiences of the vows of younger women religious side by side is an act of pulling both something old and something new from the treasures of the storeroom, to borrow an image from the Gospel of Matthew (13:52). The newness is a claiming of the vows for younger women religious, even as I recognize that the vows are a part of an ancient tradition with a meaning that will likely evolve throughout my life. The story of Hannah's vows offers one such example of an ancient vow that provides insight for women religious today.[1]

Hannah's Vow

Vows in the Old Testament were made in times of turmoil or distress[2] in order to beg God for success in battle, as was the case for Jephthah (Judg 11:30), or to negotiate pleadingly with God for a child, as was the case with Hannah (1 Sam 1:11), or to ask for safety in returning home before heading out on a long journey, as was the case with Jacob (Gen 28:20-22). Old Testament vows were conditional promises made by people in distress and were a kind of bartering with God.[3] The vow of the individual was only upheld if God followed through

[1] It is, of course, completely anachronistic to look at the vows of women religious in light of vows in the Old Testament, as there were no women religious in the Old Testament. However, Scriptures are always a source of possible reflection and insight, so we will rely on insight as an opportunity for reflection here even though no perfect correlation between the experiences is reasonably possible.

[2] Ronald T. Hyman, "Four Acts of Vowing in the Bible," *Jewish Bible Quarterly* 37, no. 4 (October 2009): 231-38, accessed March 20, 2016, http://0-search.ebscohost.com.grace.gtu.edu/login.aspx?direct=true&db=rfh&AN=ATLA0001743204&site=ehost-live.

[3] Tony W. Cartledge, *Vows in the Hebrew Bible and the Ancient Near East* (Sheffield, England: Sheffield Academic, 1992), 2.

and granted the petitioner's request.[4] It would be quite a stretch to claim that there is a direct correlation between the vows of biblical figures asking for success in battle or pleading for a child and the vows as lived by women religious today. Women religious do not make vows to plan for war or have a child! In spite of obvious differences, biblical vows still can offer points of insight or reflection into the way women religious live their vows.

A closer look at Hannah's vow demonstrates she is truly in distress. Although her husband loves her, she is taunted and abused by her husband's other wife because she is childless (1 Sam 1:5-10). Hannah pleads fervently at the shrine of Yahweh at Shiloh for a child (1 Sam 1:11):

> Hannah vowed a vow to Yahweh of hosts,
> "If you look upon the affliction of your servant
> and remember me,
> and do not forget your servant,
> and give your servant offspring,
> then I will give him to Yahweh all the days of his life
> and a razor will not be brought upon his head."[5]

Both Old Testament vows and the vows of women religious rely on a vow formula and are made within the context of prayer. Old Testament vows follow a typical formula:

Individual's name +	"vows a vow" to God/Yahweh +	a conditional statement
Hannah +	vows a vow to Yahweh +	If you look upon your servant . . . then I will give him to Yahweh

[4] Yael Ziegler, *Promises to Keep: The Oath in the Biblical Narrative* (Boston: Brill, 2008), 4. Vows are distinctive from oaths, which are promises that have a curse imbedded in them. For example, I will do this, and if I do not, let this curse happen to me.

[5] All translations are by the author from the Hebrew text. *Westminster Leningrad Codex (WTT)* (Philadelphia: Westminster Theological Seminary), BibleWorks, v.9.

The vow formula signals the solemn nature of an event, highlighting that this not an everyday occurrence. In common parlance the word "vow" is reserved for serious, life-changing circumstances that affect a person's identity. Marriage is the most familiar example of people's understanding of vows. In this case, Hannah vows a vow to God,[6] then she makes a conditional statement detailing what she will do if God acts on her behalf. If God gives Hannah a child, she will dedicate her child to God. Hannah names her identity here as "your servant" three times. She repeatedly claims a relationship with Yahweh in a manner that demonstrates her dependence on God.

Hannah addresses her vow to "Yahweh of hosts," where "hosts" is another word for "armies." Hannah uses a military metaphor in her naming of God because she is vulnerable. As a woman, she will be unprotected by society should she outlive her husband without having children. She is also publicly shamed by the other wife.[7] Hannah is calling on the God of armies to defend her and fight on her behalf. This is uncomfortable imagery—and it would be inappropriate if Hannah were in a position of power. However, because she is in a vulnerable position, it is understandable and appropriate that she would call on God in this manner.

It is worth noting that all biblical vows are made to God.[8] Vows are not made to human beings because it is only God who can change the desperate circumstances of the person making the vow. Only a relationship with God can lead to the total transformation of circumstances Hannah seeks. Hannah is calling on a God whom she hopes will reply to her. She further emphasizes her position as she asks that God remember her and not forget her. This repetition demonstrates that

[6] I am using "Yahweh" and "God" interchangeably in this chapter.

[7] Philip F. Esler, *Sex, Wives, and Warriors: Reading Biblical Narrative with Its Ancient Audience* (Eugene, Oregon: Cascade, 2011), 127.

[8] Cartledge, *Vows in the Hebrew Bible*, 17.

Hannah has a relationship with God. It does not make sense for Hannah to plead that Yahweh remember if there is no prior relationship. Therefore, she is calling on God to remember the history of their relationship.

Religious women also have vow formulas when they make their professions that might go something like: "I, (name), in the presence of (congregational leader and community) vow to God forever to live poverty, chastity, and obedience according to the Rule and Constitutions of (the community's canonical name)."[9] As with Hannah, our vows are addressed to God, rather than human beings.[10] Religious communities' vows also include the individual's name, the content of the vow, and are addressed to God. This indicates a relationship with both God and the community. Choosing a life that means living with strangers, with whom we might not have much in common besides our commitment to living the vows, is definitely an example of vulnerability. When we are in formation, we experience an abundance of the gift of transition and live with people of all different ages (though rarely our own age) and different cultures. This plentitude of differences means we are blessed with endless opportunities to annoy, frustrate, and baffle one another. The commitment, honesty, and vulnerability this requires breaks us down and builds us back up if we stay. Arriving firmly grounded in our relationship with God allows us to call on God to remember us.

[9] This example follows the vow formula of the Sisters of St. Francis of Dubuque, Iowa. Poverty, chastity, and obedience are the three most common vows among women religious.

[10] At one time the earliest members of my community did vow to individuals in addition to God, Mary, Francis, and the saints. The gradual move over time to vowing to God and *not* individuals within our vow formula likely reflects a shifting relationship with authority and the growing understanding of the concept of power as being with people rather than power over others. I have not done a thorough survey of vow formulae across congregations, but I imagine other communities have undergone similar changes.

A Faithful Woman

Hannah prays silently to herself (1 Sam 1:10-13) when her husband does his yearly duties (1 Sam 1:3) at the shrine at Shiloh, though her prayer is witnessed by Eli the priest (1 Sam 1:13). She weeps profusely as part of her prayer (1 Sam 1:10). Eli first misunderstands her and accuses her of drunkenness (1 Sam 1:14) but then adds his wishes that her prayer might be fulfilled (1 Sam 1:17). This is an affirmation of her character and faithfulness even before God responds to her request. While Hannah's vow is private and directed only to God, her prayer and its intensity are witnessed by someone else.

God's fulfillment of Hannah's request is a sign that God chooses to be in relationship with Hannah.[11] After she receives her longed-for child, she must then fulfill her vow and give her child back to God as she promised. Hannah's petition for God to act on her behalf is a plea for a change of her desperate circumstances, as childless women were considered cursed.[12] Her lack of a child had socially oppressive consequences for her. Sarah (Gen 11:30) and Rachel (Gen 29:31) similarly lack children for a time and suffer the consequences (Gen 16:4, Gen 30:1). Their suffering contrasts with their change of circumstances once they have a child. Hannah's prayer for a child is a prayer for life. When she receives the gift of a child (1 Sam 1:20), the gift of new life, she does not hang on to him. All the problems Hannah faced due to her childlessness would again return when she gives her child up to God at the shrine in Shiloh. She would still face an uncertain future if her husband died.[13] Yet, she fulfills her vow and gives her son back to God to be raised at the shrine in Shiloh (1 Sam 20:24). Hannah's fulfillment of her vow ensures her future vulnerability. She does not cling to what she has been given, but fulfills her responsibilities faithfully, as she set out for herself when she made the vow. Hannah's

[11] Hyman, "Four Acts of Vowing," 232.

[12] Robert Wilson, "Child, Children," in *HarperCollins Bible Dictionary*, ed. Mark Allan Powell and others (New York: HarperOne, 2011), 128.

[13] Esler, *Sex, Wives, and Warriors*, 129.

vow is a prayer of petition for the gift of new life and God responds to her. But the answer to Hannah's prayer is not a gift for her to keep for herself. In order to fulfill her vow she must let her gift of life go. She gives up her security. Hannah demonstrates her ability not to grasp, but to lean into the abundant wideness of God's generosity. She receives further life in the form of more children as a result of her faithfulness, though she did not know this would occur. She was willing to take a major risk, trusting in her relationship with Yahweh. Hannah's gift of a child is not only a gift for herself, but a gift for all of Israel. Her generosity flowing from the generosity of God leads to one of the greatest prophets of Israel's history.

Our Witness to Faithfulness

The risk younger women religious take as they begin living this life today is different from both Hannah's and previous generations'. Women religious make public vows, which carry responsibilities and witness value to the larger community. Younger sisters experience the public nature of this commitment early on in their formation, often well before they take vows—before they are anchored in the vow relationship as Hannah seems to be. In fact, it is not unusual for a young woman entering religious life today to receive a significant amount of media attention, to be interviewed multiple times and across different types of media even as she enters the community and well before she professes her first vows. If someone were to google us, our life stories are readily available online. There is a weightiness to this reality. Even before we profess vows we are becoming public people and carry a great responsibility to the people we serve. When we introduce ourselves as "sister," then we cannot be lazy in our relationships—even if we believe we will never see these people again. No one should snap at someone else because they are having a bad day, but the impact could be greater when we represent God or religion for people as sisters. We become representatives of the vows—even before we make them.

Hannah's Prayer

Hannah's petition and the fulfillment of her vow by giving the gift of life she received back to God may be considered a prayer. The words that we say in prayer—when we pray with words—reveal something about who we are and who we believe God is. Hannah's prayer following the fulfillment of her vow further demonstrates her relationship with Yahweh and broadens even to reflect her understanding of Yahweh's desire for right relationship in our world (1 Sam 2:1-10):

> Hannah prayed saying,
> My heart rejoices in Yahweh;
> my horn is exalted to Yahweh.
> My mouth is wide against my enemies,
> for I rejoice in your salvation.
> There is no one holy like Yahweh,
> because there is none except you
> and there is no rock like our God.
> Do not continue speaking so very highly,
> nor let arrogance go out from your mouth
> for the Lord is a God of knowledge
> and by God deeds are weighed.
> The bows of the mighty ones are shattered
> and those who are stumbling are bound up with strength.
> Those who are satisfied with bread hire themselves out.
> Those who are hungry become fat,
> while the one without offspring gives birth seven times,
> and the one with many sons becomes weak.
> Yahweh causes death and brings back to life,
> brings down to Sheol and raises up.
> Yahweh makes poor and makes rich,
> brings low and raises up.
> Yahweh[14] raises the poor from the dust.
> Yahweh raises the needy ones from the dung heap
> to cause them to dwell with nobles.

[14] I have chosen to translate this text inclusively. Therefore, when the Hebrew uses a masculine pronoun to refer to God, I have usually substituted "Yahweh" instead.

> Yahweh causes them to inherit a throne of glory
> for the pillars of the earth belong to Yahweh,
> and Yahweh set the world on them.
> Yahweh guards the feet of Yahweh's pious ones,
> and the evil ones in darkness are made silent,
> for not by the strength of humans does one become great.
> Those who conduct a case against Yahweh will be shattered.
> Against them Yahweh will thunder in the heavens.
> Yahweh will judge the ends of the earth and give strength to
> Yahweh's king
> and raise up a horn to Yahweh's anointed.

Vows, prayer, and relationship with God are woven together as part of the fabric of this narrative. Hannah first demonstrates her relationship with God by calling on God in her time of distress (1 Sam 1:10-13). Then God affirms a relationship with Hannah by granting her petition for a child (1 Sam 1:20). Hannah again reaffirms her relationship with God in her ten-verse response of praise for God (1 Sam 2:1-10). Some aspects of her prayer are simple praises to God, which affirm that God is greater than any calamity that human beings might experience. For Hannah, God is singular and holy. God's power and strength are demonstrated through the metaphors of rock and thunder (vv. 2-10). God further guards the feet of pious ones like Hannah (v. 9). This song of praise is firmly grounded in Hannah's experience of who God is. There are elements of her prayer that seem to be a reversal of the situations of the world that are unjust for the pious and vulnerable people in it. The bow of the mighty is shattered; the weapons of war and oppression are broken, so the tools that the mighty used to oppress others are no longer available (v. 4). Conversely, those who are stumbling are bound up with strength (v. 4). These are opposite images that imply a reversal of fortunes. Further into the prayer, "those who are satisfied with bread hire themselves out. Those who are hungry become fat" (v. 5). So, those who were presumably comfortable and did not need to work will now have to toil for food, while those who have gone hungry will be satisfied. This is another clear reversal of how the world works. But in God's vision, this is precisely what is accomplished. Then "the one without offspring gives birth to seven children, while the one with many sons becomes weak" (v. 5). Each of the reversals of expectations leads up to the precise reversal of fortunes that Hannah experiences. God is interested in the personal turmoil in which her vow is made. The number seven expresses totality and fulfillment, suggesting that she is fulfilled, regardless of the actual number of children she has. These verses may be read as God's vision to turn the expectations of the world inside out. No one expects those who are powerful to become weak, and the weak to become powerful. Instead, those in power usually gain more power. No one expects that those who have plenty are suddenly toiling for what they achieve, while those who were hungry are now full. Instead those who have more continue to gain more, while those who have less, seem to have less and less and struggle to survive. But Hannah rejoices and aligns herself with God's vision, and her experience is utterly transformed by God's way of acting in the world.

While younger women religious do not make their vows out of intense personal turmoil, as is the case with Old Testament characters such as Hannah, women religious do make their vows in the midst of a world in turmoil. The vows of poverty, chastity, and obedience are each countercultural and profess an "alternate" way of living in the world that is radical.[15] It is this alternate vision that God has for the world that makes sense to those of us in religious life. We know when we commit to this journey that there are so many ways that saying "yes" to this life makes no sense. It's not practical. We will not make money in this way of life. We "give up" sex, a spouse, and there will be no seven children for us. Everything about this choice seems to be a reversal of expectations akin to the

[15] Sandra Schneiders, *Selling All: Commitment, Consecrated Celibacy, and Community in Catholic Religious Life* (New York: Paulist, 2001), 109.

reversals found in Hannah's prayer. Furthermore, our older wisdom sisters are all going to die, and there will not be very many of us left. Some of us have even joined communities in which we have no peers at all. Who signs up for such a life? How can this be life-giving? It makes no sense by any worldly measure. Yet, for us intrepid few, we know this is where we belong. It is somehow in the midst of these impossible situations that God will gift us with life. Hannah's prayer demonstrates that God likes to do the impossible and unexpected. The reversal of expectations for our lives is part of our manner of embracing a relationship with God. We who align ourselves with such a program find ourselves professing that we wish to walk the unexpected pathway of poverty, chastity, and obedience forever. Scholars have long noted that Hannah's prayer acknowledging the unexpected way God works in the world is the basis of Mary's canticle (Luke 1:46-55). It is the maternal ancestor of Mary's prayer, as Mary's mother's name is traditionally known as Anna, and the Hebrew form of that name is Hannah. (It takes a whole history of such women to give birth to a child like Jesus! We continue this lineage through our own witness to God's unexpected actions in our lives and in the world.)

Another closer look at Hannah's prayer, and the portions of the prayer we identified as carrying the weight of a reversal of expectations, allows us to peel back another layer of possible meaning. The aforementioned passages may indeed be read as a reversal of expectations, as mentioned above. However, I would like to suggest that they might also be read as Hannah's celebration of her experiential understanding of God's preference for equality among people, as opposed to injustice. Breaking the bows of the mighty and strengthening the weak might be read as destroying the tools of oppression and leveling the playing field. In essence, this might be seen as God's desire for restorative action, which is also mirrored in the concept of the year of Jubilee (Lev 25:10), where land is returned to those who have lost it in times of disaster or distress. After all, it is the bows—that is powerful weapons—that are smashed, not the people themselves. "Those who are satisfied with bread hire themselves out; those who are hungry become fat" (v. 5) might merely mean that all people need to work for their bread and those who are hungry may now be fed through a more just distribution of resources. It could indicate the reversal described above, but could also be another example of leveling the playing field. Then, of course, Hannah's personal experience of fortune reversal follows: the childless one has children, and the woman with many sons "becomes weak" or "wastes away" (v. 5). We do not have to read this as wasting away, which would clearly indicate a reversal of fortunes. Instead we could also read it as "grows weak," which could indicate that her power as the only one with children has ended with the offspring of the once-childless woman. This then might be read as another example of "equalizing" the circumstances between the women. Such a program toward equality serves to both prevent and redress increasing imbalances of power as an issue of justice in God's eyes. This suggests a program for women religious today as they enact their vows in a world that does not value poverty, chastity, and obedience.

Furthermore, God is acknowledged as having control over life and death and rich and poor. Specific mention is made of those who are poor, lowly, and needy being raised up (v. 8). However, those who are mighty are not punished here, but their weapons are destroyed (v. 4). The interest of these verses seems to be to raise up the vulnerable and stop oppression, but not to punish enemies (v. 6). Pious ones will be guarded and evil ones will be silent, but again, this does not have to mean they are punished (v. 9). This second, equalizing reading might offer a point of reflection for women religious. Not only does our life call for a reversal of expectations in our world, but we also are working toward equality, which is God's desire for the vulnerable people of the world. Equality is not equality for its own sake, but a recognition of God's care for those who are vulnerable is often achieved by restraining the powerful.

I have found I am constantly educating others by simply existing and introducing myself as "sister" in the ordinary encounters of everyday life. People's expectations are overturned when they meet a young nun. Every time I acknowledge my identity as "sister" I am professing my vows anew and publicly holding myself accountable to these words I have committed my life to. Whenever I find myself in circumstances that challenge me to respond as my best self, I touch the ring I received at my vows—a ring that identifies me as a Sister of St. Francis of Dubuque, Iowa. This simple action grounds me in my vows and connects me to the women whom I share this life with. It is a reminder of who I am called to be in the world with and for others.

Theological Anthropology and the Vows of Poverty, Chastity, and Obedience

Juliet Mousseau, RSCJ

The glory of God is the human person fully alive.
(St. Irenaeus, second century)

Who are we? What does it mean to be human? Who is God? How do we find fulfillment in this life? In every era, people strive to answer these questions, searching for meaning and purpose. In today's Western world, human fulfillment might be sought through family relationships, financial stability, material possessions, social status, or notches on a bedpost. These societal answers often leave people dissatisfied and still searching. Religions try to fill the void by connecting human life to transcendent realities. In our Christian tradition, we learn that God created human beings in God's image and likeness. Yet we also learn that human beings, having been given freedom, make mistakes which remove us from the goodness for which God created us. Our fulfillment comes as we, step by step, freely choose the good and in doing so cultivate the image of God in our lives. As women religious, we choose to live the vows of poverty, chastity, and obedience as a means to direct our human freedom more clearly toward the good.[1]

Of course, we women religious do not live in a vacuum—and apostolic religious do not live in a cloister. Our vows find a place within the context of human life at a particular moment in time, within a distinct cultural context. I write from the twenty-first century as a white woman in the United States. Thus, the culture in which I live is shaped by Protestant and secular tendencies, individualism, consumerism, and materialism, a national identity that is at the same time a "melting pot" and one deeply suspicious of outsiders, and inundated with the broad use of sexualized imagery and sexism. On the other hand, the United States is also a place of great optimism, democracy, and philanthropy that upholds equality and justice as primary ideals. All of these characteristics interact with my understanding of religious vows and how I attempt to live them.

In this essay, we will explore what it means to be human, to be created by God, and to be women in relationship with God; that is, we will explore the theological anthropology that expresses our faith-filled understanding of who we are. Following this, we will survey the meaning that our Christian understanding of the human person gives to the vows of obedience, poverty, and celibacy. Though a centuries-old tradition, religious vows are shaped by our cultural and historical context, and living them out in a rapidly changing world provides a prophetic witness for the possibility of a better world.

Humanity in the Context of Creation

A Christian theology of creation is based in the book of Genesis. In two allegorical stories, we learn that God created our world out of nothing and that everything God created is

[1] While some religious orders make different vows, in this essay I will focus on these three most common vows.

good. The cosmos, the earth and the water, animals of all kinds, plants, and finally human beings, were created and organized according to God's vision. God created human beings in God's own image—male and female, endowed with body, mind, spirit, and desire, predisposed to relationships. Human beings were created with the desire for union with God. Creation is the outpouring of God's love, a love that cannot be contained in the infinite God! God freely decided to create without compulsion or need, and God created us to be in relationship with the earth, with one another, and with God. This Christian mutuality of relationship with the earth and one another directly confronts the societal use and destruction of earth's resources and the tendency to disregard another's needs in favor of one's own desires.

In the image and likeness of God, we mirror God's freedom and love, and we become cocreators with God. We are explicitly given stewardship or care of all of creation, which directs us to right relationship with other living beings. As cocreators, we tend God's creation. We depend on the earth to provide us with all that we need to survive and to thrive. We seek out shelter, harvest food, use earth's goods to clothe ourselves, and we delight in the beauty of the world around us. Created by God, the cosmos bears the image of God as well, allowing created things on earth and in heaven to become a book by which we understand who God is to the degree we are capable.[2]

In creating us male and female, God reflected the communitarian relationships of the Trinity. As we understand the Godhead to be Father, Son, and Holy Spirit in a reciprocal and intimate communion, so too we understand ourselves to be

[2] The idea of the "book of the world" that reveals God to us is a common medieval image, used especially in St. Bonaventure's writings. See especially Bonaventure, *The Soul's Journey into God, the Tree of Life, and the Life of St. Francis*, trans. Ewert Cousins, Classics of Western Spirituality (New York: Paulist, 1978).

social creatures. Like God, we reflect the Trinity in the intimacy, reciprocity, and union of our relationships with other people. God created woman to accompany man in the garden, and so too we accompany one another on our life's journey. The communitarian nature of our creation provides a powerful counterbalance to the individualism of Western society. Additionally, to understand other human beings as our companions and supports prevents us from using others as objects and requires that we recognize each one as a free human being, likewise lovingly created by God.

Human beings are spiritual beings. Implanted in us is the desire to be united with God in prayer and at the end of time. Union with God is our ultimate happiness, the fulfillment of our seeking.[3] It is the highest calling of all human beings. God created us out of love, to be loved, and God delights in us for who we are and for how we embrace our identity as children of God. In the famous words of St. Augustine, "Our hearts are restless until they rest in You, O God."[4] Perhaps the frenetic pace of our world today is a reflection of the restlessness many feel because they do not know where to look for God.

The second story of creation found in the book of Genesis emphasizes the creation of human beings and their fall from grace. In this story, we see our origin as relational beings, created for one another. Our freedom includes the possibility that we can choose *not* to live out God's desire for us. Turning aside from God's vision impacts not just our own lives but also the lives of our descendants and those around us. God created us, but with such love and freedom that we are set free to make choices, even if those choices lead us to reject our Creator and harm one another. A return to the intent of our freedom means we act only when we have considered how we are connected to one another and to the earth. We counter individualism and

[3] Thomas Aquinas on happiness. ST I.II.2.1-5, on "Man's Last End."
[4] Augustine, *Confessions*, bk. 1, chap. 1.

unhealthy attachment to personal gain when we weigh our actions against their impact on others.

While God created only goodness, the freedom human beings were given allowed us entry into life shaped by sinfulness as well. Human beings long for meaning and purpose in life, and yet we are easily distracted by earthly concerns, desires, and possessions. In confusion and sinfulness, we often choose the opposite of what we long for.[5] Additionally, human sinfulness pervades society as a whole, not just in the sins of individual human beings, but also in the sins that have been institutionalized in our world's structures, including harmful economic practices, racism, destruction of the environment, and the exploitation of human beings. These sinful structures lead to unjust circumstances for many people, especially for the vulnerable and for those who find themselves on the peripheries. Even the divisions between the powerful and the powerless point to the injustices caused by personal and social sins.

Though we are sinful, God created us good, and we are called to seek out the good. We strive to let go of the things that call us away from goodness. In seeking out the good and rejecting the evil, we model and encourage in one another the wholeness that is God's dream for humanity. What a profound gift of hope and joy we bring to the world because we know this truth in our hearts! Following the teaching of Jesus, we seek God's kingdom, both in the life to come and in the here and now. Knowing that as human beings we have both gifts that we are called to share and limitations that we are called to overcome, we strive to live as best we can. As religious, we do this in a very deliberate way, through our prophetic witness to God's desire for us in the public vows of poverty, celibacy, and obedience.

[5] *Gaudium et Spes* (Pastoral Constitution on the Church in the Modern World), 10.

Obedience

In my congregation, obedience is placed first among the three vows, and so I place it here. I am called to obey the voice of God in my life, which I can hear only through a life of prayer and discernment. The voice of God calls me from my own heart, from the people I meet, and from the earth itself. It means obedience to the voices of those who are in need, whether they be the sisters I live with or the refugees fleeing violence in Syria. In addition, it means trusting that the Spirit works not only in my own heart but also in the hearts of my sisters, especially those in leadership.

Discerning the call of God in my own heart requires a deep and steady life of prayer that facilitates careful listening. I began to hear God calling me to religious life ten years before I was able to heed the voice and formally enter the process of discernment with the Society of the Sacred Heart. At first, the outside voices of those who did not understand the call of religious life kept me from hearing. Later on, my own desire for continued education and independence led me down different paths. Finally, when my desire to study theology had been satisfied and I was surrounded by supportive friends who could reflect my heart's desire, I was able to discern and obey the voice of God calling me toward religious life. I could hear in my heart the deep desire to offer myself and my gifts to the needs of the world around me. Finally, following this deep desire brought me peace and joy like nothing I had experienced before.

Obedience has a very negative image in our society. Popularly, obedience is viewed as self-denial at the whim of another, which is what I felt about a midnight curfew when I was a teenager. Not able to understand the meaning behind their rules, I was supposed to obey my parents blindly. In religious life, I have found obedience to be something very different. While I do not always understand the reasons for some of the things I have been asked to do in formation, they are usually presented in the context of community discernment and wisdom. It certainly demands faith that my leadership, too, are listening to the call of God in their own hearts, in the world, and in my voice. In my experience, their discernment for my life has led to my own growth and well-being.

We are not called to blind obedience. This is an important area of growth in most religious orders today. Because my human dignity includes the capacity to reason and understand in the image and likeness of a rational and understanding God, obedience requires that I use those capacities in discernment. As a young woman still figuring out religious life (even after nine years in it!), this means it is important for me to voice my thoughts when I am asked to do something and to listen to the wisdom of other sisters. I must voice my thoughts because my sisters do not know my heart or my hesitations unless I tell them. These vulnerable conversations are incredibly fruitful.

An example of this experience in my life came a few years ago, when I was about three years into temporary vows. I was asked to spend a month in Spain to experience ministry among the poor and to practice speaking Spanish. I had hurt my ankle several months before I went, and the physical therapy was not helping it heal. I was very anxious about going for such a long period of time, but I did not feel like I could question the will of my formation director and our leadership team. With the encouragement of trusted friends, I brought it up to my formator, and we talked about my anxiety, my fear that my ankle was not healed, and my uncertainty as to whether I was allowed to change plans. In the end I did not go, and I had to have ankle surgery as well. My formation director did not know that I was anxious and in pain. With that further information, we discerned together a better path. I learned that in order to know what I really need and where God is calling me, I must first listen to my heart, and then I must share what I discover within myself with my sisters.

Obedience calls me to right relationship and generosity with those around me. The vow of obedience affects not just major life choices, but also simple daily actions. When I spend more time than I want to with a sister or student who needs to talk, it is because I know in my heart that relationships with others are more important than other things I have to get done. Obedience frees me to be entirely present to others when in other circumstances I might be distracted by the things on my to-do list. Thus, obedience helps me to live both the freedom and the relationships that are integral to human identity. In those relationships, we human beings reflect the Trinity, God's innate relatedness. This connection to others is the impact of God's unity on the world.

The vow of obedience also calls us as a community of women to discernment together. When we make decisions in the congregation about leadership and priorities for the next few years at our general chapter, we listen together to God's call to us as individuals and to us as a group. In the writing of this book, we, who are from all different congregations and charisms, discerned together, listening to the thoughts, prayers, and experiences of one another to help us gain a broader image of religious life. As members of a community, the voices of other sisters and of our greater communities challenge our assumptions and articulate what God is saying to us. Community discernment can either affirm or correct some harebrained idea I might have.

Above all, obedience to the voice of God in my life is a source of great freedom. Just as God freely created the world out of love, so too I am called to freedom and to creativity born of love. The vow of obedience taken in the context of community allows me to act in courageous ways to follow Jesus in making present God's kingdom here on earth. It means that even when I am the only one acting on something, I do not act alone but with the support of my sisters. It means that when one of our sisters stands up against the violence of nuclear weapons or with migrants crossing national borders, I am with her as well. This sense of communal identity and obedience to the will of God is both empowering and a humbling expression of my humanity. Our voices in concert are significantly more powerful than my voice alone.

Poverty

The vow of poverty reminds us that everything we have and need is gift. God created the universe, including the oceans, plants, and animals that we rely on for life, and we, too, are counted among God's creation. Our wholeness as human beings is interdependent on God and on all God created. In the face of an individualistic society, this interdependence challenges our self-perception and requires us to be vulnerable. In the face of materialism, we come to learn that happiness does not come through having more and costlier possessions.

While we call this vow "poverty," I find it difficult to discuss because in my community we are anything but genuinely poor. Unlike those who are poor, we do not have to worry whether our most basic needs will be met. We have access to education and to people in powerful positions. The choice of voluntary poverty is more about putting our gifts at the service of others, living simply, and advocating for or working with those who are materially poor.

I saw material poverty in a very real way last summer while living in the *altiplano* of Peru. Our sisters there live far simpler than I do in St. Louis, yet even so they too have their needs met without worry. The poverty of the Peruvian highlands leads people to work the land, to walk miles upon miles to get to school, church, or the market, and often to leave school before receiving a basic education. I could see the years of working the land on the sunburnt, wrinkled faces, backs bent with heavy burdens, and dusty sandaled feet. Yet I also saw great joy and a hospitality that revealed the value of human relationships in their lives. The poverty I brought to Peru was not material, but rather the poverty of being unable to communicate in the native language, Quechua, of having suitcase space for only the essentials, and of being too far from cell and internet to connect with my loved ones at home. In certain moments, I felt very keenly the poverty of being unable to connect on a deep level with people I cared about, limited by language constraints and the remoteness of our location.

I learned in that experience to see the richness of human relationships, of the joyful love freely given by children—even to this big *gringa*—and of the deep connection to working the land. While my poverty was more spiritual, I began to see material poverty and the reality of daily struggle.

In the act of creation, God gave humanity the role of steward over creation, reflected in the way Peruvian men and women cultivate their fields and care for their animals. Just as God cares for all God created, so also we have a role to reflect God's care. In religious life, we do this through limiting our use of the resources available to us and minimizing our impact on the environment. This living out of the vow of poverty takes place in communal living. The members of the household share what they have in order to meet the needs of each person. We do not each need to have a separate home and all of the resources that go into it. Sharing resources means that we use fewer of them collectively and that we are challenged to use less individually. We are called to "live simply that others might simply live."[6]

Care for creation is a hot topic among women religious, due in part to this value placed on God's creation and in part because of the close connection between the well-being of the most vulnerable and the health of the planet. Throughout history, religious have deliberately tried to live simply, to touch the earth only lightly. Throughout the twentieth century in the United States this trend increased exponentially. Now, women religious run farms, petition the government to fight climate change, and seek out ways to make their properties dependent

[6] This quotation is attributed to Mahatma Gandhi, Mother Teresa of Calcutta, Elizabeth Anne Seton, and bumper stickers everywhere.

on renewable energy. These actions both stand against the destruction of the environment and the effect of that destruction on the most vulnerable people in our world. Thus, concern for the integrity of creation is at the same time a move toward compassion for those at the peripheries.

Not only does a vow of poverty place us in right relationship with the things of this world that we depend on for our well-being, it also gives us a freedom of holding lightly what we have. When I remember that all I have is gift, that everything comes from the generosity of God, I am humbled by my gratitude for this gift. I also know that it is not mine to hold onto tightly, but that I am given these things so that I can share them with others. Just as I am given talents and skills that I must share with those who need them, so also the material goods that come to my use are only mine for a short time. Plus, if I do not claim things as my own, my time and energy is not spent in protecting them or keeping them for my exclusive use. I am freed from the restraints of too many things so that I can be available and present to others. It is like travelling with suitcases that I cannot carry: if I hold on tightly to things because I think I need to have them with me, I miss out on the freedom of easy travel where I am able to carry my necessities on my back.

The vow of poverty counters the constant advertising we face daily, which tries to convince us our happiness lies in purchasing yet another thing. We learn to be empty of material possessions and not to cling to our own desires so that Jesus can take over and guide our lives. Rather than being empty because all I have has no meaning, instead my emptiness is filled in relationship with God and others, and with the great gift of the love of God.

Our identity as human beings with a share in God's stewardship for the earth both informs and shapes the religious vow of poverty. The vow helps us direct our attention to what really gives us life—to the relationships with others and with God that bring us fulfillment.

Celibate Chastity

Christianity teaches that human beings are called to chastity—this is the call to remain faithful to commitments. For married people, chastity refers to fidelity to a spouse. For women and men religious, the vow of chastity is really a vow of celibacy—that we commit ourselves in fidelity to God, not to any human person. This is contrary to what we learn in Genesis about the human person: God did not create us to be celibate. God created men and women to be together, to unite their bodies and their hearts, so that they are not alone and are not lonely. Men and women are called to unite and to bring children into the world.

My best friend married the same year that I began discerning a call to religious life. We both were seeking something more, a commitment to life that drew us out of our single lives. While Christine looked to the future and saw family life and children, I looked back at previous relationships and realized that they were not fulfilling to me. I chose to live a broader love that freed me to serve many people and many children. Our world needs both of these kinds of love, for both of them echo the love God has for us: love that rejoices in the particular person each one is created to be and love that widely embraces all types of people, all of humanity, and all of creation.[7]

We learn in Genesis that God did not create human beings for celibacy, so why do we as religious seek to live celibate lives? Theologically speaking, the reasoning from the Scriptures emerges in the New Testament belief that the Second Coming was right around the corner. Paul tells us basically to remain as we are—if we are married, stay married; if we are single, stay single—because Jesus is coming again right away and we should not radically change our lifestyle in that way

[7] Timothy Radcliffe spoke of the love of chastity in comparison to the love of marriage in this way at a symposium at Catholic Theological Union, Chicago, Illinois, February 6, 2016, entitled "Community Life and Mission: Toward a Future Full of Hope." The video can be accessed here: http://www.ctuconsecratedlife.org/videos/ (accessed April 1, 2017).

in order to be ready for him. It's as if Paul says that marital status doesn't matter at all in the coming kingdom of God, and so there's no reason to make any big changes when time is so short.

Of course, the Second Coming was not nearly as immediate as Paul and the other first-century disciples of Jesus thought it would be. Yet their writings and traditions remain our own. Paul's acknowledgement that celibacy and marriage were essentially equal when moral questions are considered was one justification for celibacy among Jesus' first followers. Additionally, in our tradition we hold that Jesus himself remained single throughout his lifetime in order to devote all that he had and was to his salvific mission. His life of faithful celibacy provided another example for us as we strive to follow him more closely. After his death, early Christian martyrs displayed holiness in their willingness to die for their faith. When martyrdom became less common, Christians turned to self-denial as a demonstration of holiness, and celibacy was given yet another purpose.

While celibacy began as a way to devote a life of prayer to God in a monastic or hermetical setting, it spread to become a symbol of holiness among those called to ministry in the church. Only in the twelfth century did celibacy become universal law for ordained men. Thus, in today's world, we have a celibate priesthood, so that those who serve the church as ordained ministers and the women and men religious who devote themselves to lives of prayer and service both embrace celibacy. While it is often perceived as a sign of holiness among those who don't live it, for the celibate religious I know it is viewed as a path of freedom in order to live fully for God, open to making a wider difference in the world.

Celibacy today is no less a radical choice than it was for Jesus and Paul. So much of our Western culture tries to convince us that sexuality is the pathway to fulfillment. Celibacy in the context of the vow of chastity challenges our culture by seeking out fulfillment in other ways. As human beings, we remain sexual beings, but we place physical sexuality in proper proportion to other aspects of human intimacy. Rather than seeking wholeness only in the body, we seek wholeness in a balanced life of relationships, prayer, ministry, and physical expressions of joy. Human beings are physical, emotional, and spiritual wholes: overemphasis of any one of those areas can make us lose our equilibrium.

Genesis calls us as human beings to cocreate with God in our world. One way to do so is, of course, through family life and parenthood. Religious find creativity and generativity in other ways: through nurturing life in all its forms and stages, through education and healthcare, through ministry to those who are marginalized or on the peripheries. Regardless of the situation and the ministry, the central gift of religious to the world is in *who they are*. Religious are called to manifest God's loving presence in the world, no matter what they do on a daily basis. This nurtures life. This nurtures wholeness in others. This is love, lived in the image and likeness of God.

Just like everyone else, religious women need to find intimacy in relationships and ways to be creative. Both of these are necessary for human wholeness. In my life, creativity comes out in a number of ways, all of which must be nourished. As a teacher, I find certain parts of teaching, such as creating course plans and presentations, to be creative. In my personal life, I like to make things for others, such as baby blankets for my friends as their families grow and delicious meals for my community.

Intimacy among religious is a more difficult topic to discuss. We are human beings, and we need intimacy, but at the same time we vow not to have the physical intimacy of a sex life. Intimacy, luckily for us, comes in other forms. First, we need the physical touch of other human beings. For me, I love the sweet cuddles of little children when I visit my friends' homes or my niece and nephew. Expressions of affection from my community members and friends, and a healthy yoga practice, help me remember that I, too, am a bodily creature. Secondly, we find intimacy in the depth of relationship we have with others. Though many of my friends and all of my family live far from me, we have regular conversations that deeply touch me at the core of who I am and what is important in life. In conversations with my brother, we remember our family history and discuss our relationships with other family members. When I talk with Christine, I feel comfortable revealing my self-doubts and we can talk at a deep level about the meaning of our lives and vocations. I am able to meet regularly or talk by phone with other younger sisters, and we share the struggles we have with religious life, and the joys that we find there in a way that my family and friends (and even older sisters) cannot relate to. These intimate relationships help me to remain deeply connected to the people I love, and they help me remember my identity as a woman in relationship with others.

The vow of celibacy offers us freedom to love. We are freed from the particular love a spouse offers to his or her family so that we can share love in a more general way for the world as a whole. This speaks to the relational identity of all human beings. Celibacy is not to deny us relationships, but it shapes and molds the precious relationships we hold. We are called to a depth of relationship that is not physically sexual. Because we have different commitments than most families do, we often have an availability for intimacy that others do not. That intimacy takes the shape of deep spiritual connection, time spent at critical life stages such as deaths and births, and friendships of mutual emotional support. These faithful friendships come with a freedom for both involved, seeking mutuality and honoring each person as an individual with particular needs and desires. Friendship in this context is healthy, not dependent or manipulative.

Conclusion

The meaning and purpose of our lives as men and women religious emerges from our identity as human beings created in the image and likeness of God. Above all, that image and likeness marks us as connected to all of creation and to God. All human beings are created in this way—and yet all are constantly seeking fulfilment. As vowed religious, we live with a deeper awareness of God's image and likeness, choosing obedience, poverty, and celibacy daily. Through our vows we become people of loving presence, of peaceful hope, who focus our lives on relationships. It is through these peaceful and loving relationships that religious promote the dream God has for humanity.

Seeking the kingdom of God means not just the big picture, but also seeking out the wholeness of each individual. This includes ourselves—how are we fully integrated, fully living as God created us to live? The vows give direction to our lives and our energy, and help us to find wholeness. They remind us that only in God can we find our fulfillment.

So who are we? We are women listening attentively for the voice of God within our hearts, in the cries of the earth, and in the suffering of human beings. We are women who know our wealth comes not from our material possessions, but from the priceless care and compassion we share with God and others. We are women who find our fulfillment in loving relationships marked by inclusivity and tenderness toward all human beings. As we live our vows with passion and intensity, we become prophetic witnesses, showing the world a glimpse of God's kingdom.

The Vows and Jesus' Radical Mission: The Power of Celibacy, Poverty, and Obedience for the Reign of God

Tracy Kemme, SC

It was a few minutes after five in the afternoon when my cell phone rang. I had just changed into a T-shirt, winding down from a full ministry day. As I jostled the phone from my purse, I saw that the caller was a friend who works for a local Catholic outreach agency and who seldom contacts me.

He didn't make small talk but got right to the point.

"Tracy, we have a woman from Honduras and her baby here at the office. She's fleeing a situation of abuse, and we're helping her sort it all out, but the office is closing, and we haven't found anywhere for her to stay tonight. The shelters are full. Do you have any ideas, at least for one night?"

He wasn't asking directly if we could host, but in my heart, I knew that the invitation was for my community. A tinge of resistance fluttered in my stomach. I considered briefly how offering our house could alter the week ahead, but then purpose flooded me and erased any hesitation. I smiled as I remembered a line from my congregation's mission statement: "We dare to risk a caring response." I somehow knew that our answer would be "yes" even before I checked with my housemates. Both of them replied, "Of course," and my heart swelled with gratitude for my vocation. *Of course.*

In an hour or so, my friend pulled up, and a beautiful teenage girl climbed out carrying a plump baby boy. In came blankets as well, along with a plastic grocery bag of clothing, a baby bag, and a car seat. We knew that Mary and Jesus had come to seek refuge with us.

The next few days were sacred and exhausting. We heard our houseguest's painful story and fell in love with her chubby-cheeked son. We warmed tortillas and learned how she likes her scrambled eggs. We held the baby while she showered, and I went through my clothes to add a few more outfits to her meager wardrobe. Later in the week, a spot in a shelter opened up, and the sweet duo disappeared from our lives as quickly as they had come. We found our hearts broken and filled simultaneously. What a privilege to have had such an encounter; what sorrow for the young girl's uncertain future and for knowing we wouldn't see her again.

Sitting on the couch in our living room which felt strangely quiet without the sounds of baby cries and laughter, a community mate and I pondered the visit. We both confessed a bit of relief that we would no longer have to be "grandma" and "aunt" at home alongside our regular ministries and commitments.

"That was hard," we agreed, thankful for the freedom to admit those feelings.

Then, not a second later we affirmed, "We would do it again in a heartbeat." We agreed on that, too.

I cherish the "of-course-ness" of the whole situation. We didn't stop to weigh the risks, challenges, and inconveniences. Mission called. We knew how Jesus would respond. Our religious vows confirmed our answer before the invitation even came.

The Vows and Mission

As a younger, newer member of a religious congregation, I feel urgency in my vows. Coming of age in the twenty-first century, opportunity lay before me. I sensed a call to use my life for good, but there were many paths I could have followed. Before entering religious life, I volunteered for two years in Ecuador and considered graduate school for pastoral ministry. I explored a life-giving romantic relationship that could have led to a sacramental, mission-centered marriage. I did not need to become a sister to make an impact.

When I came to religious life, then, I came with hunger. I came to live the passion I felt in community. My commitment is imbued with a sense of what might be described in contemporary secular terms as "go big or go home" or "#YOLO"—you only live once. In other words, with so many other options before me, I choose religious life because I want to live it intrepidly.

The vows have had something important to offer society in every age of religious life's evolution. It is no different today. Our loving God plants in each sister's DNA that which is needed for the time and place in which she dwells. I look at our world in desperate need and am convinced that our vows, lived in communion by women religious across the globe, hold transformative power. As Pope Francis insisted in his letter for the Year of Consecrated Life, we can "wake up the world."[1] We make vows not for ourselves, but for the reign of God.[2] The vows are mission.

Entering a congregation of mostly aged women as a young adult is both a privilege and a struggle. My beloved sisters have given their lives in ministry, and now many are in retirement or nursing care. As I peer into the possibility of my vowed life, they grapple with end-of-life questions. God calls them to channel their mission-energy in different ways than me at age thirty. My young heart pulses to the beat of the

[1] Francis, Letter for the Year of Consecrated Life, November 29, 2014, accessed May 11, 2017, http://en.radiovaticana.va/news/2014/11/29/pope_issues_letter_for_year_of_consecrated_life/1112885.

[2] Throughout the essay, I use the phrases "reign of God" and "kingdom of God" to indicate the kind of community toward which Jesus worked. I don't find the royal connotation of the phrases helpful in today's context, but as they are used in Scripture, they seem the best word choices.

beckoning Gospel, fresh with the ardor of a newly made commitment. The example, wisdom, and mentorship of my elder sisters inspire me to follow that beckoning. At the same time, the fire I yearn for takes shape most evidently in gatherings with religious life peers from across congregations.

When we young sisters assemble and reflect on religious life, the word "radical" surfaces frequently: radical in the sense of something countercultural, extreme, and comprehensive. It strikes me that "radical" comes from "root." The dictionary defines radical as first, "fundamental," and second, "something that transforms social and political systems."[3] I see a profound connection between those two meanings. To live the vows as needed today, we must seek our roots—that which is most central in our vowed lives. Such seeking will steer us to mission with the power to heal and transform in sweeping ways.

The deepest root of our call to vowed life is, of course, Jesus. A man who walked the earth over two thousand years ago lived mission so intensely that millions follow him still today. This Jesus is not a soft and static recollection that could be contained in a black and white mantel photo. He is living, breathing, and, hopefully, disturbing. Too often, Christianity wilts into a lukewarm obligation that can be checked off a list. We accept a religion that praises Jesus but ignores his message that true praise is lived. Jack Jezreel said in a workshop I attended, "Jesus spent his whole life passionately pointing toward the reign of God, and we ended up passionately pointing at Jesus."[4] As I discerned religious life, I saw that women religious don't buy watered-down, feel-good Christianity; they passionately point toward the reign of God with Jesus. I had to be part of it.

[3] Google dictionary, accessed April 1, 2017, https://www.google.com/webhp?sourceid=chrome-instant&ion=1&espv=2&ie=UTF-8#q=google+dictionary+definition+for+radical&*.

[4] Jack Jezreel, "On Social Mission," Gather and Send workshop, Cincinnati, Ohio, August 13, 2016.

For those of us called to the vowed life, there is freedom and glowing joy in presenting our lives to Jesus in a quite final, complete way, as embodied in St. Ignatius' *Suscipe*: "Take, Lord, receive, all my liberty, my memory, understanding, my entire will."[5] Our lives single-heartedly are about Jesus' saving mission, who meets our fidelity with faithfulness beyond comprehension. Do we grasp the enormity of the responsibility and possibility in our vows?

The context in which I bring my total self-gift to religious life is complex and distressing. The world is wrought with unspeakable violence. There are appalling numbers of displaced people and heart-wrenching destruction of Earth. Small numbers of wealthy people rule society as the gap between rich and poor expands. Trafficking and abuse turn human beings into commodities and objects. Many among us are hungry and hurting.

In the United States, racism persists and hate crimes terrorize while many in the majority choose denial and silence. Immigrants and refugees find not welcome but the sentiment of "no room in the inn." A cavernous ideological divide impedes the "one nation, indivisible," that our pledge expresses. Mainstream culture favors greed, materialism, and instant gratification. Sex is not sacred but an empty instinct sprawled across movie screens and magazines. Technology, with all its wondrous impacts, contributes to constant noise and diminished depth of relationship.[6]

Now is not the time to be wishy-washy. The world needs radical people, people who are rooted in the mission of Jesus Christ and given unabashedly for the transformation of society. Women religious must be those people.

[5] "Christ Our Life." Suscipe Prayer Saint Ignatius of Loyola, accessed March 24, 2017, http://www.loyolapress.com/our-catholic-faith/prayer/traditional-catholic-prayers/saints-prayers/suscipe-prayer-saint-ignatius-of-loyola.

[6] See Susan Francois, "Religious Life in a Time of Fog," pp. 182–203.

The following sections will explore how our religious vows embody Jesus' mission of love for this particular time and place.[7] There will be overlap, as the vows intrinsically intertwine. I hope these reflections lead us to frank conversations and courageous discernment about how God calls women religious to live radically today. All of our charisms, though richly different, point to Jesus as our driving force.[8] When we vow Jesus' mission together, we can indeed be energy of transformation and seeds of the reign of God. It is essential for our time.

Celibacy and Mission

I never thought I would be writing about the beauty of the vow of celibacy. During my discernment years, I resented celibacy. I saw it as part of the package—the necessary sacrifice alongside the aspects of religious life that drew me. Watching friends walk down the aisle in my twenties surfaced a sting in my heart, a longing for the kind of love I'd been introduced to through various romantic relationships but would never experience in marriage.

Many find it baffling that a young woman of this day would forgo not only marriage but also sex for her entire life. It's a rare choice in a society that portrays sex as the fulfillment of all human desire, a society of which I am a product. As I grew up, sex-drenched media infiltrated me and left residue of illusion in my bloodstream. I spent my teenage years seeking validation in relationships with men. Subconsciously, I staked my own identity on whether or not I was loved by a partner. I knew the relationships were missing something, but I figured I simply hadn't found the "right" one yet. Imagine my heart-

[7] For theological, anthropological reflections on the vows, see Juliet Mousseau, "Theological Anthropology and the Vows of Poverty, Chastity, and Obedience," pp. 31–46.

[8] See Mary Perez, "Local and Global: Charism of Religious Life Today," pp. 67–81.

ache when, at a more mature point in my life, I met the man I had been waiting for, but something inside nagged, declaring that it still wasn't enough. My abdomen lurched in pain as I felt the call to let go of that relationship and move into religious life.

Now I know that celibacy is not a cutting off but a flourishing. It was never about "giving up" love; it was about living into all-encompassing love that would feel restricted in a marriage of two people. Jesus' commitment to celibacy freed him to be uniquely God's instrument. Raising a family ultimately would have detracted from the forward-moving energy he knew was all for mission. And so it is for me. Somehow, my heart has been made to hold the world. The love I yearn for is big, and deep, and universal. Of course, all people are driven by this yearning for God's love. The difference is that I, as a woman religious, feel it imperative to make that kind of love the primary focus and force of my life. My heart pounds with awe when I ponder the power of groups of women vowing such devotion to a world in need. Celibacy, like all the vows, is mission. We don't vow it out of a warped glorification of virginity but because of what it makes possible: further incarnation of the reign of God.

Celibacy is about true human connection and mature relationship, both of which our world lacks. Multitudes flounder through life, never knowing real intimacy. Rampant independence governs; we have forgotten how to rely on one another and how to work together. On the contrary, Jesus was a person who genuinely encountered others. He peered into people tenderly, and he revealed himself to others, too. He journeyed in community, always figuratively and literally walking with people. Yes, Jesus slipped away for private prayer and communion with his *Abba*, a nonnegotiable in all of our lives of mission, but he operated predominantly in relationship.

The kind of relationship modeled in Jesus is an important contribution to our hurting world. In fact, intentional community is imperative to celibacy and mission today. As is true in my experience, women coming to religious life today seek to live love-in-action in community. Don Bisson says, nobody is coming to "trade an apartment, a car, and a paycheck for an apartment, a car, and a paycheck."[9] The difference is doing it together. When we commit to live together as adult women under one roof, we challenge the prevailing paradigm. Communion is possible. What's more, although it may not always be pretty, we know that negotiating differences and sticking with it helps us grow and makes us better ministers. Walking with people in the rawness of their lives, we need the skills of compassion and deep relationship.[10] Although we don't have families of our own, we will be much more authentic if we, too, are working out messiness in our homes.

Also urgently important for our vow today is radical hospitality. Intentional community allows us to create spaces of welcome where love can be deeply shown and shared. In the middle of the twentieth century, the strength of religious life was the large numbers that allowed us to go out and permeate the structures of society, reaching a lot of people. For apostolic communities, no matter how big, our charism will always include the call to be "out there." However, the strength of our smallness will be the capacity to focus and to build communities that are centers of mission and immersion—places where seekers are invited in.

The spirit of community and hospitality is what got me to religious life. As a discerner in my early twenties, I went to live with Sisters of Charity Carol, Janet, and Peggy at Casa Caridad on the US-Mexico border. I knew so few sisters that I needed to experience how religious life felt on a day-to-day basis. As these three sisters have done for many young women over their twenty-five years on the border, they invited me to live and serve with them, no strings attached. Watching them cook together in our kitchen, or tenderly embrace a child, or

[9] Don Bisson, Audio CD "Intentional Community," Workshop Series #49.

[10] See Amanda Carrier, "The Compassion the World Needs Now," pp. 147–58.

speak out for justice, a flicker in my heart grew into a flame. As we grew in relationship, I grew in awareness of my vocation. Celibacy, lived well, attracts others to join us in mission, whether as sisters, associates, or collaborators of all kinds. Collaboration is key for transformative mission.

Three fellow sisters and I have now created Visitation House, another intentional community with extra bedrooms for discerners or those needing shelter. Our shared vow of celibate love allowed us to say "yes" to the afternoon phone call that brought our young Honduran friends into our home. Each month, we host a meal and evening of reflection for young adult women. We are prepared to welcome women for longer periods of time so they can catch the community spirit and try it on for themselves like I did at Casa Caridad. And of course, when God calls, we will continue to have "room in the inn" for the homeless and refugee.

Celibacy propels us to be leaders in the kind of inclusivity and bridge building desperately needed in our world. Ronald Rohlheiser posits in *The Holy Longing* that the ache of sleeping alone was an important part of Jesus' solidarity with the poor.[11] He identified with the struggles of the oppressed and lived shockingly close to those his society denounced and disregarded. Our vow of celibacy today urges us to similar prophetic action of inclusivity and relationship with those who are left out. In the face of poverty, hatred, violence, and racism, our title, "sister," indicates a keen awareness of the kinship of all. It impels us to collaboration with immigrants, refugees, indigenous peoples, people of color, prisoners, homosexual and transgendered people, and more in changing the systems that keep them down. Sometimes, it might mean being on the front lines of advocacy. Sometimes, it might mean getting out of the way so that others have a place at the table and can speak for themselves.

[11] Ronald Rohlheiser, *The Holy Longing: A Search for a Christian Spirituality* (New York: Doubleday, 1999), 207–8.

Celibacy demands working for right relationship, and it should start at home. Within our congregations, we must be honest about where we fail to be inclusive. Do we work to end division among religious communities? In most cases, we stay in our ideological corners as staunchly as society at large.[12] Do we honor and nurture the multiculturalism that we know is our future?[13] In many cases, we operate on autopilot out of a white, European-influenced paradigm. We say that all are welcome, but we cling to the way we've always done things. Do we admit our complicity in racism? For our mission to be authentic, we've got to examine our own biases and closed-mindedness.

In all areas of our lives, women religious must be bridge builders. Jesus ate with lepers and showed preferential love for the poor, but he built relationships with all. Living at the US-Mexico border taught me this concretely. A few times a week, we loaded up the car and crossed the checkpoint into Mexico, entering into the reality of cardboard homes and drug shootings on dusty neighborhood streets. After our day at Proyecto Santo Niño, a Sisters of Charity center for kids with special needs, we returned. Our US passports were our unearned ticket to the privileged, comfortable side of the border wall. The contrast was dizzying, but we knew we had to straddle both worlds.

Now, ministering in a traditionally white Cincinnati parish with a newly flourishing Guatemalan population, the call to build bridges is strong. Last year, I began hosting story-sharing potluck meals in the parish house. English and Spanish speakers alike come to share food and conversation with the help of interpreters at each table. Over tamales and German potato

[12] See Virginia Herbers, "Communities in Communion: Shifting into New Life," pp. 1–17.

[13] See Madeleine Miller, "Creating a Culture of Encounter: Finding Life in Intergenerational and Intercultural Community," pp. 110–27; Christa Parra, "The Bridges I Cross and Las Hermanas Who Built Them," pp. 128–46; and Thuy Tran, "Searching for Identity through the Paschal Mystery," pp. 96–109.

salad, Eucharist happens. They see each other as human beings. Encounter slowly chips away at prejudice and ignorance, but it will take time.

Standing in the tension is where my vows call me to be. Fellow writer Teresa Maya[14] told me that I have a "bilingual corazón." Isn't this the truth of celibacy? We have hearts made to hold everybody and spirits bent on creating a world that does, too. Radical celibacy is essential to mission for today.

Poverty and Mission

It is the age-old question: how can we dare profess a vow of poverty when we know that we are far from being economically poor?

My first real encounter with poverty came through two years as an international volunteer. I lived in community with other young people on the outskirts of Guayaquil, Ecuador, where the streets were dirt, the houses were small and frail, and the people were resilient. Each of us recent college graduates spent our days working at local outreach organizations, and in our free time, we grew close to our neighbors. Saturday mornings usually found me in stifling kitchens, talking with faith-filled women about how things looked from their vantage point. Their openness taught me about my privilege, and I grew in just anger at unjust systems.

Jenny, a favorite Ecuadorian neighbor, threw me a zinger over a plate of rice one day. "I want to know something. You come down here for a while, you live like us in our poor neighborhood, and then you go back. We're still here. It happens year after year," she pronounced, head cocked and eyes inquisitive. "So what?"

I gulped, and I still do. The question confronts all of us who profess a vow of poverty. Sometimes we say that it is an orientation of the heart, a stance and way of being in the world.

[14] See Teresa Maya, "Called to Leadership: Challenges and Opportunities for Younger Members in Leadership," pp. 159–81.

Sometimes, it is simplicity and frugality. Sometimes, we talk about creating an alternate economy in which all is gift and all is shared. So what? What does it mean for the world and the ongoing manifestation of the kingdom if we do this?

I wrestle with these questions. For the sake of full disclosure, the vow of poverty remains the most elusive to me; I struggle to put words around it. Across congregations and within them, there are a myriad of differing interpretations and expressions of poverty. Clearest to me right now is the motivation for the vow as it relates to mission. At the core is our conviction that no one should be poor. Our rich tradition of Catholic social teaching affirms the dignity of each life, and human beings cannot be fulfilled with basic necessities missing. Like Jesus, we must cultivate an unapologetic laser beam focus on healing wounds and upsetting oppression. I don't know if I will ever be able to answer Jenny's question with full integrity, but I must give my life trying.

In a time of great inequality, our vow of poverty calls us, in addition to relationship, to physical presence "on the margins." The places that most people would choose to avoid? Those places beckon us! When my current community mates and I were searching for a home for "Visitation House," a friend told us about a possible rental. Pulling up the driveway, we noticed rows of nicely trimmed lawns and well-kept houses, indicating a quiet, middle-class lane. Even before touring, we knew it wouldn't work. Location is vital in our living of poverty today. The house that God eventually directed us to is in a mixed income neighborhood at the same time rich in diversity and plagued by poverty and crime. I told my cousin, a police officer, about our new home, and he scrunched his nose in incredulity. "Are you kidding me? That's where all the action is." "Exactly," I replied.

Our religious communities are blessed with inspiring women who have shown us a "vocation of location."[15] They

[15] Kyle Kramer, *A Time to Plant: Life Lessons in Work, Prayer, and Dirt* (Notre Dame, IN: Sorin, 2010).

stayed in countries where their lives were in danger because they identified so much with the struggle of the people among whom they served. It wasn't risk *por gusto*, just for the heck of it, but for mission. The purest expression of the vow of poverty as related to mission, then, might be the raw realization that not even my life is my own. In humility and simplicity, our only aim is moving forward the reign of God. Yes, conversations about house budgets help us to steward wisely and recognize our shared possessionlessness,[16] but the most compelling living of the vow of poverty seems to be based in an utter, all-encompassing surrender.

I dare say that women coming to religious life today know a lot about surrender, in different ways than preceding generations. Unlike our senior sisters' stories of coming right out of high school, women now enter at various stages of life, often after beginning a career and owning property. Previous experience of financial independence informs our transition to the "gift economy"[17] of religious life. It can be difficult to adjust to a system of accountability and shared resources after living autonomously. At the same time, many women coming have lived the "rat race" and reject it; we are looking for something deeper. We know how our act of surrender can evangelize the world. For this reason, women today come ready to pitch our tents amid destitution. We know we may forfeit comfort or stability. Even though we might struggle with it, we long to sacrifice our wants for others' needs. In poverty, we loosen our grasp on security and control, and we encounter the everflowing strength of God within.

Our vow of poverty says a resounding "no" to the dominant economy, to greed and exploitation, to excessive consumerism and a system that oppresses producers. Perhaps most important for the time in which we live, we can denounce the raping of earth that fuels a fearfully selfish, unsustainable lifestyle in

[16] Sandra Schneiders, *Buying the Field: Catholic Religious Life in Mission to the World* (New York: Paulist, 2013), 232.

[17] Ibid., 233.

the richest countries of the world. However, if we are to be people of mission, saying and denouncing cannot stop at our lips. We can proclaim congregational stances until we're blue in the face, but unless our vow takes flesh through investment and action, we're hypocrites.

As we live in community and create centers of hospitality, the vow of poverty urges us to be close to earth, to use only the resources we need, to cultivate our own food, to compost, to move toward alternative energy in the places we dwell, and more. We couple living simply with advocacy for policies that redistribute wealth and upset the balance of power. As we invite people into our spaces, we should be modeling green living and green activism as mission. We should be leading the way to incite change if we want a future for "children who are now growing up."[18]

The vow of poverty insists that the only claim on us be Jesus' mission. Acutely aware of our oneness with and responsibility to the whole human family and all of creation, our poverty must be a wholehearted surrender. We vow poverty toward a world where no one is poor. We must do whatever it takes for justice and peace, as Jesus did in the stark poverty of the cross.

Obedience and Mission

I was sitting on a quiet beach during my first year in Ecuador when the notion of a call to religious life first slipped into my consciousness: You should be a nun. It was a voice, not that I heard out loud, but inside of me. At first, I tried to stifle the alarming new thought, but it only persisted and intensified. My frequent prayer became an angry and reluctant, "Why me?" I didn't know a single young nun! Over several years and with the help of many friends and mentors, I came to peace

[18] Francis, *Laudato Si'*, Encyclical on Care for Our Common Home, 160, accessed March 24, 2017, http://w2.vatican.va/content/francesco/en/encyclicals/documents/papa-francesco_20150524_enciclica-laudato-si.html.

and eventually joy with the fact that my life would not be as I had once dreamed. As my experience of religious life deepens, I find myself whispering a different kind of "Why me?" It is wonder-filled gratitude that I get to participate in Jesus' mission so profoundly. In vowing obedience, we know that God's call is not always easy, but it is worth it.

Jesus' utter obedience to the divine will within impelled him, at all costs, to create a reign of love and justice. Our vow, then, is one of absolute compliance with the kingdom. In her 2016 address to the LCWR,[19] Pat Farrell wisely offered that when it comes to Jesus' mission and our religious lives, "Nothing matters more." Obedience encompasses deep listening for this mission, both in our own hearts and collectively. When we vow obedience, we commit to a lifetime of pressing our ears earnestly to the heart of God to find out what piece of the great work is ours to do.

Authentic living of obedience means risk. In these extreme times, I sense that the vow of obedience will call us to extreme places. And the grace to respond generously is imprinted in us by the God who calls us. Newer, younger religious come to obedience with willingness to risk in our bones. Discerning religious life in this society has prepared us for uncommon paths and letting go; as stated in previous sections, we choose it because of its radical potential.

When I entered the world of religious life in my twenties, yearning for mission, I was startled to find how much emphasis can be placed on salary. It merits to be said that my congregation and others offer subsidies for sisters called to work in low- or no-paying ministries. But my honest reaction to that as a young discerner was consternation. "Wait a minute," I thought. "Sisters have to get special permission or fill out

[19] Pat Farrell, "Leading from the Allure of Holy Mystery: Contemplation and Transformation" (Assembly of the Leadership Conference of Women Religious, Atlanta, Georgia, August 9–13, 2016).

extra applications and evaluations so that they can work with the poor? Isn't that why we become sisters in the first place?"

As has been written many times, the way women religious minister looks and will look different from the way previous cohorts served. Our vow of obedience demands that we follow the Spirit's lead. In many cases, God seems to be urging us to more flexible ministries that offer freedom to respond to needs and engage in pressing social issues. The most critical contributions women religious can make at this moment may not come attached to a large paycheck and benefits. We should not fear this! I understand that there are real needs and considerations that must be made to sustain our communities, but if a desire for security takes precedent and impedes our prophetic response to needs, who have we become? Our vow of obedience drives us to look outward, letting the mission poured into us through Christ be that which dictates who we are, where we go, and what we do.

Mission is demanding. I know that even as we are driven by the question, "What would Jesus do?" we aren't Jesus. A wise spiritual director once told me, "Honey, the Savior already came, and it isn't you." In this sense, balance is essential to our lives. Burnout is a real thing. This is where discernment is indispensable; it keeps us from being unhealthy or busy for the sake of being busy. At the same time, we must not let our inclination to self-care obstruct our mission instinct. We must be willing to be interrupted and stretched beyond our own perceived ability and resources when mission calls. We have to step up and stick our necks out if the Spirit nudges. Maybe we'll cross the line, but playing it safe would be more of a tragedy. As T. S. Eliot writes, "Only those who will risk going too far can possibly find out how far one can go."[20]

We need only look to our congregational roots for examples of radical commitment to the vow of obedience. Our earliest

[20] T. S. Eliot, preface to Harry Crosby, *Transit of Venus: Poems* (Paris: Black Sun, 1931), ix.

founders did gritty and thankless but valiant work, sometimes around the clock. Their strategic plan was a response to the needs God placed in front of them. Small numbers and uncertain finances did not prevent them from making transformational impacts. I know they had to be creative about how to raise funds, and they had to be wise and prudent in administering the funds they had. I know they went without, sometimes surviving treacherous situations. Thinking about such sacrifice makes me squirm, but I know deep within me that, at all costs, mission must come first and maintenance second. That is obedience.

Our commitment to mission at all costs has sometimes led to tension throughout the history of religious life, particularly with the Church hierarchy. Being in relationship with those on the margins, standing on the side of the poor, and obeying deep communal discernment give us a perspective both challenging and essential to the universal Church. Pope Francis has affirmed this prophetic aspect of our global charism, asserting that "prophecy makes noise, uproar, some say a mess."[21] It may cause strife, but we embrace the prophetic nature of our life because we know it moves forward the mission of Jesus. We love our Church and simultaneously want it to continue to evolve for the better.

Ironically, even as we have been prophets in our Church, religious communities tend to suppress the prophets in our own congregations. We are humans, and as such, we are guilty at times of replicating the kind of behavior we criticize. This can be true in our congregational response to young women religious, who today enter as adults with rich life, ministry, and discernment experience. Sometimes, when we young sisters bring forth ideas that spring from deep listening to the

[21] Anthony Spadaro, "A Big Heart Open to God: An Interview with Pope Francis," *America Magazine*, September 30, 2013, accessed May 11, 2017, http://www.americamagazine.org/faith/2013/09/30/big-heart-open-god-interview-pope-francis.

Spirit, they meet resistance or closed doors. Congregations must be careful not to dismiss our vision or deflate our enthusiasm. It is possible, as we know from our experience with the institutional Church, to both deeply love and reverence a tradition and at the same time want to change things about it that are no longer helpful or add things that will help it to thrive.

Being true to the vow of obedience requires openness and courage in all of us. Younger women religious must trust our voices.[22] It is not that our voices are the only ones that matter, but they can easily get drowned out by those of much larger cohorts. When we sense the Spirit's unmistakable prompting in us, it would be wrong to be silent, even when what we speak may cause tension. Leadership teams and formation directors must trust our voices, too, and guide us with a spirit not of control or fear but of joy and hope. Particularly in formation programs, we have made strides but still regress to outdated models that stifle true obedience. We must listen to each individual woman and collaboratively craft a program that allows her to become more truly herself[23] and prepares her for life as a contemporary apostolic religious. Formation should point to mission. In our collective obedience, we must keep these questions before us: What will help each woman be who God calls her to be, and what will help us build the reign of God in our day?

Jesus' selfless fidelity to the kingdom led him to unsettling places. In his humanness, he weighed and felt the weight of the probable consequences to his prophetic actions, evidenced by his prayerful agony in the garden. However, he discerned sincerely and chose to trust. Obedience for mission requires of us this same commitment to a lifetime of discernment. Sometimes our seeking might point to mission that leaves us trembling in quiet and confounded mystery like Mary's "How can

[22] Maya, "Called to Leadership," pp. 159–81.

[23] See Desiré Findlay, "In the Garden of God's Love: Cultivating a Vocation," pp. 82–95.

this be?" at the Annunciation (Luke 1:34). At other times, it might fill us with joyful awe and ardent gratitude like Elizabeth's "How does this happen to me?" at the Visitation (Luke 1:43). In whatever situation, we know that the posture in our innermost being is one of "yes." Jesus' profound fidelity to his mission led to resurrection. Our authentic discernment and vulnerable trust will lead to great good for the world that God created and loves so much.

Wisdom figures have shared with me that the vow of obedience is the foundational vow; it is the unconditional offering of our lives that allows us to live celibacy and poverty with integrity. The vow of obedience, then, is the fount of mission for every generation. We have the Gospels as our compass and a deep commitment to listening to God, one another, and the cries of the poor as our map. If we are open, the Spirit will show us how to live religious life in the present and well into the future.[24]

Conclusion

A few weeks after our Honduran guests left Visitation House for the shelter, her case worker texted me a photo of the two of them at the airport. The young girl had decided to return to her home country with the baby in order to avoid more complications in the United States. Knowing the instability of Honduras, my heart sank, but what could I do? I smiled through my tears at the two beautiful faces, images of God. She wore my shirt and a backpack; he cuddled up to her with his hair slicked over and his pudgy legs protruding from tiny new gym shoes. She looked so brave. I savored the picture and said a prayer for them. Then, in my heart, I entrusted them to God's hands. I had to let them go, but I knew God wouldn't.

[24] See Deborah Warner, "'Traveler, Your Footprints, Are the Only Road, Nothing Else': Reflections on the Future of Women's Religious Life," pp. 204–21.

We women religious inherit a precious, powerful gift in our vocation. It is a gift not to be guarded for us but shared for the good of all. We live the vows the best we can, and eventually, as with our Honduran friends, we let go. What is true about the vows for me at this particular moment in time might be insufficient in just ten years, according to the signs of the times and the vision of new members that God will continue to call after me. I know I will someday be one of the older, wisdom-figure sisters, learning to live mission differently, perhaps from a nursing home. I will be called to let go of the way I did things and trust the young to carry the work forward as God guides them.

It is only natural that the way we live the vows is both ever-changing and ever the same.[25] The times are unruly and unpredictable; therefore, mission must adapt. Our constant is Jesus Christ. Come what may, women religious will always be deeply connected to our abiding roots in him. Although the expression of our vows will surely and appropriately evolve, they remain timeless channels of divine love; the pursuit of the reign of God transcends the ages. What a gift; what a responsibility! I pray that, individually and communally, we can be zealous in living celibacy, poverty, and obedience in our time and place. If we do this, with God's grace, we will continue to bring radical transformation to the world. The mission of Jesus and the "of-course-ness" in our hearts will not lead us astray.

[25] See Sarah Kohles, "Something Old, Something New: Hannah's Vow Touches the Lives of Women Religious Today," pp. 18–30.

Local and Global: Charism of Religious Life Today

Mary Therese Perez, OP

A picnic lunch amidst verdant trees in Prouhile, France, remains my favorite meal from summer 2016. Though the fresh bread and soft cheese linger in memory, what still captures my heart is the profound encounter with my Dominican family from around the world. I was one of a hundred young Dominican sisters and friars on a pilgrimage in the footsteps of St. Dominic. Every element of the journey—the places, the people, the prayer, the preaching—touched something in me and deepened my sense of being Dominican. It was that July afternoon in Prouhile that made real the profound relationships available in sharing charism.

As I sat with a nun from Spain, apostolic sisters from Colombia, Gambia, and the United States, and a Little Sister of the Community of the Lamb, we shared stories in English and Spanish of what it is like to be a Dominican in our different realities. Breaking bread in the place where St. Dominic first gathered women in 1206, we encountered each other as daughters of Dominic, inheritors of a mission to preach God's truth of love. My heart responded to their stories because, in them, I heard the same desire to pray, preach, and love that lives in me. In our diversity, I saw unity, and I felt connected as sisters, even though we were practically strangers. This moment resonates with my hopes for the future of women religious: to be rooted in our charisms and connected in a global sisterhood that honors diversity and seeks unity to meet the world's most pressing needs.

Global Sisterhood

We know that religious life today thrives in a setting of collaboration. Crossing the boundaries of orders and congregations, contemporary women religious live a global sisterhood, "created by partnerships—not only in what we do, in our works, but also in our relationships—how we think, plan, organize, learn, believe and hope."[1] These partnerships are animated by the unique manifestations of our charismatic witness and enlivened by the practices communities have developed to follow the Gospel and address the world's needs. Through her work in the Conrad N. Hilton Foundation, Sr. Rosemarie Nassif, SSND, has witnessed the vitality of a global sisterhood that is united across diverse realities. She proposes that focusing on the development of this global sisterhood will strengthen the work of global human development.

I am excited to live a religious life that thrives in partnerships generated by mutuality and concern for the world. My experience in Prouhile and on pilgrimage with Dominicans from around the world gives me hope for such a future. I experienced a taste of what Joan Chittister, OSB, describes as a "felt oneness of heart and wholeness of spirit and common care for the people all of us serve."[2] As I engaged in conversa-

[1] Rosemary Nassif, "Supporting the Emergence of Global Sisterhood," (presentation, Plenary Assembly of International Union of Superiors General, Rome, Italy, May 9–13, 2016), accessed March 1, 2017, http://www.internationalunionsuperiorsgeneral.org/wp-content/uploads/2016/01/Rosemary-Nassif-CN-Hilton-Foundation.pdf. 5.

[2] Joan Chittister, "The Global Sisterhood: Nowhere and Everywhere," *Global Sisters Report*, April 23, 2014, accessed February 16, 2017, http://globalsistersreport.org/column/where-i-stand/trends/global-sisterhood-nowhere-and-everywhere-381.

tions with the other sisters on pilgrimage, I sensed a unity in our desire to preach through our service. I also experience this unity when we gather as sisters in Giving Voice. A grassroots organization for women religious under fifty, Giving Voice offers a space for younger sisters to encounter each other in unity of spirit and heart. When we gather in large or small groups formally and informally, we find a common desire to offer ourselves as Jesus' followers committed to building the kingdom of God. With my sisters in Giving Voice, I experience a "global charism," a charism animated by discipleship and marked by a commitment "to a life of spirituality, simplicity and sacrifice of the self for the sake of the poor."[3]

In getting to know sisters in a variety of apostolic communities in the United States, I have come to see that each of us deeply identifies with the charism of our communities. We resonate with the vision of our foundresses and founders. This vision animates our call to follow the Gospel. Our charisms are sources of vitality, inspiration, and motivation. They help us to tune in, to lean into the call of the Gospel. They are the lens through which we focus to encounter and serve the world around us.

I view our charisms as places of encounter, not boundaries. In our relationships with sisters across charism families, we have opportunities to expand our worldview. We can share with each other the rich vision of the world that our charisms offer. In the interactions between charisms of specific orders and the "global charism" of religious life, we enrich the meaning of our own congregation's charism.

What Is Charism?

Our charisms are profound gifts from God to the church and to the world. Like all of God's gifts, they are freely given, wrapped in Mystery, and overflowing in fecundity. They are "particular facets of the likeness of God that people or groups

[3] Ibid.

reflect in particular ways."[4] In living out our charisms, we help God become visible in our world. Our charisms are not ends in themselves—we don't live them in order to make them or our founders better known. Charisms always point to God.

The description of charism in *Finding the Treasure: Locating Catholic Religious Life in a New Ecclesial and Cultural Context* by Sandra Schneiders, IHM, offers a helpful framework for understanding the theological reality of charism. Drawing upon a definition of charism as "a grace given for the sake not only of the recipient but also and primarily for the upbuilding of the Church,"[5] Schneiders proposes four interrelated expressions, or "levels," of charism that are always at play. Her elucidation of these levels illustrates the polyvalence of the term "charism" and its use in describing the multifaceted reality of living religious life. First is that religious life is a gift from God to the church. Although mediated by human experience, religious life is of divine origin. For the second level, Schneiders goes on to write that this gift is lived in distinct forms of life that equate a charismatic reality. In exploring the distinctiveness of the contemplative and apostolic forms of religious life in North America, she proposes two alternate terms that highlight the nature of the lifestyle as defined by its "touchstone" for discernment: "stable monastic lifestyle" and "mobile ministerial lifestyle."[6] The third level of charism is that of the particular order or congregation. In this regard, she appeals not to the "charism of the founder," but to the ensuing deep story developed from the moment of founding throughout the community's history. The final level is that of the individual. Each individual has a vocation that is a charism, a gift of God for the sake of the church. These levels illustrate that charism is

[4] Mary Pellegrino, "Life on the Margins: Charismatic Principles for Modern Religious," *America Magazine*, October 16, 2013, accessed January 8, 2017, http://www.americamagazine.org/issue/life-margins.

[5] Sandra Schneiders, *Finding the Treasure: Locating Catholic Religious Life in a New Ecclesial and Cultural Context* (New York: Paulist, 2000), 283.

[6] Ibid., 305–6.

simultaneously lived as an ecclesial, communal, and personal reality.

To help us live our global sisterhood, we look to the unity that we share in the charism of religious life, Schneiders's first level. As a gift of God to the church, religious life provides a path for organizing our lives to focus on the God-quest.[7] In the God-quest we see our shared desire to manifest God in the joys and struggles of our lives and our world. Focusing on the giftedness of religious life allows us to understand that living charism is about stewarding God's gifts with a sense of gratitude and purpose. Then we grow into the sacredness of our shared purpose of making ourselves available for God's work.

Schneiders's framework also helps us understand that living the charism of religious life necessarily involves living the particularities of our chosen form of religious life, our community's deep stories, and our personal vocations. The third level, which Schneiders designates as the "ongoing deep narrative" of our communities deserves particular attention in fleshing out an understanding of charism. It is at this level that communities find their distinctive identities that have developed from their founding inspiration. The use of the term "deep narrative" places the focus of this identity on the historical process of development of the charism, moving away from a singular focus on the founding moment. Schneiders writes:

> It is not so much a full-blown vision at the moment of initiation that has worked itself out over the history of the group but it is the ongoing "deep narrative" developed throughout the community's history with its attendant myths and symbols, outstanding events and persons, struggles and triumphs, projects and challenges, that the group has been developing from its origins to the present that has become the inner heritage of each member down through the years, giving them a shared identity.[8]

[7] Ibid., 228–29.

[8] Ibid., 288.

With the companionship of the Spirit, our founders initiated a response to the world that has continued to take shape as ensuing generations leave their mark in this deep story. Our shared identity is found not solely in the lives of the founders but in the deep narrative that has developed through history.

Bernard Lee, SM, also writes about the distinction between the founding moments and the ensuing deep story. His sociological understanding of charism highlights the sociohistorical reality in which charism arises. For Lee, charism is contingent upon the particularities of time and place: "Charism is the social reality that provides the setting for a new religious order. It does not exist in the founding person alone, or in the followers, or in the aspirations of the age, or in the style of life proposed, but in the mutual complicity of all these together."[9] Lee is particular in his use of the word "charism," allowing it only to refer to the historical reality of time and place. Although I do not find this terminology helpful given common parlance of the word, I do find it useful to distinguish founding moments from the deep story.

The emphasis on the historical particularities of the founding moments implies that in order to understand my community's charism, I must understand the circumstances in which it came to life. It also tells me that if my community's charism is to be fully alive now, we must clearly understand our current context and its needs. Living our charism today is not about reliving the past but continuing and developing the deep story.

Surplus of Meaning

Reflecting on the continuation of deep story as the living of charism, Paul Ricouer's theory of surplus of meaning can be

[9] Bernard Lee, *The Beating of Great Wings: A Worldly Spirituality for Active, Apostolic Communities* (Mystic, CT: Twenty-Third Publications, 2004), 27.

helpful.[10] Although Ricouer's theory is rooted in written text, it offers useful ideas to help us mine the depths of meaning of our lived texts, the deep narratives of our charisms. Foundational to surplus of meaning is the theory of "ideal meaning." Ideal here does not refer to the best or optimal meaning, but rather to the objective standard by which we can judge a valid interpretation, or in the case of charism, a valid actualization of living charism.[11] The founding moments of our congregations offer us the shape of the charism. They begin a story that continues to develop. They provide the ideal meaning of the charism. But the founding moments are not just to be replicated in each new time and place. The distinctiveness of each new reality offers deeper, fuller meaning to the charism.

This idea of richer, fuller possibilities of meaning is Ricouer's idea of surplus of meaning. In Ricouer's theory, written text has semantic autonomy from its author and originating circumstances. Although the author penned the text, the text is distanced from the meaning that the author may have intended for the original audience.[12] This allows the text to mean more than it meant at its creation.[13] As such, there is never one correct interpretation of a text but many possibilities: "Texts are susceptible of endless new interpretations as different interpreters, with different questions and different backgrounds, interrogate the text."[14] All of these possibilities are the surplus of meaning. The text can mean more than it meant at its originating moment and more than it meant in a previous interpre-

[10] My understanding of Paul Ricouer comes from Sandra Schneiders, *The Revelatory Text: Interpreting the New Testament as Sacred Scripture* (Collegeville, MN: Liturgical Press, 1999). In particular, see chapter 3 for ideal meaning and chapters 4–5 for surplus of meaning. For a fuller treatment, see Paul Ricouer, *Interpretation Theory: Discourse and the Surplus of Meaning* (Fort Worth: Texas Christian University Press, 1976).

[11] Schneiders, *The Revelatory Text*, 92n22.

[12] Ibid., 153.

[13] Ibid.

[14] Ibid.

tation. But openness to endless new interpretations does not mean that anything goes. This is where the importance of ideal meaning comes into play. Ideal meaning helps gives shape to what is possible: we look to the ideal meaning of a text to see whether our interpretation is on the right track.

Each of our charisms has a surplus of meaning: each can mean more than it meant in its originating circumstance. As we live our charisms, we bring to life new meaning, richer meaning, than was present before. For example, my congregational foundress came to teach German immigrants in San Francisco; today my sisters not only teach but minister in pastoral and health care, the arts, and justice work in the United States and Mexico. Each of our communities has abundant examples of how the ministerial expressions of charism have developed since the founding moments. There is a dynamic interplay between those who live the charism and when and where they actualize it. Surplus of meaning enables us to see that our charisms will continue to develop and mean more than we have thought that they meant.

Deep Story

A global sisterhood will be strengthened by the intentional living of our congregational charisms and purposeful sharing of it with each other. As younger sisters who desire to do this well, it is important for us to know the deep stories of our charisms. In Ricouer's terms, we must understand the ideal meaning of our charism in order to live into its surplus of meaning.

Our foundresses could not have imagined the contexts in which we live today, and it takes careful historical work to understand the complexities of the times in which they lived. We are indebted to the historians of our communities for the profound gift of their work. As we consider the historical context, we ask: what did our founders emphasize as fundamental to their project? What in their living or teaching was the core to the life of the newly established community?

When I look to the founding moments of the Dominican family, I turn to St. Dominic's itinerant preaching of the Word and Truth, rooted in a communal life of prayer and study. The founding moments were not ones of formal plans, but moments of preaching and listening to the signs of the time. When I look to how I am living the Dominican charism today, I consider these questions as essential touchstones for the choices I make: How well I am engaged in my communal life of prayer, ministry, and sisterhood? Am I open to sharing and preaching the fruit of my contemplation? How aware am I of the realities of my neighborhood, city, state, country, and the world? As I ponder these questions, I realize that my context offers historical particularities that are distinct from Dominic's context. I preach God's love to teenage girls overwhelmed by unrelenting expectations of excellence and bombarded with a reality of social media that tears at their self-worth. The fruit of my contemplation takes shape in a confirmation class of teenagers from East Los Angeles who seek to glimpse God in the everyday moments of uncertainty and change. I also recognize the places for growth in my daily living, in my relationships, and in my study. Although my context differs from Dominic's, the shape of my preaching finds a touchstone of authenticity in the shape of his.

However, my preaching also differs in many ways from Dominic's. Primarily, I am a woman preacher, and in his time (and for many centuries of the Order) women were not itinerant preachers like the men. Does this mean that my preaching is invalid because there were not women preachers at the beginning of the order? No! The deep story that has developed since Dominic's time has given fuller meaning to the Dominican charism. The myriad narratives of apostolic women's congregations that came into being to meet the material and spiritual needs of God's people have added to the polyvalence of meaning in the deep story of the Dominican charism.

The particular stories of my congregation's beginning hold an essential place in my understanding of deep story. The stories of three brave, young, Dominican sisters traveling from

New York to the wild west of San Francisco in 1876 are foundational to my congregation's understanding of meeting needs in unexpected places. The stories of the faith and courage of my congregational foundress, Mother Maria Pia Backes, are always retold with awe and admiration. The ensuing deep story of preaching for the Dominican Sisters of Mission San Jose has taken shape in teaching and serving the young, the poor, and the vulnerable. Stories like my congregation's give a richness to the meaning of our charisms. We can all look to our charisms to see how they have been enriched in previously unforeseen ways by sisters who attended to the needs of their contexts. Our founding stories inspire us to meet God's call with faith and enthusiasm.

As I have learned stories of faith-filled women of my congregation who served the young, the poor, and the vulnerable, I have come to make these stories my own. The witness and bravery of my sisters in Mexico at the time of the Revolution, the dedicated service and humility of the sisters from Germany who spent their lives in the United States in kitchens and laundries, the devotion and prayer of my sister musicians and artists, and the untiring preaching of my sister educators, nurses, spiritual directors, chaplains, peace activists, justice workers—these stories all shape who I am becoming as a Dominican Sister of Mission San Jose. The witness to God's love in our stories continues to shape me and my vision as I look at the needs of the world.

Through our immersion in our deep stories as younger religious, we begin to see with the consciousness of our community and to notice how our lives might contribute to the continued telling of the story. We need to know where we have come from, including the difficulties and challenges our sisters have faced. We need to hear of the hopes and visions held at critical junctures in our history. It is equally important that our community hears our stories. They need to know where we have been and what has shaped us because the iterations of charism into the future will be mediated by our stories, our lives, our gifts.

It is critical that I speak to my community about my desire to serve God's people. I must share the stories that have shaped my life and brought me to this place of joining my life to the congregation's. Since my personal vocation is now a part of the charism of my community, I have a responsibility to share my gifts, my contemplation, and my deep story with my community. Through this process, I begin to join my story to the deep story of my community. In offering my story, my prayer, my service, and my gifts, I join in the sacred task of bringing my congregation's charism to life.

Hope

Living a global sisterhood necessitates that we live our charisms with enthusiasm and hope. If you are looking for hope for the future of religious life, you need only go so far as a newer member to find it in abundance. Communities with hopeful futures are in processes of claiming their identities, collaborating, and closely reading the signs of the times. Ted Dunn describes the elements of refounding that he distills from his experiences of accompanying congregations. In the process of communal refounding, communities commit to a "process of personal and communal conversion initiated in response to God's call to choose life."[15] Applicable here is the second element of Dunn's process: the reappropriation of charism. He writes that communities who desire to refound must "reclaim their authentic inner voice and act in accord with it."[16] I appreciate Dunn's understanding of charism as the community's inner voice.[17] To hear this inner voice, we must attend to our deep story, to the story that we are forming today, and to the hopes and vision we have for our stories tomorrow. Sometimes in these conversations, the voices of the newer and younger

[15] Ted Dunn, "Refounding Religious Life: A Choice for Transformational Change," *Human Development* 30, no. 3 (2009): 8.

[16] Ibid., 10.

[17] Ibid., 9.

can get lost in midst of the established authoritative voices. It is incumbent upon all of us to listen to each other's visions and discernment. Our deep stories will only continue to develop with attention to the personal charism and wisdom of all of our sisters. If we are to live into the surplus of meaning of our deep stories, we must heed the call of Mary Pellegrino, CJS, to go to the margins of our charisms.[18] In the margins, we will discover the gifts God is preparing for our futures, and together we can discern how we continue to offer our charisms today.

Our deep stories will continue to shape us, and we will continue to shape our stories. There is great hope in this continual growth and development of our charisms. How will we shape them together with gratitude and reverence? How will we be united in our charism of religious life?

Global and Local

Our future as women religious will be a global reality, marked by partnerships across congregations and international borders. To meet the needs of the world, this future calls us to live both globally and locally. The global realities of poverty and suffering implore us to bring forth all that we have and all that we are. In solidarity with the earth and its people, our sisterhood is "a dynamic global force"[19] that can affect the course of our world. Together, we can influence "not only the works of mercy, but the decisions, the policies, the distribution of aid, the local, national and international governments, [and] other religions in ways that everyone feel[s] loved, sought after and forgiven."[20] Through intentional collaboration, communication, and communion, we will develop a global sisterhood capable of meeting the world's most pressing needs.[21]

[18] Pellegrino, "Life on the Margins."

[19] Nassif, "Emergence of a Global Sisterhood," 5.

[20] Ibid., 6.

[21] Ibid., 5.

Each of us is called to action in creating a global sisterhood. We must commit to developing networks of relationships and collaborative ministry ventures. Our sisters in leadership are already forging bonds of interconnectedness that will shape our global future. In global charism families and in the International Union of Superiors General (UISG), congregational leaders are deeply engaged in global visioning and action. But it is not their work alone. This work belongs to us all. Locally, in our congregations, charism families, ministries, and relationships with other women religious, each of us can practice the skills necessary to interact at a global level. Our efforts in deep listening, contemplative dialogue, vulnerable sharing, wild dreaming, and mutual acceptance shape our readiness to engage in the unknown ahead.

Charism plays an integral role in the development of our global sisterhood. When we embrace God's gift of religious life for ourselves and for the world, we enter into communion with God and with each other. In this communion, we seek unity through honoring the diversity that each of us brings. Our diverse deep stories offer prophetic vision for embracing the God-quest and building the kingdom of God. Each deep story is a gift. Receiving these gifts from each other deepens our sisterhood and enriches the meaning of our own charisms. The surplus of meaning available in our charisms allows us to receive one another's deep stories without fear. Cherishing the profound faith and daring witness of other charisms offers fuller possibilities of meaning for our own. Our global sisterhood will find strength and vitality in the mutual sharing of our deep stories, as we live into the surplus of meaning of our charisms.

Engaging in true partnership offers an important path for living into this surplus of meaning. In her address to the UISG Plenary Assembly, Carol Zinn, SSJ, articulates the stances necessary for our global sisterhood:

> In order for a collaborative effort to upgrade as it were to a partnership, the very goal trying to be achieved needs to be

> mutually discerned and the resources, all of them, need to be "put on the table" and offered with no strings attached. And the outcome needs to emerge and unfold and develop as the partnership evolves. The need for flexibility, error, change of direction, shift in planning, and even the presence of failure demands a freedom, courage and fearlessness beyond what many of us are used to offering.[22]

It is incumbent upon us to share with each other from places of mutuality and flexibility, courage and fearlessness. We enter into these partnerships to mutually discern our actions and allow the outcomes to unfold. If we engage in true partnerships, we will find ourselves moving into the margins of our charisms. These partnerships will show us the freedom and fecundity available in the surplus of meaning of our charisms.

As a newer, younger religious, I have experienced religious life as a rich web of relationships. The sustaining relationships in my congregation, the inspiring friendships in Giving Voice, and the hopeful connections in the Dominican Family nourish the surplus of meaning of my personal vocation. These relationships will continue to shape my deep story and the deep story that we are creating together in our global sisterhood.

As consecrated religious, we know the importance and value of our congregational charisms and the global charism of religious life. Both are sources of our identity, our strength, and our witness. They motivate us to live more faithfully to the call of the Gospel, to open our hearts more radically to the people of God, to live more freely with mercy and acceptance. As we live into the surplus of meaning of our charisms, may our global sisterhood be united in the richness of our diversity.

[22] Carol Zinn, "Crossing the Threshold: Weaving Global Solidarity for the Life of the World," (presentation, Plenary Assembly of International Union of Superiors General, Rome, Italy, May 9-13, 2016), accessed March 1, 2017, http://www.internationalunionsuperiorsgeneral.org/wp-content/uploads/2016/04/Pl-2016_-Carol-Zinn_ENG.pdf, 11-12.

May our charisms inspire us to meet the world's most pressing needs with hopefulness and expectation in the abundance and vitality of religious life, God's gift for us and the world.

In the Garden of God's Love: Cultivating a Vocation

Desiré Findlay, CSSF

"Discovering vocation does not mean scrambling toward some prize just beyond my reach but accepting the treasure of true self I already possess. Vocation does not come from a voice out there calling me to be something I am not. It comes from a voice in here calling me to be the person I was born to be, to fulfill the original selfhood given me at birth by God." (Thomas Merton)

The Seed

So often I have heard women say that before they entered religious life they asked themselves the question, "Is this all there is?" I asked that same question. We ask because we get tired of our routines. We get tired of momentary happiness and having to achieve more every time we reach a specific goal. "Really?" we ask. "Is this all there is?" Pieces of our lives are full of promise—scholarships or hard-earned job titles—but the question remains. We feel that there has to be a greater purpose, a greater reason for working so hard and giving so much of ourselves. We ask the question, and then God so happily leans over and whispers, "Nope, this is *not* all there is."

I didn't know how much of myself was missing until pieces of me started showing up. They began to appear as I began saying "yes" to God. I began saying "yes" to different types of events such as retreats and pilgrimages. I began saying "yes" to people who strengthened my spiritual life. I said "yes" to time in adoration, "yes" to daily Mass, and "yes" to changing my fast-paced lifestyle. I didn't know I was answering any sort of special call or that God was even calling me in the first place. It was simply an energy stirring from a hidden place within me, and when I felt that energy, I would sway with it and my feet would follow. That energy, I discovered, was God. It was God guiding me to a vocation that would change my life and shape my very identity.

I had lots of ideas concerning what I wanted to be when I grew up. I think my earliest plan was to become an astronaut. I loved looking at the stars and scanning the sky for the constellations whose names were like magic to me. The moon was my favorite nightlight. By sixth grade I had a telescope so I could view its surface and feel closer to its beauty. I wanted to experience zero gravity and "fly" like all those other brave humans who had broken through the barrier of space and time. Then my affections turned toward our fuzzy friends and I decided I wanted to be a veterinarian. I wanted to be around cats, dogs, and all sorts of creatures as often as possible. Throughout my youth I owned cats, dogs, a bearded dragon, a parrot, a rabbit, gerbils, hamsters, and even hermit crabs. I figured becoming a veterinarian would provide me with endless puppy cuddles and kisses. Eventually, I made a choice as to what I would study, and I chose teaching. I enjoyed my college courses and dreamt, like most aspiring teachers, that I would change the world. I thought of all the possibilities behind the theories. I drew pictures of the ideal classroom and confidently scribbled ideas for interactive activities and lessons.

One fine day, in the midst of all my planning, I received an invitation from a friend. She told me about a pilgrimage she had walked during the summer. I had never even heard of a pilgrimage, but the way she spoke of the culture and the community made me want to be a part of whatever it was. I agreed to go without even asking any questions, and soon enough I was signed up to walk one hundred miles the following summer. One hundred miles led to three hundred more as I signed up for the pilgrimage another three years in a row. I met women who were legitimately in love with God and who wanted to maintain a relationship with him. There were teenagers on the pilgrimage, married women in their thirties, forties and fifties, and retired women who made the sacrifice of energy for their families. Their appreciation of the Mass, their strong prayer lives, their devotion to their families and to one another all inspired me. I wanted to find a way to live that every day.

When I first signed up for the pilgrimage I did not know it was a pilgrimage for vocations. We were praying for happy and holy vocations to the priesthood, religious life, and married life. It turned out that a couple of the women I walked with were women religious. I learned that they belonged to the Congregation of the Sisters of Saint Felix (or Felician Sisters), and after the pilgrimage I began to spend more time with them. I spent time with their community in prayer; we exchanged laughter and stories; I attended retreats with them, and they shared their wisdom with me. All the while God was quietly working within me. I started spending time on my own in prayer and could finally see how empty my life really was. I was on a dance team for a semiprofessional basketball team at the time, but my love for dance and who I was as a person never made it to the court. I had fun performing, but there was no point to it. During my time with the sisters I came to understand that my gifts, my interests, even my very life could have a purpose. I wondered why I had been wasting my time and decided that this place of awakening was the place for me. This community of women who had helped to stir my sleeping soul, they were the place for me.

The Roots

I had learned about the "honeymoon" phase somewhere along the line in conversations with my aunts and uncles who admitted that after about a year of marriage they'd had their fill and were ready to go home. Eventually I learned it was the same for religious life. We are full of zeal because God has called us out of our sluggish state and into a way of life where we can love him better and serve the poor until the end of time. Such beauty! Such perfection! Then we begin initial formation and we have no idea what hit us. "Is this really what I signed up for?" we wonder, but God's grace leads us along as we spend time in the silence, as we listen in prayer, and as we hover in God's great love for us.

I grew up in New Mexico, and that is where I met my religious community. I figured that once I officially joined the congregation, I would stay in New Mexico with the sisters and therefore near my family. I was wrong. That's how things had once been, but now that women were entering one at a time in isolated areas, and now that the community had just merged eight provinces into one, I had to move to Pittsburgh, Pennsylvania, for my postulancy. I was joined by three others—two from Michigan and one from Missouri—and together we made up the postulancy for the newly formed North American province. As a postulant I had to learn how to live with people who were not my immediate relatives and had to adjust to life as a member of a group rather than as an individual. I couldn't decide when I would go to Mass; it was decided for me since we all had to go to Mass together. I couldn't just order take-out; I had to actually cook a meal and make sure it met everyone's needs and preferences. We lived life on a schedule, with everything taking place at a certain time on a certain day, including household chores, personal laundry, and shopping. I also realized I was living with women who did not share my same cultural background, traditions, or practices. At Christmas there was no *pozole*, and instead of *biscochitos*, we had poppyseed rolls. We sang Polish hymns at Easter and called lunch "dinner" and dinner "supper." It was a strange world, but I stuck it out and entered the novitiate a year later.

As a novice I had to continue adjusting to the routines and the lifestyles of a community with Polish roots. There were new schedules to learn and more traditions to inherit, but I assumed it would be a peaceful and quiet two years nevertheless. Actually, it was one of the most interiorly turbulent times of my life as different types of challenges began to evolve. Not only did it feel like my heritage and lifestyle were being replaced, but now my knowledge and life experience as well. I was a young adult, but felt like I was expected to take in every bit of information, no questions asked, the way a child would. It was the same for the other women in my group, two of whom were in their forties. Both of them had held prestigious positions in their careers and had extensive knowledge about finances, technology, and the world of business. However, when we engaged in discussions during class, or talked about decisions concerning household matters, our input did not carry much weight. It was frustrating to have a wealth of knowledge—individually and collectively—but to feel like that knowledge was irrelevant. I struggled with this and with missing my family, since I had never been away from home for so long in my entire life. It is common in my culture to remain near relatives, including grandparents, aunts, and uncles, so being hundreds of miles away felt like betrayal. Fortunately I was held in countless prayerful hearts, and after an emotional two years, I made my first profession of vows.

When I became an annually professed sister, I figured it would be nothing like postulancy or novitiate. "No more evaluations!" I thought. "No more overly academic and unrelatable books to read!" I thought. "No more awkward conversations about nothing at the dinner table!" I thought. I should have known better. Besides those, I still had schedules, personalities, traditions, and household practices to which I had to adjust, and now new challenges arose as a result of my ministerial and communal obligations. Not only did I need to keep up with the daily routine of my religious community—morning and evening prayers, daily Mass, meals, and recreation—but all of this in addition to teaching full time. We had to pray every morning at 5:45 just so that I could make it to 6:30 Mass before school started at 8:00. Some days I needed to have a meal ready by 5:00 in the evening even though I didn't typically get home until 4:00. On occasion, I either ran myself ragged or had to choose between community and ministry events, such as during the Christmas season when semester exams were due. Not only was I committed to a plethora of grading and report cards, but I was also expected to attend the many parish events to which we were invited during the holidays. This was not unique to the month of December, of course; it was simply magnified during that time. Who knew initial formation would be less shaping and more stretching?

Along with each of the challenges throughout my years in initial formation, there were also many surprises: blessings that I did not know would be like little flowers in the concrete. When I had to concede my preferences for things such as when I attended daily Mass, the type of food I ate and cooked, and when I could do my laundry, I was learning how to think of others. In small ways, I was becoming aware of the fact that my every move affected someone else. Rather than think about what was simply best for me, I was learning how to think about what was best for the whole. I was also becoming aware of other traditions and how other cultures celebrated important feasts and holidays. Not only that, but because I still cared about my own traditions, I began to share them and thus helped others open up to cultures with which they had previously been unfamiliar. At the same time, humility taught me that my knowledge and input was not always necessary. I may have had life experience outside of the convent, but initial formation showed me that I still had more to learn. I didn't know everything, it turned out, nor did I always have the solution. However, feeling at times as if I was being silenced also made me determined to speak up for myself. It was never something I needed to do before, so formation provided me with the opportunity to find my voice. Missing my family gave me the chance to empathize with others who missed their families for various reasons. Balancing my life in ministry and my life in community gave me an environment in which to further develop my time management skills. Not only did I have to focus on spending my time wisely, but instead of agreeing to chaperone every dance and join every committee, I had to learn when and how to say "no." I also learned the valuable lesson of when and how to ask for help. When I felt rushed, or I didn't have enough time to prepare an evening meal, I had to ask the sisters in my house for help. Although I felt uncomfortable about it at first, I eventually learned that my sisters wanted to help. They cared about me and didn't want to see me stressed or overwhelmed. My community loved me, and I began learning how to better love them.

The Blossom

Jesus offers us a choice in each of our trials: we can either rail against what we think is unfair, or we can seek God's truth and wisdom in the midst of it all. In choosing the latter, we can find God's unveiled beauty in the depths of religious life. We can find ways to speak love, to taste eternity, and to hold Divinity. We do not merely receive a vocation; we receive God's very breath. God patiently pieces us together, and then brings us here as the place to unfold.

When I had first gotten to know the Felician Sisters, they learned that I was a dancer and asked if I would do a liturgical dance for one of their jubilee celebrations. I agreed, and that's when I discovered my gifts could actually have a purpose. When I entered, however, I did not anticipate having the opportunity to dance in my future. Like Abraham, I was ready to give this precious gift back to God, but God, seeing that I was willing to offer everything, returned it to me a hundredfold. Not only was I invited to perform at our assemblies when there was an opportunity, but in my very first ministry I was called to teach dance. I was even able to do so in Haiti one summer. I am not just a dancer anymore. I dance as a way to move with the breath of God flowing through me. It's a way for me to carry God's love, to offer that love back to God, and to share that love with others.

Through religious life, God offers us opportunities that we may have never thought possible for ourselves. We are blessed not only with countless opportunities, but also with women who dare to support our ambitious endeavors. We are all called to return our gifts back to the Giver, and sometimes we receive those same gifts back in abundance. Other times, God calls forth other gifts from us that we perhaps never knew we had. As a dance teacher I was responsible for our school's annual dance recital. I had never done anything like that before and thought my inability to be detail oriented would ruin the whole thing. I discovered instead that I was actually pretty good at working with details and ended up heading other similar projects. God calls certain gifts forth in us when, how, and where he needs them. As religious, we do not claim our gifts for ourselves. Instead, we speak love by sharing those gifts and by trusting in their development over time.

I'm an introvert, so verbal communication is not quite my forte. However, I still find words useful and beautiful and necessary. I find much joy in writing, but would not previously have called myself a writer. When I became a novice, I was required to write reflections on certain topics and books. Most often, the positive feedback I received concerned my writing ability. Soon enough, I was invited by one of our sisters in the technology department to write a blog. It gave me a place to develop my thoughts on certain issues and to process some of the inner work that was taking place throughout my trials.

Whether introvert or extrovert, religious life requires reflection. It asks that we take time each day to consider carefully what we do, what we think, and what we say. For most of us it involves an examination of conscience of some sort in the evening when we contemplate all that took place during the day. This is necessary because it allows us to encounter that which is emerging from us. We should be aware of why we are feeling content, unhappy, or even angry. We cannot address our issues by ignoring them, nor can we contribute if we aren't sure what we have to offer. We can taste eternity by dipping ourselves into the waters of self-knowledge, for it is God who dwells at our center, and if we do not know ourselves, we will not know God.

Since I don't tend to express myself verbally, I have been known as more of a listener. During my handful of years as a teacher, many of my students came to share their pain and hardships with me. While working at my desk during lunch, a student would often come in and ask, "Sister, do you have a moment?" Listening has always been easy for me, but interruptions have not. However, knowing I was called to something other than the current task at hand, I would quickly prepare myself to spend the rest of my lunch with that particular student.

We may not all consider ourselves listeners, but we are all going to be called to listen in religious life. Not only must we make time for listening to God, but we also need to spend time listening to others. We have whole religious communities to hear, and in our ministries we have colleagues and students and patients and clients who also need to be heard. Listening with intention rather than for the sake of responding and listening even during the times when nothing is being spoken are ways we can encounter the Divine. We must reverence God's voice within everyone. When we do, we carry their joy, their sorrows, their doubts, their passions, and thus we are able to hold Divinity as we rejoice with the risen Christ or console the wounded Jesus.

The Field

We have become colorful pieces in a grandiose, gorgeous mosaic, a mosaic that's alive with the breath of God's Holy Spirit. We sway with her whispers and reach for her warmth.

We are storytellers, artists, daughters, leaders, and survivors. We come from different countries, cultures, demographics, and backgrounds. None of us is the same, but we are family. This is religious life.

During my first year in the novitiate, my sister became pregnant with her first child. Being unable to leave and be present for my younger sister as she entered this new phase of life was extremely painful for both of us. I could feel her disappointment and did not hesitate to add my own grief to the weight I carried heavily in my heart each day. I had never *not* been there for my little sis. In the midst of questioning why God would ask me to be so distant from family—by miles and in support—I received a little piece of inspiration. My candidate director lived in the same city as my sister, so I thought maybe she could visit my sister in the hospital. I called her and wearily made the suggestion, thinking she might be too busy or feel too out of place. Her response was quite the opposite: she agreed with so much joy in her voice that it chipped away at the wall of pity I'd built up around myself. She went the very next day and even sent me a picture of my sister with the flowers and card she'd brought to her hospital room in my name. In that very moment, I realized just how big my family was. After that, I jumped on many opportunities to send cards to the ailing family members of Felician Sisters, or to Felicians themselves if I heard they'd lost a loved one. The Felicians made my family their family. How could I not make their families mine in return? The value that we place on familial relationships can only strengthen our bonds as sisters. We end up unable to tell our families apart from one another because we have so integrated them into our larger religious family.

In addition to placing importance on family, the Felician Sisters celebrate the gift of diversity in community. We do so collectively and are also encouraged to do so individually. I was invited to attend the 2017 National Black Catholic Congress, and as excited as I was about the prospect, I wasn't sure how easily I would be able to obtain permission. It turned out to be much easier than I thought. I sent an email to our director of formation, and after discussing it with the council, she replied less than a week later to let me know I could attend. "Just make sure you schedule your annual retreat before your summer gets booked," she reminded me. That was it. There were no questions asked about why I wanted to go or how I thought it might help me. Instead they trusted that this was part of my identity I wanted to further explore, and they had no qualms about it. Perhaps because I am part of a community who sees cultural identity as a valid piece of who we are, they can recognize how important it is for each person. When everyone was Polish, they all took great pride in their culture. Now they see that each sister still takes great pride in her culture, but most of us happen to be something other than Polish these days.

This diversity has taught me something as well. It has taught me how to catch glimpses of God in various colors, shapes, and dimensions. Just like the flowers God uses to decorate the earth, each person offers a different hue of radiance. Each person offers a different aspect of God.

The same is true for my countless favorite Felicians, some of whom have already been called to their heavenly home. One of them, Sr. Mary Claire Kehl, was a great example of God's humility and simplicity. Her love for her sisters was genuine, and her gentle care for all sorts of plants and animals reflected her very nurturing spirit. One day Sr. Claire invited me to help her tend the roses in our courtyard. I almost said no, because I am not good with plants and because I assumed we wouldn't have much to talk about. Instead of giving into my resistance, I went with her. To this day I don't remember any of the information she shared with me about the roses or how to keep them alive, but I do remember the way she taught me and the way she pruned them. In that moment, I felt like the rosebush, like she was helping to gently clear the space around my budding leaves so that new life could breathe in my dry spaces. It's women like this—women of different ages and backgrounds and ethnicities—who teach me how to live pilgrimage every day. In their own ways and with their own gifts, they help all of us on the journey toward God. As newer members, we are just as responsible for embracing diversity as our religious communities are. Our colorful assortments of sisters are like gardeners, helping guide us toward Someone greater.

The Sower

So why do we stay when others leave? Why do we continue to say "yes" to something that our friends, family members, and even gynecologists don't understand? It's because we have found that pearl of great price (Matt 13:45-46). Each of us is the desired one of God's heart. God wants us here—wants us on this earth and in this way of life. We responded to that burning love—that longing for something more—because within it, we found the desired One of our hearts.

When my mom was a young married woman, she longed to have children. She was told too many times by medical professionals that this was impossible for her. Stubborn yet full of trust in God, my mother turned toward prayer and help from the saints of heaven. Her honest plea was, "Lord, You know it is my heart's desire to have children." My baptismal name is Desiré because I was my mother's first child, the desire of her heart.

The origins of my name have played a large part in my spiritual journey. Just because my mom received the child she prayed for didn't mean I came without complications. Many times during her pregnancy that same beloved medical staff told my mother she had either miscarried me or I was going to be stillborn. Even when I was born she was told I wouldn't survive. After a painful birthing process, two blood transfusions, and several days in the hospital, my mother was discharged. I, on the other hand, was supposed to spend the remainder of my short life in an incubator until God called me home. It's a good thing my mom is stubborn. She insisted that if I was going to die, I might as well do so at home. I was discharged, and my mother brought me to the hospital a month later, unrecognizable to the doctors because I had gained so much weight.

Similarly, we acknowledge the love burning in our hearts, and God responds by gifting us with those desires in the vocation of religious life. The process is not an easy one. The vows are not some magical string of words that keep us from being human, and the communities we enter are not full of saints. We will struggle in both initial formation and ongoing formation. There will be at least one vow that stares at us and says, "You and me? Yeah, right." As much as we'd like to think our sainthood began in the womb, it didn't. Along the way, however, God provides us with the people and situations we need in order to prosper. We just need to listen and pay attention to the movement of God all around and in us. We will be given friends, peers, mentors, advice, critiques, and opportunities, and it is our job to learn from them. Religious life is not here to strip us of who we are. God does not call us here to cancel out our identities. He formed those identities! If this is truly our vocation, then this is the fertile ground where we will most fully live out those identities.

We may not all have a beginning-of-life story like mine, but I certainly believe it reflects God's call to each of us. We all struggle through turbulent times, especially in our divided and wounded world today. Many of us experience the birthing complications of a broken family or insecurities and doubt brought on by the confident lies of thoughtless media and greedy corporations. We do not escape the brokenness in religious life. We feel alone at times, especially when the media claims that physical love is all we need or when we find it nearly impossible to relate to the women with whom we live. We feel inadequate, relying on the negative voice in our heads rather than on the still, small voice in our hearts, thinking maybe we are not enough. We give in to believing that things will never change, that we'll never be able to live religious life the way we imagine it could be. All of that will try to work against us, even on this hallowed ground. Yet, God's voice is the same for you as it is for me: "You are necessary. I am calling you here and now; do not be afraid. Trust me and I will be with you in the field of your vocation where my love has the power to sustain, delight, and transform you." It's not always about changing the world. Sometimes the only world that needs to be changed is the one we carry within us.

Searching for Identity through the Paschal Mystery

Thuy Tran, CSJ

While they were eating, Jesus took bread, and when he had given thanks, he broke it and gave it to his disciples, saying, "Take it; this is my body." Then he took a cup, and when he had given thanks, he gave it to them, and they all drank from it. "This is my blood of the covenant, which is poured out for many," he said to them. "Truly I tell you, I will not drink again from the fruit of the vine until that day when I drink it new in the kingdom of God." (Mark 14:22-25)[1]

From the moment of my birth, I have been in between two cultures: Vietnamese culture and American culture. I am a religious in a primarily white US religious community. Perhaps my identity search was exacerbated because I am the first American-born child of Vietnamese refugees. I was born in 1976, less than a year after my parents, four older siblings, and other family members arrived at Camp Pendleton, California. I grew up in a Vietnamese enclave surrounded by family and

[1] *The Holy Bible: New International Version (NIV)* (Colorado Springs, CO: International Bible Society, 1984), BibleWorks, v.9.

friends who were struggling to learn survival English while holding onto their Vietnamese culture and their Catholic faith. I think that each of us at various times in our lives (frequently beginning during adolescence) asked: "Who am I—really?" "Do I fit here?" "Am I good enough for this dream?" This search for identity is not a one-time event; it is an ongoing journey throughout all of life. The search seems particularly relevant as I discern the lifestyle to which God is calling me and I begin to live God's call to religious life.

The formative years of my grandparents and much of my family occurred in Vietnam. When they left Vietnam in 1975, they came to the United States with family traditions and values, a strong Catholic faith, and experiences with the Communist government. Throughout my discernment, I have reflected on the social institutions of my family, religion, and government and the way my formative years have shaped me. My great-grandparents and other ancestors were some of the first Vietnamese persons who were converted to Catholicism in North Vietnam by French missionaries in the early 1600s. My grandmother shared stories about experiences of being persecuted for their religious beliefs. By the early 1950s many of the Catholics and Buddhists had migrated from North Vietnam to South Vietnam because of religious persecution. Their faith and religion was a place of support, consolation, and reconciliation.

In April 1975, when Saigon fell to the Vietnamese Communists, many people left the country. In the midst of changes and uncertainty, religion was a source of grounding and safety for the people. Their first glimpse of the United States came at the Camp Pendleton Marine Base. My family experienced a jumble of feelings, including relief, disorientation, powerlessness, anxiety, and grief. Holding tight to their faith gave them the stability and security of the God they had known for generations in Vietnam. My family and several other Vietnamese families were sponsored by an American family. They were taken to the desert, where they soon realized that they had become working slaves to the people who had received government money to assist them in their resettlement process.

It was November 1975 when the Sisters of St. Joseph of Orange heard about my family's situation with the sponsoring family. Two sisters, Sr. Rose Marie Redding, CSJ, and Sr. Caritas Gorski, CSJ, drove several hours to the isolated area in the California desert where our families were being held and assessed the situation. They drove back to the motherhouse and presented the problem to the congregational leadership, who readily agreed to take in all the refugees from that place. They also agreed to help them find jobs and housing. Soon my extended family of over thirty people was relocated to the motherhouse, and a few months later, I was born at St. Joseph Hospital adjacent to the motherhouse.

Paschal Mystery

The experience of my great-grandparents and other ancestors who converted to Catholicism was very different from my own experience of religion. Being raised in a loving family community, I have been able to develop my relationship with God from an early age. Through this relationship, God helped me find my vocation to become a religious sister. As a young adult, I volunteered with Vietnamese-American teenagers because I understood their suffering and confusion of living biculturally between parents and peers. My family's faith in God has been the foundation of my faith and zeal.

In the light of my faith journey, I find special meaning in my search for identity by focusing on the Paschal Mystery. I feel the need to give of myself for others—to die a little or a lot—in order to grow into the person I am called to be for God, for myself, for others. Following God involves suffering, and Jesus is the model from whom we learn how to live, die, and be renewed. By connecting with Jesus, the Paschal Lamb, I can believe that my dying, done in compliance with God's will, brings new life for myself and others far beyond any human expectation.

This paschal mystery is clear to me as I try to connect my cultural background with my religious identity. The traditional learnings from catechism classes and pious family upbringing were good for their time. Throughout my formation, my ideas and growth in appreciation of my family's history, ethnic, and religious culture has expanded and has shaped who I am today as a practicing Catholic and woman religious. I have a lingering fear that if I grow out of my childhood images and stories, I might not have anything left in which to believe, or I might be betraying my God who has always been there for me: so real, so supportive; so loving, and forgiving. I have, however, grown confident that real knowledge is not "the enemy" and that I need only to trust God who has always been faithful to me; I know that the God of my childhood is not going to abandon me.

One of the blessings of being in a religious community is the opportunity to grow in theological knowledge. It was especially meaningful to understand that Jesus is the sign and center of everything: the visible sign of God on earth, the way of knowing God's ongoing grace, forgiveness, love, and presence in the world, and the reason the people of God come together. The words of the Eucharist, "Do this in memory of me" (Luke 22:19 NABRE), center me in the whole of the paschal mystery, which I live by being in service and becoming enriched by those I serve. I have spent time reflecting on Jesus' presence with the disciples in the Upper Room before the passion when they broke bread together; Jesus wanted the disciples to experience his passion, death, and resurrection. As a woman religious and disciple of Christ, I too am called to enter the paschal mystery. Along the way I surrendered myself and came to understand who I was meant to be: holy and consecrated. Though I did not yet understand what these two words meant and what God was asking, I trusted that God would reveal their meaning in time. One day during my thirty-day retreat, after the sign of peace during Mass, everyone recited the "Lamb of God." Then the priest broke the Eucharist in half. All of a sudden, at the sound of the Eucharist being broken in two, I was overwhelmed by God's grace and presence. I became totally aware that Jesus was holy and consecrated—broken for me and the world. I, too, am called to be holy and consecrated, to give my life for our broken and wounded world. Jesus in the Eucharist invites me to be like Him. Christ in me and I in Christ—these words are true to the depth of my heart. I have been touched by God so deeply that I was, and am, willing to risk my life. I live the paschal mystery when I trust the Holy Spirit to fill my heart and soul with confidence in the voice of God from within my heart.

Growing up in a Vietnamese family, I learned to treasure my elders and ancestors. As a member of a religious community, I bring the same reverence to my older sisters and my "Sister Ancestors." Listening to their stories grounds me in God's presence in my community from the start. I want to learn and retell their stories of joy, serving, suffering, dying, and rising to the future generations of my community. The knowledge of this same paschal mystery of my own family is lost to me, partly because they were refugees and had to leave much behind. I realize too that I did not have the courage to ask my parents and grandparents about their childhood experiences in North Vietnam, and those stories are lost, for many who migrated from there have passed away.

Many of my Vietnamese religious friends had similar experiences of growing up in a Vietnamese cultural enclave, surrounded in the neighborhood and at church by like-minded, culturally similar family and friends. As soon as we moved beyond the Vietnamese culture, we realized that there is more to understanding the church, religion, and world. The mystery for me involved a growing understanding that we are part of the world, that it is our world, and that it belongs to everyone from different faith traditions, backgrounds, and cultures.

I am attentive to how the mystery of Jesus being God-with-us and God-not-distant-from-us touches me. As both human and divine, Jesus also has a dual identity. It must not have been easy when he was questioned by many people about his identity. There is a sense of comfort in my heart that Jesus is in solidarity with me in my journey. In reflecting intimately on gospel stories of Jesus' birth, ministry, death, and resurrection, I have learned that Jesus (fully human and fully divine) is love, compassion, mercy, and reconciliation for all of humanity, especially for the poor, vulnerable, and marginalized. Additionally, at significant moments in my life, receiving the Eucharist—both concrete and divine—was a signal of the ongoing presence of God and my covenantal relationship with God through the Holy Spirit.

Cultural Identity

The reality of the paschal mystery deepened for me in 2003 when I visited Vietnam. Although I had heard many wonderful and challenging stories about Vietnam, I was finally going to explore the country for myself. My hope was to enjoy the journey and to learn from the experiences. I had no idea what to expect, and my greatest hope was to arrive there with an open heart. I went to Mass early the morning after I arrived, and, while praying this verse came to me: "The Lord will give you the bread in adversity and the water in affliction. No longer will your Teacher hide himself, but with your own eyes you shall see your Teacher. And your ears shall hear a word behind you: 'This is the way; walk in it,' when you would turn to the right or the left" (Isa 30:20-21 NABRE). I remembered wanting to see the Vietnamese people with Christ's eyes. I experienced mystery during the consecration, as I felt Jesus' presence inviting me to receive communion in such a way as to embrace Vietnam and the people.

As I entered into the suffering of the Vietnamese people, I experienced Christ dying and rising. What I discovered in this country was simultaneously exciting and inspiring, as well as shocking and sad. In the midst of the stunning beauty of the land, I enjoyed the hospitality of the people, and they wanted me to learn and enjoy being with them. Throughout my stay in Vietnam, I experienced the vibrant and diverse community of people living there teaching me about their rich culture and daily traditions. I gained a deeper insight into the global community as I journeyed with these beautiful people. However, the reality of the poverty jolted me. I felt overwhelmed by the crowds, especially as both the old and the young approached me begging for money or asking me to buy things from them. I felt shocked by the poverty of the people from the North to the South. It was an eye-opening experience for me because these were my people and I felt helpless. I tried blocking my eyes from seeing the reality of their pain and suffering, but I could not escape the reality that was in front of me. If there is such a thing as divinely inspired discomfort, these sufferings of my own people have fueled a passion in me to free others from poverty and suffering.

I was stunned when I noticed people staring at me. At one point, something struck me from within, saying, "I am not Vietnamese." In every corner that I looked, I saw a reflection of myself in the people. However, my body structure and my much-less-than-fluent Vietnamese language indicated to the people that I was not one of them. I was a visitor, not a native. Here I was at the birthplace of my ancestors and family, including both my parents, and still I did not belong to this country. It was the first time that I had ever questioned my identity as a Vietnamese person. I chose to stay in the suffering of the people and the separation I felt as I realized that I was not one of them.

Identity in Religious Life

As an Asian American in religious life, I asked myself, how do I integrate my culture, rituals, and traditions with those of my religious congregation? I found the new life of the resurrection when, thirty years after the Sisters of St. Joseph welcomed my refugee family, I entered their community. When I first moved into religious life, I told the sisters I live with that I was a "twinkie" (yellow outside and white inside). As I continued to live with the sisters, I missed everything about my Vietnamese culture—from my family and friends to the food.

The movement of grace in my early journey was to notice the triggers that led me to feel certain ways. Many of those triggers involved the cultural and generational differences in my local community and congregation. I missed the Vietnamese food because at my parent's home we had rice almost daily, and we used fish sauce as a main ingredient to almost every household staple dish. I missed waking up to my parents speaking Vietnamese to my siblings and me. I realized that the cultural differences continued to be a challenge and struggle for me. I noticed that I am sensitive to the fact that the smell of the food I cook lingers in the house for days. I am proud of my Vietnamese roots, culture, and food. To celebrate a special occasion, I offered to prepare a traditional Vietnamese dish. I felt excited as I baked a whole fish in the oven. At first the sisters were surprised to see a whole fish on the table, but I remember my joy as I watched them work to assemble the fish, fresh veggies, and noodles into a spring roll wrap. This Vietnamese-American "breaking bread" came with the openness of the sisters trying something that was so important to me and their desire to learn about my food, culture, traditions, and family. By the end of my candidacy year, I could say to my sisters that I am totally Vietnamese and I am not exactly a twinkie anymore!

Being Vietnamese-American, I have the sense that I am stuck in the middle of two cultures, perhaps a bit like Jesus who had no place to lay his head (Matt 8:20) and who did not claim blood relatives as his family (Mark 3:33), but left his family home to create a path to God. Vietnamese-American theologian, Peter Phan, in "The Dragon and the Eagle: Towards a Vietnamese-American Theology," states, "To be betwixt and between is to be neither here nor there, to be neither this thing nor that completely. Spatially, it is to dwell at the periphery or at the boundaries."[2] East Asian cultures incorporate elements

[2] Peter Phan, "The Dragon and the Eagle: Towards a Vietnamese-American Theology." *East Asian Pastoral Review* 2–3 (2002), accessed April 1, 2017, http://www.eapi.org.ph/resources/eapr/east-asian-pastoral-review-2002/2002-2-3/the-dragon-and-the-eagle-towards-a-vietnamese-american-theology/.

of Taoism, Buddhism, and Confucianism, and these faith and philosophical traditions invite people to live in harmony, to practice contemplation, and to have respect for all life, in particular for elders and ancestors who impart wisdom and give life to their descendants. I come into my religious congregation with a mixture of the church of Asia and the church of the American West. Other Asian women with whom I grew up chose to enter more traditional monastic or contemplative communities. I chose to enter a ministerial community with only a wooden cross as an outward sign. Throughout my childhood, I remember seeing Sisters Rose Marie and Caritas at all of my family's cultural celebrations, including Tet (Lunar New Year). I was impressed that they were not wearing a traditional habit. From my family's perspective and traditional experiences, the Vietnamese culture places high value and regard on religious, and a priest or religious is viewed automatically as an important figure in my family's household. The fact that my family respected these two women religious who did not wear a habit opened me to see that there were other ways of being a religious in our world. This was another sign of Christ's presence in this journey between a Vietnamese culture and an American religious community.

Western religious life has offered me both growth and grace. I appreciate and love my congregation and the other religious communities I have encountered throughout the United States and world. Interestingly, my religious congregation has had two dominant cultures from its earliest days with French-speaking and English-speaking members. Perhaps this foundational diversity has helped the congregation incorporate newer members of other traditions. I am not the same person that I was when I entered my religious community, and I cannot go back to the way things were before. I can relate to the disciples as they encountered Jesus, and they were never the same after meeting and being with him. My life has flourished by the richness of being in the life with sisters from various cultures and backgrounds and appreciating different ways of expressing spirituality. I am proud to share with the many lay partners in my ministry the congregation's traditions, history, and heritage by telling the stories and inviting others to share their own stories.

My community is one hundred years old. In the first half of our existence, the community struggled to build harmony between the original French-speaking sisters and the newer members from Kansas and California. In trying to find common ground, they articulated the phrase, "She is a Sister of St. Joseph and that should suffice." Perhaps the phrase went a long way to overcoming differences, but it also allowed the community to lose the rich gifts of distinct cultures. Like other congregations, mine had an ideal vision of a perfect sister. While the phrase "according to the model at the Motherhouse," was originally used to describe the precise construction of habits, it transitioned into popular language to describe the perfect sister. Even today there are external behaviors that are remnants of the old religious life culture, such as how one cuts a piece of fruit at the table. I realized that not only am I trying to learn about Vietnamese culture and American culture, but religious life culture as well. The changes in religious life after Vatican II called communities to evaluate whether they had become cultures closed in on themselves or if they were open to the world. My community took on the paschal journey of dying to nonessentials and rising to a more Spirit-filled life in which we can see the face of God manifest in many cultures.

When I entered the Sisters of St. Joseph my mother gave me words of wisdom that she wanted me to remember: "If you disagree with an elder sister, just remain silent." Asian women often see silence as contemplative and use silence to withhold affirmation, process what is going on around them, and discern next steps. This is an active engagement and is not an act of submission. This is one element of Vietnamese culture that became disorienting when I was struggling to fit into an American community. In my family, I had learned to have respect for my elders. I even acknowledged the status of my older sister Trinh by calling her Chi Trinh, adding "chi" as a form of respect for elders in the Vietnamese culture. When the Americans asked me not to use the term "Sister" and just call them by their first name, I did not know what to do.

My greatest struggle in religious life is blending the values of silence with using my voice. The sisters encouraged equal sharing of opinions, whereas I grew up expecting I would speak last, or not at all. I realized that when conflict would arise in a group, I would become quiet. During difficult and challenging conversations in the novitiate with my fellow novices, I would sit in silence and observe the dynamics. I would remain silent for an extended time even after the meeting. When I would remove myself from the group, the other novices would become concerned. When they shared their concerns with me, I shared with them how we deal with conflict in my culture. From the Asian perspective, difficult conversations are communal, respectful, and harmonious, and here, I was experiencing just the opposite. My friends from the novitiate were able to meet me halfway in this, and I am growing. Now when I am faced with conflict I tell the sisters that I need only two days of silence, instead of fourteen days! Slowly, I am learning to find the courage to speak up respectfully and honestly in difficult situations. I am experiencing dying to self and rising to new life as I learn how to be in these conversations with my sisters, and new understandings are being created.

During my transition, there were moments I felt stressed with the demands of religious life: pursuing studies, living in community, balancing my personal and spiritual life, talking about difficult issues in formation, and having responsibilities in ministry. At times my stress level was so high that I wanted to run away or take a break from religious life. There were moments when I was thinking about leaving religious life. I felt frustrated and questioned my vocation, wondering if religious life was not for me. I always allowed God to walk with me during difficult times, enabling me to learn, to grow, and to be challenged. I continued to be honest with God, and in prayer, solitude, and silence I was able to find peace where my desires and God's desires met.

Why did I choose to stay in religious life? God is the center of my life and I believe in my vocation. I am grateful to the sisters that continue to love me and to share their lives with me. I have many moments of joy and laughter in religious life with my sisters. I love the spontaneity of going to the movies in the middle of a working day, going out to eat and experiencing different cultural food, laughing and teasing, and sharing intimate moments from late night conversations or road trips. I am grateful to have had sisters who have seen my greatest potential even before I was able to see it in myself and who have become my wisdom figures when I needed their strength and care. I love when they look at me and are proud that I am one *of* them and that I am one *with* them. Community life has taught me much about myself and has been a source of life to grow in prayer and deepen my relationship with God and the world. Finally, my heart feels at home with my sisters, and I am proud to be a Vietnamese-American sister! Transition is a difficult time for persons in initial formation; it is heightened for women from other cultures. During this time, it is important to support and love women as they work with questions of identity. During these times of transition, my deepest desire is for our sisters to mentor new members, allowing them to grow in our charism and to live it. I have created an acronym to assist in understanding and accepting other CULTURES.

Care with Compassion
Understand with Love
Listen with both Head and Heart
Trust Each Other
Understand Individual Gifts and Talents
Respect Traditions and Ritual
Embrace Differences and Similarities
Speak with Integrity

I hope more women from diverse cultures feel a sense of welcoming, so that together we can engage in the local and global world with love and respect. The greatest gifts of living in between two cultures are deepening understanding of being at the margins, as well as the opportunity to be bridge-builders. It is important to know the challenges of social justice in our church and world. Being at the margins and encountering poverty locally and worldwide continues to remind me that I am called to reach out and treat every person with human dignity.

Religious life has been for me the paschal mystery of being "betwixt and/or in between" and continues to be one of the most transformative aspects of my life. I continue to be amazed that God wants to be in solidarity with this diverse global community. The paschal mystery is our call to eucharistic life, to the love of Christ we share with each other and which will hold us together no matter what happens or how different we are. Just as Jesus shared community and the breaking of the bread with the disciples, we are called to break bread and to reach out to the pressing issues in the twenty-first century: the immigrants, refugees, people with mental illness, the economically poor and vulnerable, and all marginalized groups. We offer gifts (bread, wine, ourselves) to God who has already given them as gifts to us—hence our poverty; then we are all transformed and all one in our poverty and in our riches through Christ.

Being part of God's family is the journey of the paschal mystery. In 2015, which was the fortieth anniversary of the fall of South Vietnam, my family and religious congregation came together to celebrate my perpetual vows. I will never forget that day as the day when the East and the West finally came together to celebrate. My religious ceremony was bilingual in Vietnamese and English, and both cultures were celebrated. For the offertory, I asked two of my religious sisters to carry up the gifts to express the gratitude from my family, and countless others, who are grateful for the sisters and their services.

They represented the many religious throughout the world who have risked their lives for the mission of Jesus. I am honored to stand on their shoulders. Later that evening, we celebrated the Eucharist at my home parish with the Vietnamese community. It was the first time for the Vietnamese community in my home parish to see a religious sister without a traditional religious habit. My parents have embraced dialoguing with the Vietnamese community to help them understand different ways of expressing religious life. Now, I realize my life is richer in service for others because I have three cultures in my life: Vietnamese, US American, and religious life. Searching for identity is the experience of passion, death, and resurrection, and the Eucharist is the reminder of resurrection. With resurrection there is no death but life. I am called to choose life as my life is broken for all people, and we become ONE.

Creating a Culture of Encounter: Finding Life in Intergenerational and Intercultural Community

Madeleine Miller, OSB

"We are accustomed to a culture of indifference and we must strive to ask for the grace to create a culture of encounter, of a fruitful encounter, of an encounter that restores to each person his or her own dignity as a child of God."[1]

Introduction

In a world where everything, even the human person, is treated as disposable, we as women religious are called to proclaim a Gospel rooted in radical encounter. When religious communities successfully live this culture of encounter, the very life of the church and the world can be transformed for the better. In order to explore this graced invitation placed before us as sisters today, we will travel three paths leading

[1] Francis, "Overcome Indifference, Build a Culture of Encounter," Vatican Radio, September 13, 2016, accessed May 11, 2017, http://en.radiovaticana.va/news/2016/09/13/pope_overcome_indifference,_build_a_culture_of_encounter/1257732.

us forward. First, we will look at how to help women encounter themselves, their God, and their brothers and sisters in Christ with radical hospitality and availability. Next, we will look at how we as sisters are called to live in intergenerational and intercultural community with openness by seeking what is true, good, and beautiful. Finally, we delve into the lived experiences of women religious seeking to breathe life into the culture of encounter today despite our human limitations. As our church grows in beautiful diversity, we as women religious are called to witness prophetically to the gift of each culture, generation, and child of God.

As a newly finally professed sister, I see how desperately our church and our world need to see the culture of encounter brought to life in our religious communities. Coming from a world of individualism and consumerism, allowing Christ to transform our attitudes from fear to gratitude will make us far brighter lights in a dark world. I learned this firsthand during my recent time on mission in Brazil. Through this experience, I moved from outright terror to deep love and gratitude. While the frustrations I felt in not understanding my own sisters or in enduring the heat were real, I learned from them what it is like to truly appreciate the beauty of our missionary life and our Catholic faith lived with joy. This same opportunity is possible for each of us if we too take the risky journey of transformation.

Encounter and Commitment: Discernment and Formation

Considering religious life as young women today asks us to put ourselves in the place of Moses standing before the burning bush (Exod 3:2). God's presence wants to transform us, dramatically altering the course of our lives while leading us to wholeness. Like the burning bush, when we encounter God's presence, we are changed but not "consumed." We know that fire cannot stay still. It has to move, to grow, to shed light, and to give totally of itself. When God calls us to follow him in religious life, we are challenged to follow this same path: to move, to grow, to reflect Christ's light, and to give ourselves wholeheartedly. In the face of this daunting prospect, it is easy to be afraid. The good news is that we never say "yes" to Christ alone. We say "yes" in and with our community, and fundamentally with Christ whose perfect "yes" brings all of our yeses to perfection.

Going forward in our discernment, we might ask three key questions. First: Am I truly willing to encounter God and let him transform me? To answer this, we should look within and beyond ourselves. In the first chapter of John's gospel, when Jesus begins to invite others into public ministry, we meet two disciples who come to understand their calling gradually. Jesus asks them a series of questions, drawing them out of themselves. As they follow him physically, Jesus teaches them to follow him holistically. After they ask where Jesus lives, he tells them simply, "Come and see" (John 1:39). To follow Christ in a relationship of encounter, we need to see it in the spirit of charity, not perfection. In the process of discerning religious life, we can rationalize that it is too late for us to change or that we like our comfort zone or that we are not worthy. This is not what perfect charity is about. As Edward P. Hahnenberg explains, "The word perfection implies growth. Charity means love. Thus to be holy is to grow in love. This is our first and foremost calling."[2] God himself teaches us to love, and if we trust the process, we can let him prepare us to do great things for his glory.

The second question discernment places before us is: Am I willing to encounter my real self? Quickly we discover that discernment "is not a spiritual treasure hunt. It is less about looking out and more about listening within."[3] Turning off the noise, tuning out the distractions, and starting to foster a life

[2] Edward P. Hahnenberg, "Theology of Vocation: Attuned to the Voice of God," *Human Development Magazine* 36 (Spring 2016): 54–58.

[3] Ibid., 59.

of disciplined prayer are essential as we listen for God's whisper. The journey of self-discovery is difficult and often brings up areas to grow internally or old wounds that need to be healed. It forces us to look at our faults, our weaknesses, and our shortcomings. We also come face to face with our own complacency in this encounter. At World Youth Day 2016, Pope Francis reminded young people today of how easy it is to mistake happiness with being a "couch potato." While lazing on the couch looks like the answer to every young person's prayers, he said, "That is probably the most harmful and insidious form of paralysis, which can cause the greatest harm to young people. . . . Little by little . . . we start to nod off, to grow drowsy and dull."[4] Clearly we cannot afford to live our vocations in a mediocre way. A new sister must give everything without seeing a roadmap. When times get hard during the journey to self-discovery, we remind ourselves that the grace-filled identity we received at baptism remains alive and active.[5]

Formation gives us a paschal moment of encounter where we can overcome barriers that exist within each of us and live with radical openness. Learning to be vulnerable, allowing ourselves to be taught, being willing to actually change—these are invaluable if we want to grow into our vocation that necessitates a holistic encounter (body, mind, and spirit). Jean Vanier reminds us, "Community is a wonderful place, it is life-giving; but it is also a place of pain because it is a place of truth and of growth—the revelation of our pride, our fear, and our brokenness."[6] As we embrace our wounded selves with the help of Christ, our wounded healer, we can see how deeply

[4] Francis, "Journey to Poland: Prayer Vigil with the Young People in the Campus Misericordiae," August 30, 2016, accessed May 11, 2017, https://w2.vatican.va/content/francesco/en/speeches/2016/july/documents/papa-francesco_20160730_polonia-veglia-giovani.html.

[5] For further exploration about this journey, see the chapters written by Amanda Carrier, pp. 147–58, and Desiré Findlay, pp. 82–95.

[6] Jean Vanier, *From Brokenness to Community* (New York: Paulist, 1992): 10–11.

we are loved as we are. With this knowledge, it becomes clear that the story of our imperfect community is our story, our shared salvation history. Only when we know and love ourselves in a deep way can we love God and others in a life-giving capacity as wounded healers ourselves.[7]

The third and final question we discover at this stage in our journey is: Am I willing to deeply encounter others as they are? Formation helps us to celebrate diversity and see every brother and sister before us as beautiful parts of the Body of Christ. Encounter must also come to life in our missionary service together. There, on the margins, we can help those who feel excluded and silenced to feel accepted and loved. As Vanier explains to us, "When we welcome people from this world of anguish, brokenness and depression, and when they gradually discover that they are wanted and loved as they are and that they have a place, then we witness a transformation—I would even say 'resurrection.'"[8] We as sisters living the culture of encounter are called to a consistent posture of dialogue, listening, learning, and reverence.

As we learn to spread our wings during formation or after profession, it's essential to expect that we will make mistakes. Pope Francis again gives us marvelous words of comfort for just these moments. He reminded the young people in Poland, "If you are weak, if you fall, look up a little for there is Jesus' hand extended to you as he says: 'Rise up, come with me.' 'And what if I fall again?' Rise again."[9] Any commitment to God is a gift that starts in him and is daily sustained by him. Religious profession is a commitment we make in the church and for the sake of the church, never for ourselves or in our own human power.

[7] See the chapter by Amanda Carrier for further discussion of this topic, pp. 154–58.

[8] Vanier, *From Brokenness to Community*, 15.

[9] Francis, "Journey to Poland."

Lives of Radical Encounter: Intergenerational and Intercultural Common Life

Prayer time spent in my congregation's retreat house has led me to reflect further on the gifts of diversity and encounter. I love sitting on the cabin deck that overlooks a stream as I do *lectio divina*, listening to the water cascade over the rocks and wind around the bend towards the bridge downstream. In many ways, this sacred stream represents the beautiful diversity of religious life today. The stream we are in has its source in God; it leads us back to God who carries us along the journey with the same gentleness and love regardless of our culture or generation.

In our communities today, we find members who are in young, middle, and late adulthood. As Erik Erikson tells us, each developmental stage can express itself in healthy and unhealthy ways.[10] The work of young adulthood is to form close relationships and gain the capacity for intimate love, in tension with isolation and the pain of rejection. Meanwhile, the work of middle adulthood is to generate: to contribute to the world. Those in middle adulthood want to be life-giving, but can stray into fatalism and withdrawal. Finally, late adults, as they reflect on life and prepare to leave their legacy, love to be generous but often struggle with feelings of uselessness. These and other developmentally appropriate tendencies, both good and bad, are part of the tension in intergenerational community life today. As each sister grows in self-awareness throughout her religious life, she can grow in ways that help her express intimacy, generativity, and integrity rather than isolation, stagnation, and despair.

In order to discover concretely how to live well in an intergenerational community, we can learn from some encouraging trends. For example, in 2015 *The Atlantic* published a major

[10] Saul McLeod, "Erik Erikson," *Simply Psychology*, October 20, 2016, accessed May 8, 2017, https://www.simplypsychology.org/Erik-Erikson.html.

article about several nursing homes in the Netherlands where college students live with elders, volunteer their time, form meaningful relationships, and have their living expenses taken care of. Research cited in this article stated "for the residents, the students represent a connection to the outside world."[11] The students share their gifts of energy, new ideas, conversation, and even technological skills such as Skype. While "research links loneliness to mental decline and increased mortality . . . regular social interaction with friends and family has been found to improve health"[12] for elders. Over time, residents and students can bring life and support to each other in a spirit of communion. A similar practice has been implemented at a retirement home in Cleveland, Ohio, with a local music school.[13] There students share their musical gifts through concerts and art therapy sessions, bringing joy and beauty to their elders. Despite the large gap in age, participants in these programs can accompany one another on the ups and downs of human life in a positive way.

To live effectively in an intergenerational community, whether in the world or in religious life, we as young people need certain practical skills. First, we need to see and welcome Christ in each other. Christ, our teacher and Lord, always wants to speak to us through others. Consequently, we need to be open to learn from our elders. Pope Francis gives us clear advice: "Ask them so many things, listen to them, they have the memory of the history, the experience of life, and for you this will be a great gift that will help you on your way."[14] In listening with the ear of our hearts, we can learn how our fel-

[11] Tiffany Jansen, "To Save on Rent, Some Dutch College Students Are Living in Nursing Homes," *The Atlantic* (October 5, 2015).

[12] Ibid.

[13] Heather Hansman, "College Students are Living Rent-Free in a Cleveland Retirement Home," *Smithsonian* (October 16, 2015).

[14] Francis, "Address to the Boys of Italian Catholic Action." *Zenit*, December 20, 2016, accessed May 11, 2017, https://zenit.org/articles/popes-address-to-youth-of-catholic-action/.

low sisters have faithfully lived our charism and mission over decades of life in community. Their stories can tell us more than a formation class or article ever could.

As we receive from our elder sisters, so too we need to be willing to reverse mentor to share our gifts and skills of our youth with them. Through meaningful conversation, we can share with them what it is like to discern a vocation today. We can share our joys and struggles growing up in today's culture and how difficult it is to find our path in life with so many options before us. It can be comforting for us to see that our elders don't have everything in religious life figured out and that living with questions is normal. It leaves the door open for the Spirit to work. By entering into relationship, we as young sisters can deepen our roots in our communities, hone our listening skills, grow in compassion for those who are different from us, and see and serve Christ in new situations. As we age, our elders give us valuable models for how to age well. This spirituality can help us to go deeper, to go inward, and to surrender fully to the God who calls us and sustains our "yes" as women religious.[15] Elders can teach us how to forgive ourselves, to find our identity in who we are rather than what we do, and to be grateful for who we are together as community. As Sr. Janet Malone eloquently explained, "Gratitude involves satisfaction with life, with oneself, with one's congregation and with the world. I am enough. I am good enough. I have enough."[16]

In a compelling article, Sr. Teresa Maya recently wrote a letter to sisters in the Great Generation. She credits these sisters with being the living catechism through which she learned about the church and religious life.[17] She said, "You may not

[15] Janet Malone, "A Spirituality of Aging in Religious Congregations," *Human Development* 34, no. 2 (Summer 2013): 8–17.

[16] Ibid., 14.

[17] Teresa Maya, "An Open Letter to the Great Generation," *Global Sisters Report*, December 4, 2016, accessed May 8, 2017, http://globalsistersreport.org/column/trends/open-letter-great-generation-16171.

know this, but your lives were the first catechism of my generation—yes, your lives! Your attempts, your quest for meaning and purpose . . . your theology, your poetry, your art. Your lives were indeed our first theology."[18] Rather than trying to write our own stories alone, we need to tap the life-giving waters held in the sacred hands of our elders and dive into our shared story. Sr. Teresa calls the elder sisters not to give up on us: "My generation needs your wisdom, we need you as mentors, to counsel us, to tell the stories, to pass on your passion, to stand by our side and assure us it is OK to make mistakes, to try again, to inspire us to carry on your legacy."[19] Doing this, taking these risks will produce abundant fruit. While we young sisters need to risk trusting others, our elders need to risk entrusting their legacy into our hands.[20]

After considering the gift of intergenerational community, we now turn our gaze to intercultural community. For our foremothers, a central challenge in the late 1900s was walking through and implementing the teachings of the Second Vatican Council. *Nostra Aetate* (Declaration on the Relation of the Church with Non-Christian Religions) asked Catholics to find truth in all faiths.[21] *Perfectae Caritatis* (Decree on the Adaptation and Renewal of Religious Life) also challenged religious men and women to rediscover their roots and reorient themselves to meet the current needs of the church and the world through the lens of their congregation's founding vision.[22] Our sisters' often painful journey is part of the culture of their generation. I believe that our generation of younger women religious also has its own culture. Some key components of our culture are love for the church, hope for the future of religious life, a desire to make everyone feel welcome in God's family, and a belief

[18] Ibid.

[19] Ibid.

[20] Please see Teresa Maya's chapter for more on this topic, pp. 159–81.

[21] See *Vatican Council II: The Conciliar and Post Conciliar Documents Study Edition*, ed. Austin Flannery (Northport, NY: Costello, 1986).

[22] Ibid.

that we offer a unique gift to the world from our prophetic stance as sisters. The challenge before us is to discover what is true, good, and beautiful in each generation and culture—both within and beyond our monastery walls.

As with each generation, so too does each culture have dignity and value. Whether a sister comes from an impoverished village in Tanzania or a wealthy city in Europe, we are all in community to seek God in and through our diverse cultures together. Our rich diversity is fundamentally connected to the moment of Pentecost. As disciples of Jesus, we can stay huddled in fear, wondering where the next threat will come from, or we can allow the Spirit to breathe on us, calling us forth in our diverse unity. For instance, when a new sister arrived in my community from Asia last year, I had the graced opportunity to welcome her as my sister. When each of us responds to the call of radical hospitality, we can bring our charism to life here and now and not allow it to grow stagnant. Through this radical welcome we meet our God who, like our charism, longs for life and always wants to meet us in the present moment.

In my life as a young sister, the most profound learning experience I've had occurred in my three month mission assignment to our priory in Olinda, Brazil, in preparation for making final vows in 2015. After I got over my initial shock and concern about safety in Latin America, the heat, my struggle to learn Brazilian Portuguese, and the experience of going far out of my comfort zone, I received the greatest and most sacred gift: encounter. While in Brazil, I was immersed in the vibrant, rich, and deeply historical culture of the church there. Participating in the live passion play near Barbalha, working at our kindergarten in the nearby *favela*, and seeing the profound devotion of the people who came to Holy Mass in our chapel moved me in ways that are beyond description. Before my trip to Brazil, one of my elder sisters told me that the most important thing to do in the missions is to listen. She said of her own mission to Namibia, "When I went, I spent the first two years listening, only then did I begin to speak." This helped me to absorb and appreciate the varied cultures and generations in helpful ways without the critical voices or fearful feelings that often cloud my thinking. Because I lived out of a contemplative stance, our sisters could feel free to teach me about their lives, their struggles, their joys and the ways they bring our charism to life within their culture and generation. Thus, real encounter could blossom.

Despite the many apparent and subtle differences between my North American culture and the Brazilian culture, I grew to see the strands of unity. Every sister in every generation and culture is called by the same Lord, nourished by the same sacramental life in the church, and sustained by both her God and her community along the way. In Brazil I could learn from our elder German sisters who had been sent there on mission decades earlier and appreciate how they found a sacred middle way by being themselves yet also Brazilian. By being elders but thriving in communion with the energetic young Brazilian sisters, I saw our elders create a culture of encounter that was alive and life-giving. Their witness personifies what I believe we are called to bring to life today in our own intercultural and intergenerational communities.

As we strive to form healthy, life-giving, intergenerational, and intercultural communities, we cannot expect perfection. We will make mistakes along the way no matter how good our intentions may be. This certainty brings to mind an experience early in my formation when a sister from overseas gave me organ lessons. In her culture, lessons were formal and structured. They were not a time for friendly talk. After my first few lessons, I was convinced this sister wanted nothing to do with me. My wise novice directress helped me understand that the other sister came from a culture different from my own. My task as her sister in community was not to judge her, to run the other direction, or to try to change her. Instead, I needed to understand where she was coming from and adapt my inner stance to one of respect and learning.[23]

[23] *Rule of Saint Benedict 1980*, ed. Timothy Fry (Collegeville, MN: Liturgical Press, 1981), Prologue.

This small instance brings to life the spectrum people inhabit in terms of intercultural competence and the invitation to grow into diverse community life. Instead of staying in the places of denial, polarization, reversal, or minimization, we can move to the fruitful lands of acceptance and adaptation and even beyond to celebration. In reflecting on her own intercultural community experience, Sr. Melinda Pellerin, an African-American Sister of St. Joseph, wrote, "My cultural experiences, what I eat or how I celebrate, are things that the other sisters try to embrace. Sometimes it works out, sometimes it doesn't. We're all learning."[24] When we keep learning from one another, we remain good students in what St. Benedict calls the "school of the Lord's service," where we bring all of who we are to the table daily.

Inhabiting Encounter: Lived Experiences of Communion

Two essential questions remain before us in the pursuit of incarnating a culture of encounter. The first is: How is this lived and shared in mission? The second question is: Where do we go from here as sisters today? In order to delve deeply into the first question of how to live a culture of encounter, I brought this to members of my own community through a questionnaire about intergenerational and intercultural community life alongside the culture of encounter proposed by Pope Francis. I reflected on their profound answers and prayerfully considered their wisdom alongside that of the saints, especially St. Teresa of Calcutta. The sections that follow share some of the fruits of my reflection.

After years of living in our intergenerational and international community, our current prioress, Sr. Pia Portmann, OSB,

[24] Elizabeth Evans, "Q&A With Sr. Melinda Pellerin, on Having Two Callings," *Global Sisters Report*, October 14, 2016, accessed May 11, 2017, http://globalsistersreport.org/blog/q/trends/q-sr-melinda-pellerin-having-two-callings-40041.

recounted, "Each culture has its own unique way to express the identity. Our Congregation has its own monastic/missionary culture that unites us. . . . I learned to listen and to observe before I make a statement or judgment. . . . I have learned to let go, adjust, be flexible and to love."[25] Letting go and becoming flexible were also essential for me during my years in temporary vows. Sr. Pia, who is Swiss but served as a missionary in Tanzania and Italy before coming to the United States, was our directress during this time. Hearing her stories and seeing her lived example of the culture of encounter was a gift and a challenge. At many points I remember telling myself, "She may be older and from another culture, but her example of faithful and joyful Missionary Benedictine life is something I need to learn from, not something I can afford to discard as irrelevant." Being formed by Sr. Pia helped me to work on letting go of my idols of efficiency as I learned to appreciate the gift of the journey, the gift of God that each person is in our lives.

When asked about living with sisters from other generations and cultures, our former prioress Sr. Kevin Hermsen, OSB, described coming to learn "that everyone matters even those who drive you crazy! . . . You can live with people that God has sent to the community even though you would never choose them."[26] Often in her writings, St. Mother Teresa reminds us that our vocation is about Jesus; it is not in any one person or ministry we find in community. We make our vows to him, and only his faithfulness can sustain us. When talking about missionary service, St. Mother Teresa explained to her sisters, "How can we love God and his poor—if we do not love each other with whom we live and break the Bread of Life daily together? . . . Do I recognize the beauty of my Sisters, the spouse of Christ, at the Breaking of the Bread—in the daily

[25] Pia Portmann, interview by author, Religious Life Book Project Questionnaire, Norfolk, NE (December 2016).

[26] Kevin Hermsen, Religious Life Book Project Questionnaire Responses (December 2016).

Mass we live together?"[27] By loving God in our sisters, we become ready to welcome God in the distressing disguise of the poor whom we serve in mission.

The church teaches us that while God always seeks unity and communion, Satan stirs up division and disunity. To work toward union, God calls us to use practices such as dialogue, prayer, sharing, forgiveness, and mercy. With this, transformation happens radically. As a novice, Sarah, described, "My mind has definitely been broadened by the sisters from other cultures and generations. I have encountered anything from having a better understanding of the Depression and World War II to having my heart and mind opened to music and dance of a variety of cultures. The older generations and variety of cultures have definitely allowed me to see my prejudices and faults better and so have allowed me to strive after holiness all the more by a better self-knowledge."[28] Despite the temptation to stereotype others, we need to be open to difference as beautiful and unpredictable. For example, elders need to see that young people who desire traditional forms of devotion do not necessarily wish to return to all elements of the pre-Vatican II church. Our leaders and elders are called today to understand that we may differ in the rituals we see as meaningful in our lives; this is not an existential threat, but a chance to be opened.

After the winding journey to self-knowledge in formation, we as young sisters will consistently find opportunities to grow in holiness in community. Sr. Constance Tescon, OSB, from the Philippines similarly shared that challenges in diverse community life help us to adapt ourselves to one another's weaknesses and grow in compassion.[29] When asked what gift her

[27] Teresa of Calcutta, *Where There is Love, There is God*, ed. Timothy Fry (Collegeville, MN: Liturgical Press, 2010), 57.

[28] Sarah McMahon, interview by author, Religious Life Book Project Questionnaire, Norfolk, NE (December 2016).

[29] Constance Tescon, interview by author, Religious Life Book Project Questionnaire, Norfolk, NE (December 2016).

generation brings to community, she answered, "flexibility, simplicity, and agility."[30] Even with our many differences, with God's help we can see what makes us one. Sr. Constance affirms that being her authentic, strong self "made me creative on how to look at everyone as part of me, a part of the priory and a part of the congregation. I look at each person as someone like me who is trying and struggling to be a real Benedictine in the eyes of God."[31] The gift of seeing with God's eyes is exactly what our world needs today and a gift we are called to bring to life.

These past experiences help us consider how we can incarnate the culture of encounter in the future. When asked how our community can be more welcoming to new members, Sr. Deana Case, OSB, reflected, "Be open, stop judgmental attitudes, offer kindness and warmth. . . . Learn, laugh, and play as though Christ himself came knocking on the door."[32] We must welcome all cultures and generations who seek to live the gospel through religious life. Celebrating identity is inherently part of the spirit of communion, and this spirit is enhanced when our African sisters dance the offertory to the table of the Mass. Vanier explains, "Communion, in fact, gives the freedom to grow. It is not possessiveness. It entails a deep listening to others, helping them to become more fully themselves."[33] For us to grow into the future, we need to embrace the deep listening of communion, allowing each one the freedom to grow in her own culture and generation.

In an article she wrote looking back at her own religious life and considering future generations, Sr. Ann Marie Paul, SCC, proposed a number of practical attitudes, including these three

[30] Ibid.

[31] Ibid.

[32] Deana Case. Interview by author. Religious Life Book Project Questionnaire. Norfolk, NE, December 2016.

[33] Vanier, *From Brokenness to Community*, 17.

that help us foster freedom among our diverse sisters.[34] First, she recommends being grateful so that we might see diversity as a gift. With a touch of humor, Sr. Ann Marie said, "I am grateful for the welcome I received from the sisters and the guidance they gave me—everything from where to find the extra toilet paper to how to persevere in living my vows."[35] At the first community I visited as a new convert to Catholicism, I needed a sister to explain to me that a chaplet was not a small chapel but rather a form of prayer. Her graciousness in taking the time to explain this new language gave me courage in my vulnerable years of discernment. The smallest kindness and moment of encounter can lead us from death to life.

The second attitude Sr. Ann Marie offers to us in regards to the future is to "be the community you want to see," to live a life of integrity with a wholehearted "yes."[36] If we as young sisters want to see a culture of encounter take over our communities, we need to live it. Similarly, we need to live our charisms authentically. We are called to be true to the foundational elements of our life: prayer, community, service, simplicity, the sacraments, and lifelong commitment in the heart of the church.[37] As a young novice, it moved me to see our prioress in chapel every morning before Lauds praying with Scripture. This kind of model of authenticity taught me an invaluable lesson and challenged me to offer that to those entering now. Young people see shallow cultural icons and hypocritical figureheads constantly. They are looking for something radical, authentic, and transformative. As fully committed women religious, it is up to us to be fearless as we live into our call.

[34] Ann Marie Paul, "Gleanings from My First Ten Years," *Review for Religious* 69, no. 1 (2010): 63–70.

[35] Ibid., 64.

[36] Ibid., 65.

[37] Paul Michalenko and Dominic Perri, "Authentic Responses to the Future of Religious Life," *Human Development* 33, no. 4 (Winter 2012): 3–9.

Finally, Sr. Ann Marie calls us to embrace an attitude of solidarity. We aren't on the journey alone and cannot afford to be self-centered. When we find ourselves in a storm, we have an anchor in Christ and a road map in our charism that will take us to shore intact. Rooting ourselves in the sacramental life of the church, especially in frequenting the sacraments of Eucharist and confession, will keep us on the path to life and healthy community. When I entered our community, the monastery was in the midst of renovation. Touring the nearly finished chapel one day with my novice directress, she explained why our sisters decided to put a huge image of our Missionary Benedictine cross directly over the altar. It struck me profoundly. She said that this is our call: to bring Christ whom we receive in the Holy Eucharist to the world in missionary service. Without the glue of the Eucharist received in this moment of sacramental encounter, we would be lost. Similarly, we are upheld by the power of mercy that transforms us through confession. I appreciate that now as a final professed sister more than ever. In our busy lives, we rarely slow down and allow ourselves to be healed or loved in our brokenness. Here, in the vulnerability of this sacrament, we can receive Christ's healing love.

We also find this rootedness in our sisters. When I landed in Brazil and felt like a fish out of water, one of the main sources of hope that sustained me was the group of nine joyful and generous junior sisters I met there who embraced me with open arms. With them, I was never alone on the journey. No matter what, Sr. Ann Marie advised, "Avoid wasting time questioning how God could ever have intended this seemingly motley group to do anything together, let alone live in community and witness to God's love. Instead, praise and thank God for the wondrous diversity in which you are privileged to participate."[38] Together in our beautiful and life-giving di-

[38] Paul, "Gleanings," 69.

versity, we can meet the gift of the present moment without fear. Conflict will inevitably come, but if we practice openness, we can liberate ourselves from the prisons it can create.

Conclusion

We as sisters today incarnate the culture of encounter for a church and a world hungry for relationship and hope. We are called to help women encounter self, God, and others during discernment and formation. Our communities need to embrace encounter both practically and theologically within intergenerational and intercultural community life. The lived experiences of sisters committed to the culture of encounter in diverse community contexts gives us key, fruitful insights. Each culture and generation has its own gifts and stories. In telling our stories, welcoming those of others, and celebrating how God is moving in the church today, we will live out of the one story—the story of God's redeeming love.

In the words of Jean Vanier, Christ invites us into this one story: "Come and live with these brothers and sisters who may squabble together like the first of my disciples, but this is where I am calling you to be today. It might be difficult but it will be a place of growth in love for you. It is there that I will reveal to you my love."[39]

[39] Vanier, *From Brokenness to Community*, 42.

The Bridges I Cross and Las Hermanas Who Built Them

Christa Parra, IBVM

Hay tantisimas fronteras
que dividen a la gente,
pero por cada frontera
existe un puente.

There are so many borders
that divide people,
but for every border
a bridge exists.[1]
(Gina Valdés)

"I wish I had a warmer chaqueta," I think to myself as I try to keep up with Sr. Rita speed walking across a huge puente connecting El Paso, Texas, to Ciudad Juárez, Chihuahua. Each week this Irish hermana, in her late seventies, crosses to el otro

[1] Gloria Anzaldua, *Borderlands/La Frontera: The New Mestiza*, 4th ed. (San Francisco: Aunt Lute, 2012), 107. A glossary of Spanish words used here is included at the end of this chapter.

lado to work with mujeres at el Centro Santa Catalina,[2] a sewing cooperative and spirituality center located in a destitute colonia. We rush over the bridge to catch the bus. She gives me her scarf and I quickly wrap it around my frozen face. We arrive at the bus stop, and I realize that I don't have any pesos. La hermana asks the caballero next to us if he can spare some pesos for my bus fare. He kindly does. As I get on the bus, Sr. Rita reminds me to watch mi bolsa. We enter an old green-gutted bus and sit on a long bench on the right side. I notice how carefree this hermana seems, smiling and making conversation with las personas around her. We bounce along the bumpy, poorly paved camino. I look out the ventana and watch the city as it wakes up.

A huge billboard captures my attention. It proclaims, "¡Juárez es Amor!" with a picture of Pope Francis smiling. The message "Juárez is Love!" strikes me as ironic, considering I know about the hundreds of mujeres kidnapped, murdered, and found in mass graves in Juárez. This femicide, the murder of local women, occurred from the mid-1990s through the early 2000s. These women, hijas de Dios, worked in las maquiladoras and lived in extreme poverty.

We finally arrive at the bottom of a dusty hill where Centro Santa Catalina stands as an oasis in el desierto. We are greeted with hugs and besos by a comunidad de women en la lucha for a better vida. In the cooperative, the women work diligently at their sewing machines. Some mujeres are ironing fabric while others fold and package tortilla warmers, scarves, and tablecloths.

Everyone stops to celebrate the Día de Los Reyes Magos with Sr. Rita and me. They offer us a seat at their mesa along with cafecito and a slice of cake. I listen to the emotional stories of how Centro Santa Catalina transformed their lives from

[2] "Centro Santa Catalina—The Spiritual, Education and Economic Empowerment of Women," accessed March 4, 2017, http://centrosantacatalina.org/.

darkness to light. They share how two Adrian Dominican Sisters from the Midwest crossed the border, spent time in the colonia, a former city garbage dump, listened to the women's stories, and built something nuevo with the mujeres and their children. These mujeres of faith y esperanza are committed to being in solidarity with all mujeres fighting for freedom from poverty, violencia, and oppressive sistemas which prevent them from being fully and freely themselves. That day, Sr. Rita was a bridge, helping me understand that "Juárez is love."

A few days before the journey to Juárez, I drove to a mountain in El Paso overlooking the border cities. I admired the scene of dos ciudades basking under the same sol. I couldn't see where una ciudad ended and la otra began. However, the divide is a lived realidad for borderland people. Although la violencia has decreased in the last few years, the differences between the two ciudades are enormous in terms of economic, healthcare, educational, and employment opportunities. When I visited El Paso, the eager esperanza of the pope's arrival was contagious on both lados of la frontera. It seemed that el Papa would become another puente unifying both sides and sending a message to el mundo that we must have a preferential option for our brothers and sisters at las fronteras. On his flight back home from Juárez, the press interviewed him. El Papa les dijo, "A person who thinks only about building walls, wherever they may be, and not building bridges, is not Christian. This is not in the Gospel."[3]

Today we have an extraordinary oportunidad to courageously cross fronteras and not only build bridges but also become them. In this chapter, I will reflect on my experiencias as a young Mexican-American hermana religiosa entering a predominantly Irish and white community in the United States. By age and ethnic background, soy una minority. How-

[3] Joshua J. McElwee, "Pope Francis Questions Donald Trump's Christianity, Says Border Wall Not from Gospel," *National Catholic Reporter*, February 18, 2016, accessed May 11, 2017, https://www.ncronline.org/news/pope-francis-questions-donald-trumps-christianity-says-border-wall-not-gospel.

ever, as a Latina, I belong to a demographic that is among the fastest growing population in the United States and makes up nearly half the Catholic Church in this country. My context as a Mexican-American mujer from the US/Mexico border is helpful because la frontera represents the posibilidades of building bridges. Bridges have the power to welcome, include, and unify people by providing a means of crossing over with ease from one side to the other. Bridges can be places of hospitality and la vida nueva. I consider my vocation a journey of border crossing over bridges built by mis hermanas religiosas.

I entered la vida religiosa in the United States almost a decade ago. The more comunidades religiosas I encounter, the more I wonder why there are so few people of color, particularly in women's religious communities. Nuestras hermanas have lived and ministered in Hispanic/Latino/a, African American/black, Native American, and Asian American communities in the United States for decades. Yet, the majority of religious hermanas are white and elderly. Today I see oportunidades where we can heal broken bridges by reflecting on our own diversity or lack thereof and together dream of ways to build puentes. This way, our comunidades religiosas will not only reflect the diverse communities we serve, but inspire more women of color to discern, come, and stay in la vida religiosa.

El Comienzo

If you travel four horas northwest of El Paso along the border you encounter mi tierra, Bisbee, Arizona. I am third generation Mexican-American raised in a big Catholic familia. The border is home para mi. When I was a niña, my dad, mis hermanos, and I would cross the border to Naco, Sonora, with frecuencia and ease to go to la farmarcia and la panadería for fresh tortillas and pan dulce. During the summer, we would go to el otro lado to watch my older brother play baseball in the Mexican league. As my dad would speak en Español or

Spanglish with his amigos, I would listen intently trying to understand a language that unfortunately gets lost in the third generation. Although I wasn't fluent in Español until I studied it en la universidad, I knew my Mexican roots. Mariachi, cumbia, y ranchera musica pulses through mi sangre. When I hear these rhythms, my curvy hips, just like my nana's, can't help but dance. Each year, our tamale-making ritual indicates that the baby Jesus is coming soon for La Navidad. We have fiestas for every life event from baptisms to graduations to a homecoming after a long journey.

At the same time, I grew up in American culture. As a niña, Motown music, golden oldies, country, and hip-hop were also part of my experience. I played football with my tres brothers who are my best amigos. The Fourth of July is one of my favorite holidays as our familia has a big reunion in Bisbee. We love our country. We never take for granted the gift and la responsibilidad of our freedom. My younger brother bravely served in Iraq on two tours in the Army following in the footsteps of my dad, both grandfathers, and many tios/as and primos who also served in the US military. Me siento bendecida to be both Mexican y American.

It is also not easy being bicultural. The movie *Selena* depicts this bicultural realidad well. Selena's father names the tensions of being a Mexican-American:

> Listen, being Mexican-American is tough. Anglos jump all over you if you don't speak English perfectly. Mexicans jump all over you if you don't speak Spanish perfectly. We've got to be twice as perfect as anybody else. Our family has been here for four centuries yet they treat us as if we just swam across the Rio Grande. I mean we got to know about John Wayne and Pedro Infante. . . . We've got to know about Oprah and Cristina. . . . We got to prove to the Mexicans how Mexican we are; we got to prove to the Americans how American we are. It is exhausting![4]

[4] Gregory Nava, *Selena* (Universal Pictures, 1997).

Living at la frontera taught me that when we embrace both cultures there is paz, joy, and esperanza. Speaking Spanglish as a valid way of communication comes from this space. Our fusion of dos idiomas as it is spoken in daily life is indicative of our being at home in our bicultural realidad. I am borrowing from Latina theologian Carmen Nanko-Fernández in choosing to share my story in Spanglish.[5]

Cruzando Borders into la Vida Religiosa

My journey in religious life has been crossing one frontera after another. In saying this, I do not take lightly those who have died or experienced rape and other kinds of violence while crossing through the desert or by ocean into this country. The borders I am crossing are figurative and literal, but they are different from the extreme dangers one may experience migrating or fleeing their native country in hopes of a different life in the United States

El primer journey into religious life was the toughest. When I started discerning la vida religiosa, it was foreign land to me. We didn't have any nuns in our large familia; married life was the only vocation I knew. As a niña, I dreamed of getting married one day, with a big beautiful boda like many of mis primas had. I imagined my dad and mama walking me down the aisle to my handsome esposo. La misa would be joyful and the reception would be a delightful fiesta! I also dreamt of motherhood and raising my children in Arizona with mi familia. Mi mama, one of the strongest and bravest women I know, inspired me to want to be a mother. When I was a niña, she worked two trabajos and at one time tres jobs including cleaning casas to support my brothers and me. Like it was for her, family always seemed like it would be my path.

[5] Carmen Nanko-Fernandez, *Theologizing En Espanglish: Context, Community, and Ministry* (Maryknoll, NY: Orbis, 2010), xvi.

As I grew up and began to think about my life direction, the idea of religious life was not on my radar. Still, although I couldn't see it at the time, my call may not have been a surprise to others. I was voted "most likely to become a nun" my senior year of high school. I thought it was funny; I knew nothing about nuns except from the movies *Sister Act* and *Sound of Music*. When I was twenty-one, an encounter changed everything.

I was at a crossroads in my life. Un día, I went to pray in the Catholic church my nana and I went to every domingo for Mass. As I sat in la iglesia, I asked Dios, "What do you want me to do with mi vida?" Then, I realized that I was talking at but not listening to Dios. I got quiet. When I did, the pensamiento occurred that maybe I wasn't listening porque I was afraid of what I might hear. I resolved to be quiet longer.

At that very moment, a woman entró a la iglesia and approached me. I later learned that her name is Sr. Gabby and she had come into the church that day to pray for vocations. She found me. Without introducing herself she asked, "Have you ever thought about being a nun?" I quickly replied, "No. I want to get married and have a family." Sr. Gabby didn't skip a beat and, for some reason, invited me, "Come on, let's go to the convent!" I was hesitant, but, for some reason, I went.

The reason was el Espíritu Santo. As soon as I entered the doorway, I sensed a movement in mi alma. I felt at home in a place that I had never been before. Meeting the sisters, I was struck by how down to earth, joyful, and real they were. Sr. Gabby was a puente for me into religious life. Every week I met with her, and we became amigas. She got to know me, listened to my stories, and invited me to meals and prayer. She got to know mi familia. For six years she accompanied me, even while I held onto my dream of marriage. At one point I even got engaged and then broke off the engagement.

When I was finally ready to discern la vida religiosa, I went through an eight-day silent retreat. Until that point, I had been scared of what was on the unknown otro lado. I prayed for courage. On the retreat, I discovered that at the core of who I am is to love and to be loved. As I reviewed my grace history, the story of Dios at work in mi vida, I recognized from the time I was in my mother's womb, I was loved. Mi mama told me cuando ella was pregnant with me, I would respond to my dad's voz. He would talk to me and I would move to whatever lado he was on. I knew then and continue to know his unconditional love. This beautiful memory helped me see that discernment was simply listening for God's voice of great love and similarly moving to respond. God invited me to trust, and I found paz that impelled me to continue on el camino. After discerning with different religious comunidades, I decided to enter the Institute of the Blessed Virgin Mary (IBVM) also known at the Loreto Sisters, Sr. Gabby's community.

And so began my journey of discovering puentes into mi congregación. Sr. Christine, my director of candidacy, was one of those puentes. Fascinatingly enough, she is also the hermana who prepared me for first Holy Communion as a child. An expert on the life of our founder, the Venerable Mary Ward, she taught me our community's roots in the Jesuit spirituality and tradition, as well as about the courageous woman herself. La Venerable Mary Ward didn't want our hermanas to wear the habit, as she wanted us to be among la gente and for our dress to reflect the comunidades we serve. She was passionate about educating mujeres and muchachas who were not given the same oportunidades as men and boys. Today we are on five continents and in twenty-two países including India, Kenya, and Perú. Our core values are freedom, justicia, sincerity, joy, y la verdad—all which we live out in our various ministerios. We are a congregation of puentes.

Embracing la Diversidad in Religious Life

After candidacy, I entered la vida religiosa. On my entrance day, mi mama y yo went to Mass and then drove to the convent. I cried as soon as the door opened and the sisters greeted me with abrazos and smiles. Lloré when I unpacked my suitcase, and the sisters stopped by to tell me they remembered their own tears when they entered. As I walked my mom to la puerta to say adiós, I was surprised when a sister ran down the hall after us to invite mi mama y mis hermanos to come back that evening for my welcoming ceremonia and dinner. I wiped mis lágrimas and entered into the experience of settling into my new home. The prayer service that night included each hermana sharing her favorite Scripture verse to give me encouragement. Mi mama and oldest and youngest brother joined us afterward for prayer, hot dogs, and cold cervezas as it was also the eve of the Super Bowl. Mis hermanos had never been to el convento. They were worried that I would be triste, but instead they encountered a welcoming and loving comunidad. For a culture that so deeply values family, this was an important bridge. Their corazones were at peace and so was mine.

Moving into community, I embraced the new. I enjoyed the daily rhythm of Mass, evening prayers, meals together, and time in the community room. I picked up phrases like "that's lovely," "that's grand," "please God," and, my favorite, "céad míle fáilte," which means a hundred thousand welcomes in Gaelic Irish. I learned to drink leche in my tea and that a good cup of hot tea is the cure for everything!

I entered in 2008, only five years after the Irish Region located in Arizona merged with the North American Branch (Canada and the United States). Before the merge, a novice would travel to Ireland for part of her formation if she entered in Phoenix. Because of the merge, I was la primera novice to leave the Southwest and go to Chicago for formation. I journeyed two thousand miles from mi tierra in the Southwest to Illinois. The flat land and bitterly cold, snowy winters were a shock to this desert girl. The only blizzards I knew of before moving to Chicago were at Dairy Queen. The rhythm of prayer and community life was diferente from Phoenix, too, but I realized that every convent has its own ritmo. Las hermanas in this convento were white, mostly Irish-Americans with deep Chicago roots. The sisters went above and beyond to make sure I felt en casa.

In the years to come las hermanas would welcome mi familia with open arms when they would visit. The year I moved to Illinois my older brother, who works for the railroad, was sent to Chicago for the first time. In the nine years I was there, as Dios would have it, mi hermano would be sent for work at significant momentos in my journey including running a marathon, renewing my vows, and turning thirty. Dios gave me the fuerza and encouragement I needed to keep moving forward.

There were gifts and challenges in this new environment. One of the challenges for me was living with privileges that I didn't have before. I say this with awareness that las hermanas at the motherhouse, like many motherhouses, are older and in need of assistance. It was an adjustment for me to live in a place where people are hired to cook, clean, and maintain the grounds. I had a difficult time not helping with the cooking and cleaning up afterward; a few sisters reminded me not to when I tried.

The only place I saw the color of my skin was on the Mexican mujeres working in the kitchen and cleaning the convento. Mi corazón was happy as I walked into the kitchen each day greeting my new amigas in Español with Mexican música on the radio in the background. Sometimes I joined them in the kitchen pantry for their lunch, complete with salsa and tortillas, after I ate a lighter lunch with las hermanas. I felt at home being in the presence of Latinas who shared mi cultura and understood what it was like to be homesick, as they too had migrated to Illinois.

Our identidades are strengthened when we are in unfamiliar territory, but it takes work. Mis hermanas and I climbed willingly onto the bridge of compartiendo culturas. I am an affectionate Latina showing my love through greetings with hugs and besos on the cheek; for some hermanas, this was an adjustment. The sisters were open to learning about Mexican traditions. For Mexican Independence Day we had a little fiesta in the community room. I made empanadas and taught them a few cumbia moves. For my thirtieth birthday, mis hermanas religiosas surprised me with a quinceañera times two! The quinceañera is the traditional celebration for a fifteen-year-old. At the same time, I learned about the traditions of St. Patrick's Day and the importance of wearing verde, eating corned beef and cabbage, Irish soda bread, and knowing Irish canciones.

Even in the most open comunidades, this process of cultural bridging is more challenging for the minority than the majority. Everything was nuevo, as I was in constant transition learning about the culture of la vida religiosa and the culture of the Midwest all while being evaluated as a novice. I felt vulnerable most of the time and lonely some of the time, especially when misunderstandings occurred.

Along with the intercultural diversity, we are an intergenerational comunidad. The age gap between the majority of the sisters and myself is apparent to everyone and strange to many. However, when you are raised Latina, multigenerational living is a way of life. Every family gathering includes the older generation. We respect them, eat at their tables, enjoy their stories, listen to their música, pray their novenas, and love them. This is a gift that Latinas offer la vida religiosa. I spent nearly every weekend with mis abuelos as a child. Their casa was our casa. For my first vows, my novice director said only immediate familia could attend the vows. I said okay, but I thought this meant my parents, hermanos, abuelos, godparents, tio/as, and primos/as. That is not what she meant. Fortunately, after she spoke with our leadership team, mis abuelos and one tio were allowed to come.

For me, living with las hermanas who are much older than I am is a bendición. Mis hermanas have faithfully committed their entire beings to Dios, and that inspires me. They tell me that my vibrancy, energía, and joy give them esperanza for el futuro. I see nuestras vidas in community as a witness to the world that intergenerational relationships with their joys and challenges are life-giving. The worst part of this generational diversity is the grief we experience when our sisters die. The incredible mujeres with whom we have shared our daily experiences, meals, laughter, tears, and prayers impress their stories and presence on our corazones. I have attended more funerals than most people my age. Still, another puente emerges. I am regularly reminded of our hope in resurrection, la vida nueva, telling us that the best is yet to come. Jesus is our bridge to eternal life.

Who Is at the Mesa?

During my time in Chicago, the Intercommunity Novitiate (ICN) was another life-giving experience of crossing bridges. My novice director and I joined about thirty-five novices from different congregations for meetings each week. There were novices from the Philippines, Haiti, Vietnam, Portugal, and various parts of the United States. At our ICN, multiple borders merged into this one experience as we heard one another's stories and encouraged each other. One evening after a workshop, together we watched history being made as newly elected US President Barack Obama, another puente, gave a powerful acceptance speech in Chicago. As he talked, he used the slogan from his campaign repeatedly, "Yes we can!" This cry, "¡Si se puede!" would resonate with anyone familiar with civil rights activists Cesar Chavez and Dolores Huerta. President Obama talked about inclusivity, perseverance, and esperanza. Listening to his message, we knew it was an exciting time for our país. As a Mexican-American, I identify as a mujer of color. Whenever I see a leader who uses his or her poder to serve and unite toda la gente, especially those who are oppressed and marginalized, I am inspired. When the leader is a persona of color, I am invited to dream grande and take action. In la vida religiosa, we must remember this.

The longer I am in religious life, the more I wonder, "Donde están the minorities in la vida religiosa?" As I mentioned, our ICN group was one of diversidad. The majority of male novices were from otros países. However, out of the eleven mujeres in our grupo, only three of us were women of color. Out of the forty IBVM hermanas in the Midwest, I am also one of three mujeres of color. The other two both serve in leadership, one on the general leadership team and la otra on the provincial leadership team. They are puentes for me; their presence tells me that I belong in la vida religiosa. Still, at any gathering of women religious in our país, I am a minority by age and race. When I see a homogenous group of women that have served diverse communities for years, yet the membership does not reflect this realidad, I have to ask, "¿Por qué?"

The answer to this pregunta is complicado. I invite us to have the courage to reflect on our own historias and talk about why our faces do not reflect the comunidades we have served. I am also aware that the demographics are shifting as Sr. Teresa Maya, CCVI, president of the Leadership Conference of Women Religious (LCWR), pointed out in an address to a Giving Voice National Gathering. "The Catholic Church is becoming browner and browner," Maya said. To prove her point, she asked how many sisters in the room had been born outside of the United States. About half raised their hands, and Maya encouraged these sisters to be unafraid to speak their truth to older sisters, whom she calls the "Great Generation."[6] She is a puente for me telling me to use mi voz and speak mi verdad. We need to see más people of color in our comunidades and in our leadership positions.

There is another layer here. When we talk about the diversity in our comunidades increasing, the conversation is often focused upon las hermanas coming from other countries. We are blessed that our internationality is increasing. At the same time, let's not overlook the treasure of the rich diversity of Asian Americans, African Americans/blacks, Native Americans, and Latina women in the United States. We must appreciate the vast diversity within each group as well. Have we fully explored the posibilidad of inviting more people of color to discern la vida religiosa?

[6] Dawn Araujo-Hawkins, "Younger Sisters Preparing to Be the Change in Religious Life," *Global Sisters Report*, August 11, 2015, accessed May 11, 2017, http://globalsistersreport.org/blog/gsr-today/younger-sisters-preparing-be-change-religious-life-29156.

I began to think more critically about who is excluded from our religious comunidades after reading Carmen Nanko-Fernandez's work. She was my professor at CTU in Chicago and a bridge for me to the world of Latino/a theology. Latino/a theology was influenced by Latin American theology but differs in that it comes from lo cotidiano of the Hispanic comunidades in the United States and values the particular contexts of people here. Its methods resonate with every fiber in my being. Nanko-Fernandez encouraged me to use my voice and taught me how to theologize en conjunto latinamente. The commitment to theologize en conjunto is ecumenical y interdisciplinary and for the liberation of all women and hombres.

In her writing, Nanko-Fernandez questions the disparity between the number of US Catholic Latino/as and the number of Latino/as represented in leadership in the Church. She prophetically cries out to the US Catholic Church to wake up to the reality, listen to the people of God, critically reflect upon the daily lived experiences, and take action.[7] I suggest that our comunidades do the same. We must pay attention to who is not at our mesa and why. The key to building puentes and being bridges is to learn from the conjunto model and listen to one another, share stories, enjoy convivencia, and collaborate on our proyectos and in our ministries.

Although this is a difficult subject to reflect upon, racism is a tragic part of our history as a country and a church, and in religious life. I was horrified to learn that at one time women of color were rejected from some religious comunidades because of the color of their skin. Some who were accepted into religious life experienced mistreatment and racism. Shannon Dee Williams writes about this painful history, including the racism young black sisters encountered in religious life, in her forthcoming book *Subversive Habits: Black Nuns and the Long Struggle to Desegregate Catholic America*.[8]

[7] Nanko-Fernandez, *Theologizing En Espanglish*.

[8] See Dan Stockman, "Forthcoming Book Documents History of Black Sisters in the U.S.," *Global Sisters Report*, May 14, 2015, accessed May 8, 2017,

Roberto Treviño wrote about the Mexican-American hermanas in Texas who experienced the pain of exclusion and discrimination within their community:

> [Sister María Luisa] Valez reported that in the early twentieth century these tejanas often felt the sting of racial slurs and were routinely assigned primarily to menial tasks and excluded from educational opportunities. . . . These and other examples of ethnic animosity and discrimination among some of the Sisters explained, to a large degree, why historically there were so few Mexican-American nuns.[9]

Las hermanas at the LWCR 2016 meeting recognized the need to heal and reconcile with our past.[10] Some religious comunidades in the United States have been brave enough to go through anti-racism workshops and examine their own white privilege. I believe it is our call today to tear down walls built by bricks of fear and insecurities and build puentes of amor, mercy, solidarity, and inclusivity.

A Religious Life de Colores

When bridges of love and inclusivity are built, we must celebrate with a fiesta! The day of my final vows the festive sounds of trumpets, violins, and las guitarras flowed into every space of Our Lady of Guadalupe Church. For Mexican-Americans, Our Lady of Guadalupe evokes a sense of love, inclusivity, and justice. I prayed this Mass would embody those

---

http://globalsistersreport.org/news/trends/forthcoming-book-documents-history-black-sisters-us-25501. Williams spoke on this topic at the 2016 assembly of the LCWR.

[9] Roberto R. Treviño, "Facing Jim Crow: Catholic Sisters and the 'Mexican Problem' in Texas," *Western Historical Quarterly* 34, no. 2 (May 1, 2003): 144, 146, doi:10.2307/25047254.

[10] Margaret Alandt and Pat McCluskey, "LCWR Assembly Confronts Racism and Religious Life," Fall 2016, https://lcwr.org/publications/lcwr-assembly-confronts-racism-and-religious-life.

qualities as the congregation began to sing "De Colores." In the back of la iglesia, mi mama stood at my side, held my hand, and told me that she loved me. My dad said, "Mija, I am so proud of you." He bent and extended his arm for me to slip my hand through. Together, we walked down the aisle of a packed iglesia. My handsome hermanito held la biblia as he prepared to be a lector. I felt pretty in my blanco knee length floral print dress and fuchsia high heels. The fuchsia, orange, and bright amarillo tropical flores on this carefully chosen vestido reflected my joy. These colors complemented the permanent sonrisa on my face. My long dark brown hair was pulled back and up high on my head in a bun surrounded by carefully pinned curls. Mi nana's gold mariposa earrings matched the butterflies in mi estómago. The silver cruz hanging around my neck with the letters IBVM was still shining after nine years of formation. I was in awe of the family, friends, and religious who had traveled from near and far to South Chicago for my final vows celebration. My parents y yo stopped and bowed in front of el altar then sat in the first pew still singing about the many colors in God's beautifully diverse creation. Behind me were three rows of my IBVM sisters whose smiling faces met mine when I looked back at them. In this Eucharist, we began our fiesta of thanksgiving to Dios for God's many gifts. We gave gracias a Dios for the regalo of a vocation to la vida religiosa and for the pueblo de Dios that made it happen. We continued our bilingual celebration followed by dinner for all three hundred guests while enjoying the Our Lady of Guadalupe Youth Mariachi. After la cena of pollo and potatoes with agua de jamaica and horchata for our drinks, the baile began!

El día of my final vows we celebrated cruzando borders and sharing culturas. With the journey's joys and struggles, our fiesta proclaimed that we are una familia de Dios. Every time we cross a new frontera and venture into the unknown it is scary at first. Yet if we are open, Dios gives us the courage and grace to take risks and build relationships we never imagined.

In order to become puentes, we must identify walls that prevent us from being more inclusive and deconstruct them. Mi esperanza is that we will listen carefully to las historias of women of color and learn how to be better compañeras. My dream is that we will build and become puentes welcoming more mujeres of color to come and stay. My prayer is that we will make la vida religiosa de colores a beautiful realidad for the greater gloria de Dios. ¡Que viva la vida religiosa!

Translation Glossary

abrazos–hugs
adiós–bye
agua de jamaica–hibiscus flower flavored water
amarillo–yellow
amigos/as–friends
amor–love
bendicion–blessing
besos–kisses
blanco–white
boda–wedding
caballero–gentleman
cafecito–little coffee
caminar–walk
camino–road
canciones–songs
casas–houses
Centro Santa Catalina–St. Catherine's Center
cervezas–beers
chaqueta–jacket
cinco–five
colonia–neighborhood in Mexican city
compañeras–companions
compartiendo–sharing
complicado–complicated
comunidad de–community of
comunidad–community
comunidades religiosas–religious communities
convivencia–living together/co–existing
corazon(es)–heart(s)
cruz–cross
cruzando–crossing
culturas–cultures
De Colores–the many colors
Día de Los Reyes Magos–Three Kings Day
diferente–different
Dios–God
Domingo–Sunday
¿Donde estan– , , , ?–Where are the . . . ?
dos ciudades–two cities
el comienzo–the beginning
dos culturas–two cultures
dos idiomas–two languages
el altar–the altar
el convento–the convent
el desierto–the desert
el día–the day
El Espíritu Santo–the Holy Spirit

el futuro–the future
el mundo–the world
el otro lado–the other side
el Papa–the Pope
en casa–at home
en conjunto–with others/ together
en la Universidad–in the university
energia–energy
entró–entered
escuela–school
Español–Spanish
esperanza–hope
esposo–husband
experiencias–experiences
familia–family
fiesta(s)–celebration
frecuencia–frequency
fuerza–strength
gloria a Dios–glory to God
gracias a Dios–thanks to God
grande–big
grupo–group
hijas de Dios–daughters of God
historias–histories
horas–hour
horchata–sweet rice milk drink
identidades–identities
importante–important
justicia–justice
la Biblia–the Bible
la cena–dinner
la diversidad–the diversity
la farmarcia–the pharmacy
la gente–the people
la idea–the idea
la iglesia–the church
la luz–the light
la Misa–the Mass
La Navidad–Christmas
la otra–the other
la panadería–the bakery
la primera–the first
la puerta–the door
la responsibilidad–the responsibility
la verdad–the truth
la vida nueva–new life
la vida religiosa–religious life
la(s) frontera(s)–the border(s)
la(s) hermana(s)–the sister(s)
lado(s)–side(s)
las maquiladoras–the factories
las personas–persons
Latina/o–a person with roots from one or more of the 21 Latin American countries
latinamente–a method of theologizing en conjunto
leche–milk
les dijo–told them
lloré–I cried
lo cotidiano–daily life
Mariachi, cumbia, y ranchera musica–Mexican styles of music
mariposa–butterfly
más–more
Me siento bendicida– . . .—I feel blessed . . .
mensaje–message
mesa–table
mi alma–my soul
mi bolsa–my purse
mi estómago–my stomach
mi mama y mis hermanos–my mom and my brothers
mi sangre–my blood

mi tierra–my land
mi verdad–my truth
mi vida–my life
mi voz–my voice
mis abuelos–my grandparents
mis hermanas religiosas–my religious sisters
mis lagrimas–my tears
mis mejores amigos/as–my best friends
momento–moment
muchachas–girls
mujeres–women
nana–grandmother
niña–girl
nuestras hermanas–our sisters
nuestras vidas–our lives
nuevo–new
oportunidad–opportunity
otro lado–the other side
otros países–other countries
países–countries
pan dulce–sweet bread
para mi–for me
paz–peace
pensamiento–thought
pesos–Mexican currency
poder–power
pollo–chicken
¿Por qué?–Why?
porque–because
posibilidades–possibility
pregunta–question
primos/as–cousins
proyecto–project
pueblo de Dios–God's people, God's village or town
puente–bridge
realidad–reality
religiosas–religious
¡Si se puede!–Yes, you can!
sistema(s)–system(s)
sol–sun
sonrisa–smile
soy una–I am a
Spanglish–mixing Spanish and English words
tamale–cornmeal dough with meat filling
tios/as–uncles/aunts
toda la gente–all the people
tortillas–flat flour or corn thin round bread
trabajo–work
trabajos–jobs
tres–three
triste–sad
un día–one day
una ciudad–one city
una sorpresa–a surprise
ventana–window
verde–green
vida–life
violencia–violence
voz–voice
y yo–and I

The Compassion the World Needs Now

Amanda Carrier, RSM

At ministry one day a volunteer took me aside to share her story of cancer survival. I was surprised she would want to talk about something so life-changing with someone at least a decade her junior, especially since we did not know each other well. Then later that day, her husband took me aside to share his experience of how her illness had changed her and how that had adversely affected their marriage. I was unprepared to be invited into something so personal but did my best to listen attentively without looking shocked or uncomfortable. This story is just one of the many times people have shared their most personal and painful life events with me. I've heard stories of abuse, addiction, marital problems, and more. From this you might assume that I'm a therapist or social worker, but really I'm a chef at a soup kitchen with no professional training in counseling. Nonetheless, when people find out I'm a sister the stories start streaming in.

People look to women religious to model compassion, and I believe that as women religious we are especially equipped to answer this need of our time. Defining compassion through presence and sacramentality, we see a model which is uniquely suited to the life of women religious. Following this definition, we will explore how to develop compassion through recognizing both our vulnerability and our belovedness, and adopting particular practices in the context of our life as vowed religious.

Compassion: Presence and Sacramentality

Compassion is being with another person in the depth of their experience. This means more than feeling pity or entering into the suffering of another; it is both tender and strong in response to either suffering or joy. It is the "force that makes a bridge from the island of one individuality to the island of the other. It is an ability to step outside your own perspective, limitations and ego, and become attentive in a vulnerable, encouraging, critical, and creative way with the hidden world of another person."[1] It is also important to know that compassion is not about fixing a problem; rather it is about connection at a deep interpersonal level. This deep connection is developed through two key components of compassion: presence and sacramentality.

Presence in the moment is the practice of being fully aware of the other. Though presence might seem simple, its practice takes some effort. Being in the moment is becoming difficult in our culture, which values speed, instant gratification, and multitasking. Yet we know when we have experienced someone's full attention. My novice minister was very good at being fully present to me in our encounters. She created a safe place where I could let my true self show through the gift of her presence. After a difficult conversation in the midst of a challenging situation with another sister, I walked into her office on the verge of tears. My minister set aside what she was doing, lit a candle, and sat with me. It is hard to describe the feeling of knowing when someone is being fully present. I notice these encounters of presence and compassion as palpable moments of warmth, safety, and acceptance. When my

[1] Mary NurrieStearns, "The Presence of Compassion: An Interview with John O'Donohue," *Personal Transformation*, accessed May 8, 2017, http://www.personaltransformation.com/john_odonohue.html.

minister sat with me it was that kind of encounter; I felt her caring and listening spirit in her attentiveness towards me. I wish I could express exactly how this is accomplished, but I am only beginning to understand it myself. I can say with certainty that my novice minister was solid in her understanding of herself and her relationship with God. She was courageous in her own sharing, which let me know that whatever I needed to share with her would be welcomed and safe. She was also very good with her own boundaries—healthy boundaries are a must for vibrantly lived religious life but that is another book.[2] These gifts which I saw in her are ones I have admired and continue to seek within myself; acquiring them is a slow process but I am not discouraged. She saw the light of God within me at those times when I had lost sight of it in myself. Her gift of presence reminded me of my sacred truth as beloved of God and called it forth from within me again and again. Now, as I practice the gift of presence that I saw in her I hope to do the same for others.

While presence is a fundamental piece to showing compassion, so is the ability to see the sacramentality of the world and people around us. As I practice presence in my encounters, I try to find how God enters into those moments. This is sacramentality. In Celtic spirituality, the "thin place" is such a place, where the divine and the earthly touch. If we encounter each person as a thin place, we see in them a sacramental presence of God. We each carry the Divine within us as the traditional Hindu greeting "Namasté" highlights. This greeting literally means "may the Divine in me honor the Divine in you." Upon reflecting on this phrase, I have adapted it to my own purposes and now pray, "May I recognize the Divine in myself and the Divine in you." It is not easy to think I have the ability to create a thin space in which God can be encountered. I am just me after all, and I know all of my shortcomings, growing edges,

[2] For further reading I recommend Henry Cloud and John Townsend, *Boundaries: When to Say Yes, How to Say No to Take Control of Your Life* (Grand Rapids, MI: Zondervan, 1992).

and failures. Nonetheless, we are claimed by God like Jesus at his baptism as beloved daughters on whom God's favor rests (Luke 3:21-22).[3]

Women religious answer the world's need for compassion in a unique way. Sisters have many gifts, including the long history of religious life with its many examples of compassionate sisters. As women religious we look to these examples to guide us in our lives. We are also guided by the many sisters who form us while we are in initial formation and those who continue to form us through our daily experience of community. Women religious answer the need as models of compassion not only because of the gift of our formal education but also by our emphasis on following in the footsteps of Jesus. Jesus' example as a compassionate presence not only gives us a path to follow as individual sisters; his life also calls us to a prophetic witness we can only achieve as one corporate life form.

Following Jesus' Example of Compassion

Jesus was moved with compassion. Though we are familiar with the stories of the Gospel, it is easy to overlook how Jesus' compassion often brought him into unexpected situations. Because he was a man of compassion, he met and interacted with lepers, outcasts, people afflicted with illnesses, and all types of suffering, often sidelining his plans. No matter what other tasks were calling him, he remained present to those who sought him. As women religious, we take Jesus as our example in our lives and we seek to cultivate a stance like his which is characterized by openness to the needs of the present moment.

The volunteers I minister with and the people I feed often challenge me to look beyond my basic ministry of feeding the hungry to respond to a prevalent hunger for compassion. My experiences at ministry remind me of the prelude to the feed-

[3] Henri J. M. Nouwen, *Life of the Beloved: Spiritual Living in a Secular World* (New York: Crossroad, 1992), 30.

ing of five thousand. Jesus left to be alone so he could mourn John the Baptist's execution. "Hearing of this, the crowds followed him on foot from the towns. When Jesus landed and saw a large crowd, he had compassion on them and healed their sick" (Matt 14:13-14 NIV). He stopped what he was doing, put aside his needs, and was present to the people. Jesus habitually responded in this way when stopped by people in crowds, called aside on his way, asked for healing, pressed upon to preach. I identify with similar expectations as a sister; people assume I have words of wisdom or consolation, interminable patience, or profound theological insights. It can be challenging to fulfill both my responsibilities as chef and as sister during my work day. Jesus is my model for responding to these demands.

One day a mother brought in her family to prepare a meal in honor of her daughter who had recently passed away. We had much to do, but everything took a back seat when the mother began to cry as she described her struggle of grieving for her daughter while attempting to reconcile her loss with her faith in God. Many members of the family were moved to tears that day as they honored their lost relative on what would have been her thirty-third birthday. This is what happens during my day: I may be in the middle of preparing a meal when a volunteer needs to talk about a friend she is concerned about, a relative who has passed away, or a wife suffering from cancer. Listening and being tender in response to the other's vulnerability is just as important in my ministry as feeding the hungry.

As women religious who seek to follow Jesus, we, like Jesus, are called to give prophetic witness to the world. We encounter many situations in community and in our ministries which call for compassion. It is evident that compassionate living and a prayerful stance in life are no longer social norms. Therefore, when someone acts and lives in a compassionate way it is prophetic simply because it shows the world a different way of being. Furthermore, because women religious act and live as one organism, the prophetic witness of this organic life-form becomes amplified. Our public vows and shared life in community become a visible and public witness to God's love breaking into the world.[4] Just as Jesus was prophetic in his life and ministry so too are women religious called to be prophetic today.[5]

As we women religious answer the call of God to bring God's love into the world, our prophetic compassion often meets resistance. There are stories of sisters who have been rebuffed, silenced, attacked, and even martyred for their actions and deeds, especially in cases where a sister is one with those who suffer. Such risk is required if we wish to be prophetic. Sisters, because of our vowed commitment to one another and to God, find freedom to risk more. We risk when we speak truth to power, we risk when we reveal our authentic selves to others, and we risk by breaking out of our historical norms into new areas that call out for our prophetic voice.

Learning to Be a Presence of Compassion in the World

Compassion takes practice. Sometimes we feel like we are not giving enough or doing enough, but the truth is that a capacity for compassion grows over time. What helps to deepen my compassion for others is becoming comfortable with my own vulnerability and recognizing my inner truth as beloved of God. In addition to these two areas there are many prayers and practices which can help to cultivate a compassionate stance, not least among these being the practice of self-compassion.

[4] Sandra Schneiders, "Tasks of Those who Choose the Prophetic Life Style," *National Catholic Reporter*, January 7, 2010, accessed May 11, 2017, https://www.ncronline.org/news/global-sisters-report/tasks-those-who-choose-prophetic-life-style.

[5] Sandra Schneiders, "Call, Response and Task of Prophetic Action," *National Catholic Reporter*, January 4, 2010, accessed May 11, 2017, http://www.ncronline.org/news/women-religious/call-response-and-task-of-prophetic-action.

One day, I risked stepping out of my kitchen and my comfort zone to sit with a guest in the dining room. He shared his story and the moments in his life which led him from a bad situation to homelessness and addiction. I was grateful to be present to him and receive his courageous vulnerability. By stopping to give him just a moment of my attention, I honored his story and his worth as a child of God—something which he could no longer see in himself.

Most of us feel like we are not "enough" and many of us know the experience of hiding who we feel we truly are out of fear of rejection. Sound familiar? Whatever it is in life that says, "You're not enough," lied. We might believe it when that voice whispers into our ears, and we sometimes build walls to protect ourselves. We can recognize vulnerability as that feeling of having those walls breached. It's that feeling we get when someone sees who we really are—not who we say we are, not the negative things we have come to believe about ourselves, but the real selves underneath all of those layers.

Vulnerability is not always that uncomfortable feeling of being found out; rather it has the potential to be a remarkable feeling of freedom which comes from being truly seen. Occasionally we encounter people who can surprise us and catch a glimpse of the real and beautiful in us. However, most people will not see past our walls so it falls to each of us to do the sacred work of taking our walls down brick by brick and letting go of that which holds us back. Vulnerability is an especially important skill for women religious because we must be authentic women if our voices and our lives are to impact the world positively. Without the authenticity which comes from accepting vulnerability, the people we meet in ministry will have no reason to trust us, and those who listen to our cries for justice will have no reason to hear us.

The walls which shield us numb pain and fear, but they also lessen joy, growth, connection, and spiritual life. Brené Brown, psychologist and researcher, reminds us that "vulnerability . . . is not as dangerous, scary, or terrifying as getting to the end of our lives and saying, 'What if I had shown up?'"[6] As women religious, we are challenged to show up and to be an example to the world of living fully awake rather than sleep-walking through life. Many people have noticed our vibrancy, joy, empathy, connection, and compassion. In fact, these qualities in the sisters I met attracted me to religious life, and I have begun to grow into them as I learn to integrate vulnerability and authenticity. Sisters who have become comfortable with their authentic selves are examples of lived compassion. They show me the gifts that come when I learn to let go of my ego's walls and live into who I truly am.

Through vulnerability, we come to know the truth of our belovedness. It is not meant to be a great secret that each of us has "been seen by God from all eternity and seen as unique, special, precious beings."[7] It will take a lifetime, maybe longer, to live into and fully integrate this reality, but once we begin, once we are reminded of who we were from the beginning of time, we can never completely go back into our comfortable ego shells. Here, we find a risk: to keep going is to never be the same, but to turn back means to live our lives without exploring the possibility in our interior life.

These risks are evident on our journeys as women religious. I have just begun to explore my interior life and have already confronted many such crossroads moments. At each turning point in my vocation story, I have had to remember that I am beloved and that God's call for me is one that leads to my most authentic self. That helps me say "yes," even in the face of risk and loss. Still, moments of embracing authenticity can come with fear. As I change, I wonder, "Will my loved ones be able to stay deeply connected to me, even as my inner life shifts?" I have not kept all of my meaningful relationships. I have

[6] Brené Brown, "Why Dr. Brené Brown Says It Takes Courage to Be Vulnerable," Oprah's Life Class video, 2 min., 53 sec.; accessed May 11, 2017, www.oprah.com/oprahs-lifeclass/why-dr-brene-brown-says-it-takes-courage-to-be-vulnerable-video.

[7] Nouwen, *Life of the Beloved*, 53.

drifted apart from some people, as I knew I would. However, the alternative would be giving up on what is authentic to my most inner being, the heart of my heart. This is the place where God dwells and where I seek to reside beyond all else. Understanding my true self is the same as understanding that I am beloved of God.

Once we have caught a glimpse of our own belovedness it must become "enfleshed in everything we think, say, or do."[8] As such, women religious can model this belovedness for others. We stand together in our countercultural life not only as a prophetic voice preaching love to the world but also to one another. Henri Nouwen, in his book *Becoming the Beloved*, stresses the importance of finding people who keep us grounded and affirm our chosenness.[9] I have found this in my community, the Sisters of Mercy, and in Giving Voice.[10] I was first attracted to both of these groups because I saw how the sisters related to one another. What I had witnessed in these sisters was the lived reality of women who had integrated their belovedness. I could not have named this at first, but now I understand that the more I claim belovedness for myself, the more I want to share this reality with everyone I meet. Fear and judgment dissipate. I want each individual to know that they are loved dearly by God and carry the divine within them.

There is no course, practice, or routine that will do the work of our own personal spiritual journey for us or keep us fresh and ready to respond to God's call. We each find little practices which facilitate our connection with the great truth of God's love and our own chosenness, but it is attentiveness to that inner truth, rather than the practices, which will keep us fed. Seeking the next big thing, be it a book, speaker, or retreat, will

[8] Ibid., 45.

[9] Ibid., 59.

[10] "Giving Voice is a peer led organization that creates spaces for younger women religious to give voice to their hopes, dreams and challenges in religious life." "Giving Voice," accessed March 12, 2017, https://giving-voice.org/.

only wear us out.[11] It is important to know what practices feed our souls, what truly fosters an intimate relationship with God, and which friends will have no problem reminding us of who we truly are when we feel lost.

It is important to know that no one is born perfectly compassionate, but we are each called to grow in compassion throughout our lifetimes. I try not to worry that I am only at the beginning, because there is no finish line on this journey. In initial formation, I have encountered many ways to learn and practice compassion. The Metta prayer from the Buddhist tradition, sometimes called the prayer of loving kindness, helps me find compassion by praying for myself, others, my enemy, and the world.[12] I also pray and ask God to reveal the true self of another, whether a loved one or an enemy, and ask to see him or her with God's eyes and to begin to love this person as God loves them.[13]

When I came to realize conflict was unavoidable in one of my relationships, I knew I had to confront the feelings churning up within me so that I could face this person and attempt to work things out. A sister reminded me how important it is in those moments to be grounded in the inner self. So, I began in prayer, and I recalled how God loves me, which reminded me that God loves this other person just as much. There were no great fireworks or revelations in my prayer when I asked God to help me see God in this person, but I could not believe the peace I felt as I entered the conversation later. I noticed I did not feel aggressive, defensive, or as if I bore a grudge. The fruits of this prayer have deepened my relationship with God as well as my human relationships.

[11] Nouwen, *Life of the Beloved*, 36.

[12] Center yourself and pray: May I be filled with loving kindness, May I be peaceful and serene, May I be happy, May I be healed. Then repeat these mantras slowly for some other people in your life, for an enemy or someone you hurt, and finish with praying for the world and/or creation.

[13] Julie A. Collins, "Celibate Love as Contemplation," *Review for Religious* (Jan.–Feb. 2000): 84.

A deeply personal prayer life is fundamental for growing in compassion. Silence and listening for the small whisper of God (1 Kgs 19:12) foster an intimate relationship with God and develop the gift of presence. There is no need to be afraid of what we will find when we delve deeply into our souls.[14] When I have had a bad day and find myself wrestling with something unsavory, I notice how difficult it is for me to show up in prayer. It is often these times when I fill the silence with words and processes. When I find the courage to stop and listen for God instead, I hear not curses but rather the affirmation of my belovedness[15] in spite of my brokenness.

In these moments when God has affirmed my belovedness, it is crucial to turn back to God in gratitude. Practicing gratitude is another way to foster the gift of presence, for presence is itself "attentiveness to blessings."[16] There are many ways to practice gratitude, from the traditional examen, to lists and notes, journaling, mantras, and any number of exercises which foster attentiveness to blessings. I find it hard to remain attentive to all of these things in my daily life which, like so many, is full to bursting with activity. I have used Thich Nhat Hanh's bell meditation[17] while I am at my ministry in order to call myself back to mindful presence every time the doorbell rings. Taking the time to stop in my busy-ness is hard but essential. The doorbell used to be an annoying distraction, but then I chose it as an intentional moment for compassion. Now, instead of sighing in frustration when the doorbell rings, I stop, breathe, and become as present as I can to whatever is currently happening. This has helped me deepen my attentiveness, stay connected with God's call in the chaos, and respond with love to the surprise encounters of God present in the other.

[14] Nouwen, *Life of the Beloved*, 76.

[15] Ibid.

[16] Ibid., 79.

[17] Nancy Corcoran, *Secrets of Prayer: A Multifaith Guide to Creating Personal Prayer in Your Life* (Woodstock, VT: SkyLight Paths, 2007), 65.

In the novitiate I reached a point one week where I had done some challenging inner work, one-on-one sharing, and was preparing for faith sharing as a community. I stopped and went to my director for help because of the raw interior feeling I was experiencing. To me it felt like exhaustion, as if sandpaper had scoured my inner self. Even though the work I had done was good and important, I could not bear the thought of doing anything more that week. Self-compassion is just as important as all the other work we do in community and ministry. Doing our own inner work, participating fully in our community lives, and living up to our ministerial demands can leave us feeling drained—even though we are called to this life and find it fulfilling. Finding people in our lives who remind us of our belovedness and allowing their presence to nurture us with compassion is an important part of being able to practice compassion ourselves. We cannot give what we have not first received. In this way, community life keeps us sharp, fresh, and ready to respond to our God who calls to us through others.

In Summary

Our call to model compassion is clear. As Frederick Buechner stated: "The place God calls you to is the place where your deep gladness and the world's deep hunger meet."[18] Women religious today are particularly called to meet the world's deep hunger for compassion by modeling vulnerability, authenticity, and openness to encounter as we strive to follow Jesus. United in the vowed life, women religious become a prophetic witness to Jesus' own compassion and a sacramental presence in a wounded world.

[18] Frederick Buechner, *Wishful Thinking: A Seeker's ABC* (New York: HarperOne, 1993).

Called to Leadership: Challenges and Opportunities for Younger Members in Leadership

Teresa Maya, CCVI

"For Wisdom is mobile beyond all motion, and she penetrates and pervades all things by reason of her purity . . . she renews everything while herself perduring; passing into holy souls from age to age, she produces friends of God and prophets."
(Wis 7:24, 27)

"No hay mas cera que la que arde" (often translated "what you see is what you get," or "that is all there is"). These were the only words Sister María de Lourdes had to offer when I sought her counsel after being called to discern congregational leadership. With these words, she made me aware of the plain fact that there are fewer younger members for any leadership position in our community, and that I should not take myself too seriously in this process despite the intensity of any election season. I learned a hard lesson that day. Whether our communities are ready or not, whether younger members are open to leadership or not, the transition of formal authority to the next generation has begun. A new journey in our understanding and appropriation of leadership and, more importantly, of

authority has quietly begun despite ourselves and our concerns.

Questions linger in my heart as I consider this new reality: Do we trust God's Wisdom is in motion, passing into the souls of the next generation, producing new friends and prophets, calling them to leadership? We have been so busy mourning the loss of one of the great moments in the history of religious life that we may be failing to notice that God's Wisdom is beginning to renew everything in the leadership of those few brave younger members in our midst. The time is ripe for us to genuinely welcome, nourish, and cherish this gift among us. New leaders are very different from what our religious communities are accustomed to: we are at home with a smaller religious life, never having been part of the large cohorts of the generations that precede us, and we were formed in collaboration from our early years, having forged friendships among the few in our age groups across our congregational spectrums. Our DNA has a different composition; our leadership style will also be different. At this unique, critical juncture in our history we have the privilege to serve side by side with mentors, sisters with leadership experience from almost every generation, who have navigated other transitions and have been wise companions on the journey. This moment will never happen again; the average age of these sister mentors who pioneered the changes of the Second Vatican Council, who opened religious life to the future, is rising fast. How do we embrace the opportunities this unique moment in history offers with more intentionality?

Over the last ten years, religious communities in the United States began electing to leadership women who entered in the late 1980s and 1990s. We are not part of that brave cohort that lived the first changes of the council, although we have a great debt to these women mentors. Most of us belong to Generation X, the smallest demographic not just in religious life, but in the places where we serve. We are a bridge generation that has significant contributions to make to religious life, our

Church, and the societies we minister. The women called forth today are barely silver jubilarians, and some have become eligible for election only recently.

We are also hesitant leaders. This is our first experience in leadership. We are keenly aware that we lack the competencies of the seasoned leaders with whom we serve. Many among us accept leadership afraid that leaving a beloved ministry will disconnect us from real need. Some younger leaders express they are resigned to "serve their time" in congregational administration or institutional ministries for the sake of the whole. As younger leaders, we tremble as we hear current leaders speak of the sacrifice and the toll the service to their sisters is taking on their health and energy. More often than many of us would dare to admit, we have assured one other that we will never accept leadership, or we will not accept it yet, and more painful still, that we do not feel capable or called to the care of elder members. This is not an attractive ministry to sisters who long to serve people in the margins.

But with full transparency, our congregations also need to accept that our older generations are likewise not necessarily attracted to the idea of having younger members in leadership. Some communities struggle with the election of younger members. Younger leaders share stories about having been the last on the ballot, or feeling like the token younger person elected. More seasoned sisters sometimes say things like "they do not love us," or "they are not willing to sacrifice anything." Stronger statements show up around dinner tables and board rooms, such as "we cannot expect much from the younger sisters." The generational divide and the challenges it offers to younger members in leadership is addressed awkwardly and sometimes painfully. While these attitudes may have happened to every generation before us, they all had peers to support them. Younger leaders today are often one of a few in their age cohort.

As a younger member, new to leadership, I have realized that the expectations of the community are very challenging.

Not only did I lack experience, but I also am missing the history of situations and issues. I am not sure when hearing expressions like "I can't believe you don't know that," or "you wouldn't know because you weren't around," began taking a toll on me, making me feel incompetent for my role. I realize that my experience of community began after the great achievements of the former generations. With no recollection of Vatican II, I know I cannot fill these expectations. But I have also had to work through feeling excluded from table conversations where I had no shared memories.

With other younger leaders, I have come to understand that our experience of the life and our gifts will bring a leadership style particular to newer generations that is not always welcome in our congregational cultures. After all, our younger members are technological natives and very much at home with diversity, to name some particular characteristics of this style. Yet here we are, at the crossroads of our life form, called to leadership. This is our generation's time to assume the responsibility to tend to the whole. We will lead through uncertainty with a hope rooted in the call that brought us to love this, our life, in the first place.

The Challenges

"If you please, my Lord, I have never been eloquent,
neither in the past nor now that you have spoken to your servant;
but I am slow of speech and tongue." (Exod 4:10)

As younger religious called to leadership we face seemingly insurmountable challenges. No amount of planning or Mercer actuarial tables has equipped us to face the present. Faith alone holds the resilience required to remain in this call today. There are days, even months, when nothing else but hope gets us out of bed—to face another funeral, close a beloved hospital, or meet with the finance committee!

Trust is perhaps the most significant challenge. Congregations must acknowledge that while members elect younger women to lead, their trust in these younger leaders is often qualified or even half-hearted. They perceive us as not having proven anything in our congregations and institutes, not having had to struggle for anything, that we did not carry the bricks to build that school nor serve three shifts in the hospital without rest. Many of them believe, and openly share, that we came to religious life and were served with a silver spoon throughout our initial formation. They think we were allowed to move forward with shortcomings that would have sent us back home in the old days. As far as religious life is concerned, we are coming to leadership having benefited from the sacrifice and hard work of our elders and have yet to prove equal to or deserving of them. We are seen by some as undeserving heiresses who will squander what we could not possibly cherish. Worse still, some elders are afraid that we do not love them enough to care for them as they enter the most vulnerable stages of aging. The pain of this lack of trust is acute for us and it requires a special brand of courage.

The leadership teams to which younger members are elected, or appointed, can often represent another significant challenge. Many of our team members have had previous leadership experience in which they were exposed to the humanity of our sisters, and so they already understand the obligations of the ministry. In contrast, we begin leadership without that same history. The learning curve for younger members is steeper when their counterparts take on the responsibilities with seasoned skills and widespread networks in the ministries and in other religious congregations. While often willing to mentor us in the beginning, their patience can wear thin when we have questions about corporate structures, canonical obligations, or the history of a certain individuals. Younger leaders need to keep up, stay alert, and learn faster and more effectively than their teams ever had to. There are many unwritten customs and traditions of which younger members are not even aware.

I still remember my first experience of a sister's death while I was in leadership. Sr. Clarita, our retirement coordinator, called me to the room in the retirement center where a sister had died of an unexpected heart attack. Stunned, I asked what I was supposed to do, not having been briefed about this yet: "Do I pray something, is there a formula or a pronouncement that must be read?" With a puzzled look Sr. Clarita asked me to let the sisters know. Diligently, I rushed from one sister to another in the retirement center, risking more heart attacks every time I burst in with the news that Sr. Isabel had died. With the task accomplished, I returned to Sr. Clarita who asked me if the rest of the leadership team had been informed. Dumbfounded, I reported I had only told the sisters in the house. Although half smiling, she looked at me incredulously explaining that when a sister dies the first to be notified should be the members of the leadership team. Poor Sr. Isabel, former provincial secretary! I got it all wrong the day she died.

Another challenge is age difference. For the most part, younger leaders serve on teams that mirror their experience of community, collaborating with sisters at least twenty years their senior. This difference of one or two generations creates a cultural divide that shows up in unexpected places, like shared references that range from music and the arts to their experience of Vatican II. In addition, the energy and pace at which younger leaders can work as well as their use of technology is often off-sync with the rest of their team. This loneliness is then exacerbated because leadership itself isolates us from the few other younger members in our communities. Our role now makes us suspect. We are caught in the in-between space as we live outside of our leadership team's shared congregational stories—including their own shared leadership stories—and outside of our own age cohort within the community. True, we all have mentors in our community willing to listen, and always mindful of us, but that is not the same as having peers. Finding peers—other younger members who are in leadership— becomes a spiritual and survival task of utmost importance.

Heart-wrenching challenges appear as we navigate our appropriate role as leaders in the pastoral care of elder members of our communities. When I attended one of my first leadership workshops, a sister shared she had accepted election only after she had clearly explained to her community that she was not to be the retirement coordinator. I still cannot forget how I felt that day, empowered, *valiente*, to take the same stand: I am not responsible for our aging issues, that is why we have appointed coordinators at our retirement centers. I kept repeating to myself, my task is to focus my energy on visioning and midwifing the future. But as my intimacy with these beloved elders deepened, my conviction waned. Elderly sisters would send cards, all kinds of cards: thank you cards, birthday cards, thanksgiving cards, and more significantly "hang-in-there" cards. They cared: about our community, about me, about the future. Gradually a "we" understanding began stirring my heart on. True, I was not the retirement coordinator, but just as true, I was one in community with my beautiful wisdom sisters. The proper role of a leader no longer seemed so clear and now I had to also attend to the surge of emotions I experience as these women decline. How do you sit at the bedside of a dying sister and attend one funeral after another without wearing your spirit out in the process? How many more times will I go to the chapel and sit with those silent tears of fear, recognizing that I cannot do this anymore, that I am afraid of the day they are all gone, that I miss their words, their cards, their presence terribly. The communion of saints has come to mean something so profound as my elder members quietly slip away from our lives.

Leadership today involves stewardship of the grief. There is no way around it. I dare to believe that even though what is passing affects the entire body of religious life, and indeed the whole church and the people we serve, it has a unique effect on younger members in leadership. What is passing is not just the religious life we grew up with—the sisters we encountered in parishes or Catholic schools, or who inspired us for the work of social justice—but our mentors, advisors, and counselors. What are we going to do when the legacy, the stories, the wisdom they hold passes? Who will we have to go to? The invitation to live this Holy Saturday experience for all religious and especially for us as younger members in leadership requires a deep conversion. This historic moment is apocalyptic and requires more than optimism. It requires absolute faith and trust in the paschal promise.[1] Are we ready for it?

Another challenge for younger leaders has to do with the contraction of the institutionalization of religious life. Particularly in North America, religious communities during the course of the twentieth century created the most complex ministry and congregational structures in the world.[2] Diminishment is such a big part of our conscious and unconscious leadership role precisely because the contraction is so much more dramatic in this region of the world. Facing the daunting task of transitioning these ministries and resizing our congregational structures can make any experienced sister run away from leadership. Now imagine being a younger member and trying to learn about sponsorship, or mergers and Public Juridic Persons (PJPs), without the background institutional history and process that created them!

Certainly, the great transition to lay leadership and this divestment began more than twenty years ago in most of our religious communities. Ours is the simple task of completing the endeavor, as I was reminded by a sister seasoned in sponsorship issues. After all, our ministries are already being led by qualified visionary lay leaders. Simple. Yet schools, hospitals, and ministries of direct service to the poor all have sisters serving on the boards. Our communities have remained en-

[1] Simón Pedro Arnold speaks of the Apocalyptic symbolism: "Por este motivo me inclino a caracterizar este momento histórico desde la simbólica apocalíptica: tiempo de confusión, de dolor enorme, de amenaza grave para la esperanza, pero, por eso mismo tiempo de desafío y de utopía renovadora, tiempo de gracia, en definitiva." *A Dónde Vamos* (Lima: Ediciones Paulinas, 2012), 52.

[2] Patricia Wittberg, "Institutionalized Ministries and Religious Life" in *Creating a Future for Religious Life* (Mahwah, NJ: Paulist, 1991), 115–35.

tangled with them at all levels, ranging from the emotional to the legal. Every year, we review sister board membership trying to find qualified sisters, even for those ministries which are now independent PJPs that are supposedly not under our purview. Younger members often come to this task wholly unprepared, both because we did not come from the ministry ranks, not having served in sponsored ministries as they grew up into complex institutions, and because we simply did not experience a call to religious life through our ministries. We did not enter because we wanted to be teachers or nurses. Many of us even did that before entering. Our call is not rooted in the apostolic works of our sisters in the past.[3] The fact is we simply do not share the same emotional attachment to our apostolic works, however big or small they are, whatever part of the sponsorship spectrum they operate out of. In so many ways we need to be grateful for that! We must also recognize that we are building on the shoulders of the giants who laid foundations for the future structures of our sponsored ministries.

The challenge of divesting our communities from the trappings of ministry has become critical for leadership at this time, and it is daunting for younger leaders. We are challenged to empathize with the loss and grief this means to most of our sisters, and we never imagined ourselves leading with the corporate intricacies our organizations entail. I have begun to hear terms like "stewardship of the great decommissioning" or the "deinstitutionalization" that we are being called to at this time.[4] Called to accompany the grief of withdrawing from

[3] "The charisms of the communities were more salient: a particular ethnic flavor, a few unique customs, and above all, a ministerial focus on a specific set of institutions." Patricia Wittberg, *Pathways to Re-Creating Religious Communities* (Mahwah, NJ: Paulist, 1996), 73.

[4] Susan Francois in her chapter in this book explains that one of the tasks for this time of religious life is to embrace the great decommissioning; see pp. 182–203. Sr. Mary Pellegrino, CSJ, shared with the LCWR Assembly in August 2016 that one of the greatest challenges of leadership was the "deinstitutionalization" of the life.

this parish after at least a century of service, or closing that school where our alumnae are appalled that we could not find sisters to serve there, or moving out of our stately motherhouse requires a spiritual strength that younger leaders will need over and over again in the next two decades. This does not mean we do not trust or even embrace the potential of our lay collaborators or coministers, but regarding our congregational relationship and influence on apostolic works, those of us called to leadership today will stand as guardians while our fall turns to winter, when all the leaves finally fall off our trees. Then we will be called to the time of the greatest pruning of North American religious life, a time of deep faith in the promise of the resurrection.

The Gifts

"They said to Jesus, 'Five loaves and two fish are all we have here.' Then he said, 'Bring them here to me.'" (Matt 14:17-18)

Religious communities have begun timidly trusting that God's Wisdom is making all things new by calling younger members into leadership in all kinds of roles. Some of us have become the first elected leaders of our generation, and others are being appointed to internal or ministry positions. A brave new world awaits us, and we are risking all we have on these precious few. Who are we and what gifts do we bring to this call? We need to assume and appreciate the unique gifts our generation brings to leadership at this time, gifts that may not appear to be so at the outset, such as not having a long history with the congregation or social networking.

Speaking of a lack of congregational memories as gift, I recall a recent conversation at a social gathering in my community where one of my sisters said to me, "You missed everything." I was not there when they celebrated the Mother

General for three days with handmade gifts for the congregational benefactors and three full days of recreation. "You missed everything" has been ringing in my heart for years. Even twenty years ago, I knew I had missed everything—the greatest moments of our congregational history, when our schools had twenty sisters, when the sisters went to Peru, when we had brave sisters going to live among the poor, and when we were pioneers in nursing and education. I missed everything. My lamentation finally turned to revelation the day Sr. Nancy Schreck, OSF, passionately repeated at the LCWR New Leaders Workshop, "What if the most important contribution of religious life has not happened yet, what if?"[5] Finally, I saw my lack of memories as blessing and realized that younger members bring this very special gift to leadership at this time. We have no lived experience of the good old days, no emotional attachment to this school or that mission. We have never known anything else but small, frail communities. We did not fall in love with this life because it was big, or grandiose, or in "missionary conquest" mode;[6] it was the vital energy of the charism that called us to this community. I dare to believe that as younger leaders we are more capable of shepherding our communities through the loss of all that gave us identity—institutions, influence, prestige, numbers—because we have no memory of them! And we are encouraged in this painful task by the witness of the generation of leaders who preceded us. They took the first courageous steps of entrusting our congregation's valued ministries into the hands of qualified and committed lay coministers.

We also grew up in a different church, which blesses us with a very different understanding of this life—church made thus

[5] Nancy Schreck, LCWR New Leader Workshop, February 2015.

[6] "Perhaps the most substantial shift of all is that of transcending the metaphor of the hero that has underpinned so much of our patriarchal domination and the religiosity of empire building." Diarmuid O'Murchu, *Religious Life in the 21st Century* (Maryknoll, NY: Orbis, 2016), 3.

by our very own sisters. We are old enough to have witnessed the great transition of religious life from the monastic enclosures to the incarnational life that has been the hallmark of our communities. These women religious modeled and made us fall in love with the life of insertion, commitment, community, and contemplation in action that they adopted so fully and authentically after Vatican II. We know the church as the people of God not through our reading *Lumen Gentium* fresh off the press, but rather through the first catechism classes we attended. There, our church as the people of God was not a new discovery. It was a fact. The new music, the new liturgy, the fresh images of God and church and mission were part of our childhood. Even the diversity the church was attempting to embrace rang in our elementary school songbooks: "What Color Is God's Skin?"[7] This legacy, this seed, planted by enthusiastic men and women bringing forth a church with open windows is the fresh air we grew up breathing. Now is the time when it will bear its fruit. Sisters before us planted; we must tend to the harvest. We have received into our hands the heart of the renewal that shaped our religious communities.

Our new generation of leaders also brings a different experience of initial formation. There are those among us who are the first generation to have gone through the newly minted formation programs after the initial years of experimentation. We were formed in the charism and heritage of the congregation from the very beginning, reading the newly printed histories and learning from the first sisters to work on the legacy of the founders. We were introduced to the heritage much earlier than any of the older generations in religious life today. Moreover, much of our initial formation took place in the midst of insertion experiences among the poor. Many of us were among the first cohorts to move out of our motherhouses into inner city neighborhoods or rural areas. During our initial formation, many international congregations included a pro-

[7] Up With People Incorporated, 1964.

longed period of missionary experience in the global south. Living among people in poverty so early in formation embeds a commitment to the world's disenfranchised that as leaders we could never forget, despite the ministries and places we were called to later in our journey. In addition, many of us were never part of large cohorts of entrants. Instead, we are among the first alumni of the intercongregational formation programs redesigned after the council. And again, I draw a distinction with the very first generation of sisters now well into their sixties who experienced the turmoil of the renewal process, while I also see a distinction with the experience of the Sisters Formation Conference that shaped the previous generation. While it is true both released incredible energy which allowed for expansive collaborative efforts, the experience of intercongregational formation of the newer generations is qualitatively different. Perhaps more significant is the fact that these programs often became the only vital sacred space to form peer relationships. The collaboration and appreciation for the diversity of charisms that we thus experienced prepared us for openness to collaboration at levels we have yet to see in religious life.

With the generation that preceded us, we have known nothing except the experimentation of new models of governance as well as the evolution of our understanding of leadership and decision-making. The resilience we have developed as a result of deepening our commitment to the life precisely during a time of constant experimentation and change has given us unique gifts for mobility and flexibility. From the beginning we have known that structures are temporary, and thus we have developed a high tolerance for the ambiguity brought about by the rapid changes occurring today in religious life. Unlike older members in our communities, we are more likely to have lived in international, intergenerational, and intercultural settings from the very beginning of our journey in religious life. We identify easily with missionary sisters who understand firsthand the many challenges and adjustments required of us by intercultural living. The gifts of resiliency and openness that we have developed will serve us well as we are required to exercise bold, risk-taking leadership. We understand that structures, congregational geographic boundaries, and ministries can be in flux provided we remain rooted in the essential call of our charisms.

Newer generations also have an ingrained understanding of the connectedness of all of life. We grew up in a time of awesome discoveries, where science began revealing the deep mysteries of the universe both at a macro and micro level. Our science classes already spoke of expanding universes and we were the first generation of children to watch Carl Sagan on *Cosmos*! The recognition that human beings are only one tiny part of the ecosystem has always been a given for us.

In fact, my generation has found the divine in nature when driven from our churches immersed in scandal or divided by ideology. Some of our first experiences of contemplation and mysticism happened there. Our sensibility to the fragility of nature was marked by the Exxon Valdez spill and similar disasters. We grew up in the Carter years and learned about energy conservation in the backseats of the family cars waiting for gas! But we also understand ecosystem at a different level. Our capacity for social networking is rooted in this understanding of social connectedness and relationality that can move easily from the virtual world to solidarity with the most vulnerable in the world.

Coming of age at a time when laity in the church were empowered, we do not see lay leadership or collaboration as something new, but rather as what is. Our experiences in ministry were always marked by the significant presence of lay leaders. The younger cohorts of leaders will hardly have had any experience of sisters or brothers in either Catholic schools, universities, or parishes. Our first formators were often these lay women and men committed to the mission of Jesus. We have always worked side by side with lay men and women, often reporting to them. We know about partnership, collaboration, networks, and cooperation because that is the church we have known all our lives. We move with ease in this relationship, denouncing both entitlement and clericalism, recognizing the unique identity of each call in the Church. In fact, we experience less ambiguity around the issue of the identity of religious life precisely because we entered knowing that we could do missionary work, pastoral care for the poor, or teaching without having to be a religious because of the lay people we encountered, loved, and befriended.

Finally, I believe that the gifts younger leaders bring to religious life are the core elements of the transformational leadership our communities require. We are at home with our vulnerability because we came to maturity at a time of fragility and diminishment in religious life, making us more likely to find and seek the help we need. We have the privilege of knowing some of the greatest sister leaders of our time, who are alive and bursting with the wisdom that will bless the next generations. Younger members in leadership are borderland people, bridge people. We live in between the new and the old. We hold the generational divide, having been in community long enough to know and love it, and briefly enough that we have an itch for the new.

The Potential

"Every scribe who has been instructed in the kingdom of heaven is like the head of a household who brings from his storeroom both the new and the old." (Matt 13:52)

Our religious communities will call younger members to leadership simply because the future is inevitable. We have choices in leadership, however, that we must discern very carefully in community. Younger members are not automatically qualified for leadership, nor should communities imagine that because they have younger members they are exempt from the task of discerning their future leadership. We can either chose the fatalistic path of resignation to the unavoidable, or we can intentionally and collectively prepare our younger members to lead, according to their gifts, into the transformation we long for. The future is the responsibility of the present, not just its consequence. Embracing this responsibility with hope and joy has to do with both how we younger women religious assume leadership and how our communities empower, encourage, and trust our leadership. Some tasks are imperative, shared by all generations currently living in the present sacred space of religious life. Our elders are called to bless, to "ben-dicere," to speak well of what is emerging. If they do this they too will experience the full circle of life that is God.[8] Current leaders—both young and old—are called to a trust that can only come from deeply contemplating the paschal mystery. Together, they must be sentinels of dawn,[9] trusting the potential of our younger members, empowering them, and allowing for a community of practice. Finally, younger members must nurture the communion for which they long by assuming the small and big responsibilities that hold our common life. Our present ecosystem must also interact with other systems around us, embracing the call to lead in the midst of desperation, displacement, and vulnerability, while energizing the charism in its participation of the *missio Dei*.[10] God calls forth prophets and leaders for every time.

To nurture the leadership potential of our younger members, we must first revise our formation, orientation, and training programs so that gifts and leadership potential are identified,

[8] "Blessing a young person when you are older is as simple as it is difficult: Do you want to bless a younger person? Step away and give him or her your job! . . . We bless others when we see them, delight in their energy rather than feel threatened by it, and give away some of our own life to help resource their lives." Ronald Rolheiser, *Sacred Fire: A Vision for Deeper Humanity and a Christian Unity* (New York: Image, 2014), 229–30.

[9] "The breeze at dawn has secrets to tell you, Don't go back to sleep." Quatrain poem by Rumi.

[10] Anthony Gittins affirms that mission is God's job, not ours, God's "job description," who God is. Anthony J. Gittins, "Mission: What's It Got to Do with Me?" *The Living Light* 34, no. 4 (Spring 1998): 8, 11.

encouraged, and empowered from early on. Sadly, while some communities have made great strides in this effort, others are lagging behind the corporate world, which has long since discovered that developing their human capital is a most valuable asset for the future. Now is the time to seize this potential in religious life.

Some of our entrants come to our common life having served as leaders in their former professional and pastoral roles. How do we break down the rank mentality that has pervaded our communities and allow newer members to serve in different leadership capacities? Formation communities need to become communities of practice for leadership just as they are for spirituality, ministry, and human development. We need to do this with every single member in community, not because we believe there is a "leader in every chair," but because all human groups need leaders, conveners, coordinators, facilitators, and—further still—prophets and visionaries. Our budgets need to reflect our decisive will to invest in the future because these programs, practices, and experiences require an investment. As elected leaders, we need to move beyond identifying leadership potential in younger members one by one, often filtering or selecting according to our own experience of leadership. Unless we broaden our vision and trust that the leadership of the future will not look like ours, we may be missing the opportunities our younger members require at this time to be ready after we are gone. Of course, we need to send participants to existing programs like the Collaborative Leadership Development Program, but that is not enough. In addition, we must encourage newer members to assume leadership responsibilities in every area of their lives: their local communities, the conferences or associations they belong to, like Giving Voice, and professional and ministerial life. Leadership is something you grow into; it doesn't just happen with an election. We have a responsibility to empower, fund, and encourage leadership development. What investment could be more precious?

The emerging future also requires religious leadership that expresses the heart of our mission. For a long time, our communities have struggled with the election of a pastoral leader or an administrative leader, often alternating leadership cycles between one and the other. Both types of leadership were needed for the internal needs of our large communities—to steward our resources, to care for members, to coordinate and organize community. But as religious communities contract to the biblical *anawim*, the organizational skills of the past need to be replaced with skills that will continue energizing our commitment to the mission of Jesus Christ, the reign of God, in this new paradigm of smallness. Therefore, the emerging leaders in our midst need to be women with hearts for the poor and focused always on what will address urgent human need. Younger religious will be called to leadership for a time such as this, where our "liquid world" finds certainty only in constant motion,[11] where in the words of Pope Francis, people are disposable,[12] where we are consuming our planet three times as fast as it takes for it to replenish our resources. These younger religious will be called to embrace the prophet within. In the words of Macrina Wiederkehr, OSB:

> The Moses in my heart trembles
> not quite willing
> to accept the prophet hidden in my being
> wondering how much it will cost
> to allow the prophet to emerge.[13]

[11] Zygmunt Bauman describes the speed: "La vida en una sociedad moderna líquida no puede detenerse. . . . lo que se necesita ahora es correr con todas las fuerzas para mantenernos en el mismo lugar . . . la velocidad, y no la duración, es lo que importa." Zygmunt Bauman, *Vida Líquida* (México: Paidos, 2015), 11, 17.

[12] Francis, *Evangelii Gaudium* 53.

[13] Macrina Wiederkehr, "Prayer Before a Burning Bush," *Seasons of Your Heart: Prayers and Reflections*, rev. and exp. ed. (New York: HarperCollins, 1991), 34.

The present generations of religious life must take to heart the sacred task of noticing, encouraging, and listening to the prophets God is already raising among us. These women, heirs of our justice-seeking legacies, are already calling us to notice the injustices in our world in new ways. They are challenging us to address causes old and new with courage and to take our stand with God's preferred people in new spaces and with nuanced styles. They stand on strong shoulders. They write blogs, work on the margins, and march for peace, and they are doing it because they have journeyed with their older sisters in community and witnessed their commitment to the cause of the poor. They do it because their men and women mentors of good will and diverse faiths have shown them that the future we long for requires the investment of all and the leaven of women religious. These new leaders will shepherd us through reconciliation from the racism that has pervaded our communities. They will open our hearts to real hospitality, embracing the ethnic, racial, and sexual diversity that surrounds us. They will gently take off our shoes so we find God speaking in all the burning bushes of our discouraged and despairing world.

We are talking about leadership in religious life, not just any kind of leadership. Imperative to our leadership is the integration of the essential core of our identity: the quest for the living God. Perhaps the most significant preparation for leadership that we can offer all generations is a constant call to a renewal of our spiritual life, a spirituality of accompaniment. In conversations with new and seasoned leaders and in my own lived experience, I constantly realize that the one thing that would have prepared me and others better for our time in leadership was not training in dealing with conflict resolution, or time management, or organizational development, but a spiritual life grounded in *lo cotidiano*[14] and always expecting

[14] Latino theologians speak of *lo-cotidiano*, the stuff of daily life as the place for theologizing, which must also be the place of religious life.

the encounter with God in all.[15] We want to share so much with younger or newer members in community, about our history, our founder, this story, and the legacy of that ministry before we go. There is such urgency in our passing on these things that we somehow fail to focus on the most essential: their profound experience and relationship with God, the one *encuentro* that allows all other *encuentros* to take place. Like Jesus in Bethany, we must remind us all, but especially our newer members, "only one thing is important" (Luke 10:42).

A discerning contemplative heart takes time, years, as all of us pilgrims in this journey well know, and yet it is the most important potential that must be developed in younger or newer members in leadership. We need to help them nourish, nurture, and care for a life of contemplation; no effort will ever be enough for the times in which we will lead. We must become communities of practice, which encourage, entice, and invite one another to become sacred spaces of deep listening and contemplation, in a spirituality of communion and accompaniment. I came to realize the urgency of this need after several younger sisters on different occasions approached me hesitantly to ask, "Tere, do you pray?" I still remember my first reaction: My goodness, was I living at such speed with such intense activism that they didn't believe I prayed? I realized, then, that my peers were sharing their own painful realization that they had lost their lives of prayer somewhere along the way. Gradually these sacred peer conversations allowed me to share my own struggles, my own distance from prayer because of my "legitimate" ministry commitments, and then my painful return to my "first love." I owned that the introduction of the book of Revelation has been mine, time and time again:

[15] Francis in *Evangelii Gaudium* explains about encounter, "It is an ongoing process in which every new generation must take part: a slow and arduous effort calling for a desire for integration and a willingness to achieve this through the growth of a peaceful and multifaceted culture of encounter." *Evangelii Gaudium* 220.

> I know your works, your labor and your endurance and that you cannot tolerate the wicked. . . . Moreover, you have endurance and have suffered for my name, and you have not grown weary. Yet I hold this against you: you have lost the love you had at first. (Rev 2:2-5)

More importantly, I recognize that I have always needed help to return to the heart of our life commitment; I have always needed community. Every single journey home has been accompanied by beautiful wisdom sisters whose names are engraved in my heart. These sisters have been gentle and stern, questioning, prodding, and encouraging but always loving in their care. As I share with my peers, a transformation begins. We offer to journey together and encourage each other to keep our eyes on *Jesús, el camino* (Jesus, the way).

Sr. Pat Farrell, OSF, spoke at the 2016 LCWR Assembly about the contemplative listening heart that is required for this time in leadership. She said we "lead by being led."[16] Leadership in our religious communities is first and foremost a leadership of following, *una espiritualidad de seguimiento*, a spirituality of following. Simón Pedro Arnold, OSB, from Peru has written extensively about the importance of returning to the Jesus story divested from centuries of trappings and customs because of the urgency of Jesus' mission for today's world: "We are urged to return to 'Jesus alone' and relearn a new adventure of discipleship";[17] his love is the requirement for the ministry of leading, of shepherding the flock. Jesus himself made this clear to Peter on the shore of Lake Tiberius. "Simon, son of John, do you love me? . . . Tend my sheep" (John 21:16). We can only lead if we follow Jesus Christ, moving beyond the *imitatio Dei* many of our predecessors were called to practice,[18] into the

[16] Pat Farrell, Keynote Address, LCWR, 2016.

[17] Original in Spanish, translation mine. Simón Pedro Arnold, *La era de la mariposa*, (Argentina: Editorial Claretiana, 2015), 51.

[18] "No se trata tanto de imitar a un maestro de manera individual y privada (a pesar del éxito duradero de esta modalidad del seguimiento desde la

dance of following (*la danza del seguimiento*) that Simón Pedro Arnold speaks about:

> Life is a most beautiful and demanding school of dance. . . . There is nothing to hold on to, nothing to grasp. We will only be saved by the art of free movement, we need to move our hips around the living spinal column of the Church: the cross of Jesus Christ. . . . How do we return to a Christ always in movement, the one Who walks on the dusty roads of Galilee, near the raging waters of the lake, and dances in the wedding at Cana? . . . In a certain way, we must be initiated into a choreographic discipleship, where we are not about imitating or catching-up with Christ in an effort of will, but we grow into his rhythm and compass.[19]

An authentic spirituality of leadership is one that has learned to love dancing with Jesus, as way, truth, and life. It takes years of practice to follow his steps of mercy, inclusion, and compassion, but we must try. This kind of leadership will help our religious communities to dance, as well, and bring the joy of the Gospel to our world.[20]

"See, I am doing something new! . . . Do you not perceive it?" (Isa 43:19) rings in my heart as I bring my reflections to an end. The God of our lives has been creating in our midst, calling women to religious life when we felt no one would be attracted to it, and calling gifted young leaders when our confidence in them was compromised. The transformative leadership our hearts long for is already happening. All of us, young

---

Imitación de Jesucristo de Tomas de Kempis.)" Simón Pedro Arnold, *La era de la mariposa*, (Argentina: Editorial Claretiana, 2015), 145.

[19] Original in Spanish, translation mine. Simón Pedro Arnold, *La era de la mariposa*, (Argentina: Editorial Claretiana, 2015), 57, 58.

[20] Speaking about the joy of evangelizing Pope Francis states: "Goodness always tends to spread. Every authentic experience of truth and goodness seeks by its very nature to grow within us, and any person who has experienced a profound liberation becomes more sensitive to the needs of others. As it expands, goodness takes root and develops." *Evangelii Gaudium* 9.

and old, must participate in its birthing. Mistakes will be made, but every new attempt moves us forward. This is something to celebrate. God's Wisdom is calling us to the dance; we cannot refuse.

Religious Life in a Time of Fog

Susan Rose Francois, CSJP

We live our religious life in an ever changing context which is clouded in fog. This is true not only in our religious communities, where change has essentially been a constant since the Second Vatican Council, but also in our local and global community where complex societal and economic forces intersect, engendering fear, uncertainty, and a general sense of unending turmoil. Millions of children and adults are displaced by poverty, war, and disaster. Families struggle to meet basic needs. Human dignity is under threat as communities are caught in cycles of division and violence. Mother Earth, our common home, is exploited and endangered. This is the mission field where we are called to minister as women religious committed by vows, to the "following of Christ as it is put before us in the Gospel."[1] The call of the Gospel looms large in this time of fog, even as religious life itself shifts from being lived on a grand institutional scale to a smaller and more intimate one.

As a younger woman religious called to elected leadership in my own congregation just a few years after I professed final

[1] *Perfectae Caritatis* (Decree on the Adaptation and Renewal of Religious Life, 1965), in *Vatican Council II: The Conciliar and Postconciliar Documents Study Edition*, ed. Austin Flannery (Northport, NY: Costello Publishing, 1986), 2(a).

vows, I often feel clouded by fog. There is the fog of shared and personal grief that is such a part of religious life at this time. This was a more generalized fog when I entered. The fog has begun to grow thicker as elder sisters I knew and respected passed on to the next phase of their life with God. More recently I have lost mentors and sisters whom I have come to love deeply, and the fog is murkier and more particular. Then there is the fog of uncertainty about who might be able to step into elected leadership after me, the challenge of meeting the needs of an aging population, repurposing buildings that are larger than needed for our current and future needs, navigating new relationships with sponsored institutions, and then of course, tending to the passion for mission in our chronologically younger and young-at-heart sisters—all of this with the fog swirling around us. Let's just say that on some days, it's hard to see the way forward. It's an exercise in trust in God, who is the way. In order to take the next steps on a path which is "hidden in fog," we "must learn to be led and to listen deeply" to the God who called us to this time and place.[2]

The path from present to future is not only foggy, it is also littered with many questions. I find that I have more questions than answers when it comes to the future of religious life. What seems clear is that the religious life I entered will look and feel substantially different in 2031, when I will celebrate my twenty-fifth jubilee at the age of fifty-nine. Many more of my religious sisters will have passed away by then, while, hopefully, some new Sisters of St. Joseph of Peace will have joined our common quest to pursue justice and seek God's gift of peace. I also know that my companions will include religious-life-age peers across congregations, even if the exact ways that our charisms, spiritualties, ministries, and community life

[2] Pat Farrell, "Leading from the Allure of Holy Mystery: Contemplation and Transformation," Keynote, 2016 Assembly of the Leadership Conference of Women Religious, 5. I first explored her image of fog in "Living, Loving, and Leading in Fog" (*Global Sisters Report*, August 26, 2016).

experiences will mix and mingle for the sake of the Gospel is at present a mystery, known only in the heart and mind of God. That unknown future excites us, and we see glimmers of it in this book.

Our founding/pioneer sisters and earlier generations responded to the unmet needs of their times and organized their common lives accordingly. What is this particular moment calling forth from the present generations living religious life? What is the gift we are being asked to become now? What witness is needed for a wounded and weary world? What are the implications for our lives of prayer and ministry lived in community, now and into the future?

These are some of the questions that keep me up at night. Paula Downey, an Irish organizational consultant who has worked with religious leadership teams, invites us to consider the future itself as "a question, not an answer."[3] That is comforting because those of us living religious life today certainly have questions. We also have the incredible opportunity, and challenge, to engage in the shared critical work of authentically living into these questions together. That is what gets me out of bed each morning as a vowed woman religious in the twenty-first century.

Seeing through the Fog—Our Reality

Like the disciples on the road to Emmaus, we cannot always see through our personal and collective fog in order to recognize the presence of God even in the messiest moments of our lives together. Nevertheless, God is with us, and we are here together, committed by vow to this life. Religious life is first and foremost a response to our creator God "who called us to follow Jesus by fully embracing the Gospel and serving the Church, and poured into our hearts the Holy Spirit, the source

[3] Paula Downey, "Religious Life for a World of Transition," *The Furrow* 60, no. 11 (November 2009): 617.

of our joy and our witness to God's love and mercy before the world."[4] This is the central relationship—the *who*—that grounds our unusual life commitment of poverty, celibate chastity, and obedience. It is significant that our vows are made not to our religious community or superiors, but to God.[5] In our case, the fundamental answer to the question of who is also the foundational answer to the what, why, and how questions of our lives as religious.

What we are about is the bringing of God's good news—the Gospel message of love, hope, joy, peace, mercy, and justice, as modeled by Jesus—to the people of God. We answer this call because we have experienced that same mix of God's presence and promise in our lives. It is only through our relationship with God that we can begin to answer the call to "practice the virtue of hope, the fruit of our faith."[6]

My friends have explored many of these questions in earlier chapters. Our communion with God and with one another grounds our very lives as women religious on mission in, through, and for community.[7] Our presence as compassionate people in a weary world is itself prophetic and speaks volumes about God's love.[8] Our vows point us toward mission and are for God and the world.[9]

We make vows which give shape and form to how we live out our call in community. I have long been intrigued by the title of Peter Block's book, *The Answer to How is Yes*. As I live

[4] Francis, "Apostolic Letter to all Consecrated People on the Occasion of the Year of Consecrated Life," November 2014.

[5] See "Something Old, Something New: Hannah's Vow Touches the Lives of Women Religious Today" by Sarah Kohles, pp. 18–30.

[6] Francis, "Apostolic Letter to all Consecrated People," 3.

[7] See "Communities in Communion: Shifting into New Life" by Virginia Herbers, pp. 1–17.

[8] See "The Compassion the World Needs Now" by Amanda Carrier, pp. 147–58.

[9] See "The Vows and Jesus' Radical Mission: The Power of Celibacy, Poverty, and Obedience for the Reign of God" by Tracy Kemme, pp. 47–66.

into the forever yes I professed at my final vows, I have also begun to think that maybe all that matters is that I continue to say "yes" each day. "Yes expresses our willingness to claim our freedom and use it to discover the real meaning of commitment, which is to say Yes to causes that make no clear offer of a return, to say Yes when we do not have the mastery, or the methodology, to know how to get where we want to go."[10] While I am sure Block was not imagining women religious when he wrote those words, I cannot imagine a better description of the journey facing those living religious life in the twenty-first century.

Thankfully, none of us is on this journey alone. Community is key and indeed is a central pull for women choosing to enter religious life today. Religious life does not have a monopoly when it comes to being about God's mission. There are a plethora of vocational and professional options for Catholic women who want to respond to God's love and make the world a better place. The committed and communal aspect of our lives—the life-long promise of the daily rubbing of shoulders for a common purpose—combined with the power of the communion of saints and the legacy and responsibility shared with the women who have gone before, gives a unique shape to who we are and how we go about mission now and into the future.

Religious life has always been intergenerational to some extent, but the demographic spread and imbalance of the present generations living religious life in North America and Europe is unprecedented. This intergenerational mix is a sign of our times that we must read honestly and hopefully as we discern the path ahead. In some ways, this mix mirrors societal trends. Those who study workplace management note that never before have there "been so many generations at work in our organizations that have experienced completely different

[10] Peter Block, *The Answer to How Is Yes: Acting on What Matters* (San Francisco: Berrett-Koehler, 2003), 27.

educational conditioning," due in part to technological advancement, globalization, and mass migration.[11]

There are now eight distinct groups of development life stages represented in the present generations of religious life: young adulthood (18–30), mid-adulthood (30–40), midlife (40–50), post-midlife (50–55), pre-retirement (55–65), young-old (65–75), old (75–85), and old-old (85+).[12] The vast majority of religious are in the three latter life stages, with many continuing to be productive community members. Typically, elected leaders are over sixty-five, with many repeating the service of leadership for multiple terms.[13] Sandra Schneiders, IHM, writes that members of her cohort "who are in their late seventies, eighties, and even occasionally in their nineties often are not retirees psychologically, socially, or ministerially even if they might be in terms of society's employment structure."[14] On the other end of the spectrum, a mere 9 percent of women religious today are under age sixty.[15] By the year 2026, the ratio of wage-earning to retired religious is projected to be nearly one to four.[16] While the intergenerational trend mirrors society, this stark demographic imbalance is particular to religious life.

Our numbers are small and getting smaller, even as the call of the Gospel during this time of fog looms large. This is our

[11] Jutta König, "Spirituality and Diversity," in *Spirituality and Business: Exploring Possibilities for a New Management Paradigm*, ed. Sharda S. Nandram and Margot Esther Bordern (New York: Springer, 2010), 104.

[12] Karen VanderVen, "Intergenerational Theory in Society: Building on the Past, Questions for the Future," in *Intergenerational Relationships: Conversations on Practice and Research Across Cultures*, ed. Elizabeth Larkin et al. (New York: Haworth, 2004), 79.

[13] For a reflection on the gifts and challenges of younger elected leaders, see "Called to Leadership: Challenges and Opportunities for Younger Members in Leadership" by Teresa Maya, pp. 159–81.

[14] Sandra Schneiders, *Buying the Field: Religious Life in Mission to the World*, (Hahwah, NJ: Paulist, 2013), 572.

[15] Mary Johnson, Patricia Wittberg, and Mary L. Gautier, *New Generations of Catholic Sisters: The Challenge of Diversity* (New York: Oxford University Press, 2014), 17.

[16] National Religious Retirement Office, "Statistical Report-August 2016," 3.

reality. I can count the number of vows ceremonies in my religious community during the past ten years on my own fingers, while I would need a calculator to add up the number of funerals during the same period.

It can be tempting to dwell on the numbers, to compare and see how many newer members have joined x or y community, and yet we do well to remember "God's dislike of statistics and census."[17] God is much bigger than that. The Scriptures tell us that God's choice is not based on the limits of human logic. Consider the promise made to Israel: "It was not because you were more numerous than any other people that the Lord set his heart on you and chose you—for you were the fewest of all peoples. It was because the Lord loved you and kept the oath that he swore to your ancestors" (Deut 7:7-8).[18]

While it is not healthy to obsess about numbers, we also do not serve the mission or future of religious life by ignoring them entirely. As tired as we have (rightly) become of the "D-Word"—diminishment—we need to look at this reality honestly with fresh eyes and holy curiosity to discern the gift and challenge of this time.[19] Religious life is in the process of transformation. That is what we know. The rest is for us to discover as we live into the questions.

In some ways, this is very familiar territory for women religious. "Religious life, even by its very name, implies the necessity for growth, change and adaptation."[20] Those words were

[17] Sophia Park, "A Reflection On Religious Vocation: The Wine Is Ready, But the Wineskin Is Not," *Global Sisters Report*, May 14, 2014, http://globalsistersreport.org/column/speaking-god/trends/reflection-religious-vocation-wine-ready-wineskin-not-371.

[18] *New Revised Standard Version Bible (NRSV)*. New York: Division of Christian Education of the National Council of the Churches of Christ in the United States of America, 1989.

[19] See my previous articles "Shifting Conversations in Religious Life" (*Global Sisters Report*, July 9, 2014) and "A Loving Gaze at Religious Life Realities" (*Horizon*, Fall 2013).

[20] Louise Dempsey, "The Function of Prudence in a Program of Renovation," (master's thesis, Summer School of Sacred Theology for Sisters, Providence College, 1964).

written in 1964 by Sr. Louise Dempsey, CSJP, who would later become the first Sister President of my congregation after Vatican II. Women religious have become experts at engaging change. It can be exciting and energizing. When I look to the future far horizon, the fog lifts as I get glimpses of the excitement earlier generations of my sisters must have felt at our founding or in the late 1960s during renewal. At the same time, "moving into unknown territory is essential and there will inevitably be a period of uncertainty and 'not knowing'—even chaos—before the new begins to emerge."[21]

Change is in the air, but we are very much living in the in-between time. "We are in a time that is simultaneously both paschal and apocalyptic."[22] In some ways, it is Holy Thursday, Good Friday, and Holy Saturday all at once, while we anxiously await the resurrection! Because of the mix of present generations, even the youngest among us are "touching what is passing"[23]—a large scale religious life we never lived ourselves—because of our relationships with elders in community and lived experience of remaining structures of institutional religious life. We are the present, living this life together now while we simultaneously cocreate the bridge to our future.

Our elder sisters bring a depth of wisdom that comes from fifty to even seventy-five or eighty years of authentically living into the questions with community. Our peers and those just ahead of us in community have a diverse mix of experiences and live into the questions with a different perspective on the future horizon. Nowhere else on earth is this exact mix of generations mingling together for the sake of the reign of God. Think about the possibility and wonder of that for a moment. This is a sacred time of togetherness that I know I will miss in the later years of my religious life.

[21] Downey, "Religious Life for a World of Transition," 618.

[22] Simone Pierre Arnold, presentation to Canadian Religious Conference 2016 General Assembly, 5.

[23] Sr. Carol Zinn, SSJ, used this phrase to describe the experience of younger generations at the 2015 Giving Voice National Gathering in Kansas.

The mission field where we are called to witness to the Gospel is also clouded in fog and uncertainty. "This is our moment. The world around us teeters on the edge of both peril and promise. Breakdown and breakthrough tussle with each other. The path forward is hidden in fog. It is your time to lead."[24] Sr. Pat Farrell, OSF, spoke these words to a room full of women religious in elected leadership, but I think they apply to each member of the present generations of religious life. Each of us, no matter our age, is on mission until the day we die.[25] The shape and function of the way we live mission necessarily shifts in keeping with our health, energy, and capacity. We may shift from being on the hospital floor, in the classroom, or social justice ministry to holding in prayer the particular and general griefs and anxieties of our weary world from an infirmary bed. It is all mission, it is all part of the call of the present generations, and the mission field is huge!

The prophetic and unusual way of life we are privileged and challenged to live itself "is a paschal act." We are called to reject the "evil reality construction" of the world—systemic social injustice and evil in all its forms—"by creating and living within an 'alternate world' which derives its coordinates exclusively from the Gospel."[26] We do not turn away from the world, but instead intentionally turn our loving and discerning hearts and minds to the critical needs of today—the global migration crisis, human trafficking, environmental destruction, income inequality, violence, and despair. Each of these ultimately stems "from the global financial crisis, issues of internalization and globalization; the threats posed by relativism and a sense of isolation and social irrelevance."[27] Going about mission in and from our alternate world, we ground our lives on shared financial resources, inclusive loving relationships,

[24] Farrell, "Leading from Holy Mystery," 5.

[25] Gemma Simmonds, "Vitality in Religious Life," Spring 2016 Assembly Presentation to the Sisters of St. Joseph of Peace.

[26] Schneiders, *Buying the Field*, 67–68.

[27] Francis, "Apostolic Letter to all Consecrated People," 3.

and a shared commitment to discern the call of God. Our very lives can be an antidote, a calming presence, and a hopeful witness to the possibility of relationships among kin based on Gospel values.

We are also called to be witnesses to the goodness of the world God created. There is goodness in the creative energy, work for the common good, laughter, and joy brought by the children of God to this thing we call life. It's a beautiful mix that yearns for our presence as women religious, bringing the gifts of our charisms to the people of God.[28] "'Reading' God and 'reading' the world are not interchangeable, but neither are they inseparable."[29] We read the "world's most pressing needs and aspirations" in the light of the Gospel, in light of God's love, and in light of the gift and challenge of our charism. We then respond as best we can, making the necessary adjustments to the shape and form of our lives together to serve the mission.

The Spirit Is Calling

The level of honesty and integrity with which we live into these questions is critical. Time is running out. The world cries out for our presence. It is up to the present generations to reshape our structures so as to breathe new life into our lives of prayer and ministry lived in community for the sake of mission. The "future is unavoidably involved in moral action. Our choices reverberate out into space and forward into time, with effects sometimes lasting for centuries."[30] It is a moral imperative that we discern the gift and witness that the Spirit is calling forth from us now and into the future.

[28] See "Local and Global: Charism of Religious Life Today" by Mary Perez, pp. 67–81.

[29] Bernard Lee, *The Beating of Great Wings: A Worldly Spirituality for Active, Apostolic Communities* (Mystic, CT: Twenty-Third Publications, 2004), 173.

[30] Daniel C. Maguire, *Ethics: A Complete Method for Moral Choice* (Minneapolis, MN: Fortress, 2010), 109.

A loving look at our reality shows us that our time is "not of triumph and glory but of decline and disintegration."[31] We know that we will not live forever and that scores of young sisters will most likely never again fill grand novitiate buildings. God is in the mix, and the Spirit is not finished but calling for transformation. This book is proof that passionate young women are still being called by God to our communities. It is not time to padlock the doors, but rather to open new ones, perhaps doors to smaller buildings where we can engage challenges and opportunities together in new ways.

I wonder if we fully realize how the priorities and choices our communities make now impact the younger and future generations. We necessarily expend large amounts of resources and energy to attend to the needs of the dominant cohort experiencing "massive and rapid aging,"[32] yet we flounder to find vibrant local communities willing and able to welcome newer members. We adopt inspirational and aspirational chapter acts calling us to new radical expressions of mission springing from the roots of our charism, but we struggle to find a critical mass of members able to respond concretely, whether because of waning health and energy or the need for active members to find paid ministry.

These tensions are real and unavoidable in this in-between time, as we shift from religious life lived on a large scale to a more intimate one. There are no easy answers. I believe the invitation is to live into the *realness* of the reality. "By putting the *real* real world at the heart" of our common life, we "would reconnect with people in the most relevant way and on entirely new terms: as equals, learning together how to restore community and renew our culture."[33]

[31] Diarmuid O'Murchu, *Religious Life in the 21st Century: The Prospect of Refounding* (Maryknoll, NY: Orbis, 2016), 2.

[32] Arnold, Canadian Religious Conference, 2.

[33] Downey, *Religious Life for a World of Transition*, 620.

Our early pioneer sisters, in many ways, had no idea what they were doing either. I cannot help but think of Sisters Stanislaus Tighe and Teresa Moran in my own congregation, who in 1890, after just three months of nursing training, boarded a train for the rugged Pacific Northwest to found a hospital. Dressed in full habit with tin pails and galoshes for the mud, they begged in mining and logging camps and sold subscriptions—an early form of insurance—for an as-yet-nonexistent hospital. They experimented, they risked, they learned, and they did it all with the odds stacked against them, together, for the sake of God and mission. As Sister Teresa in a letter to the mother general says: "Fancy two creatures like us to build a hospital. If it ever succeeds it will be by the visible power of God alone."[34] They built the hospital, by the way, and it still serves the local community. With our deep stories and rich resources, imagine what God can do through us!

Learning from Our Reality

What might we learn from the shared experience of the present generations? Religious life is lived in an intergenerational context with vowed members across a wide age spectrum. Older members, by virtue of their sheer numbers, most often interact with age peers. In contrast, as part of a distinct age minority, today's younger members are engaged daily in intergenerational relationships, technically defined as relationships between persons belonging to two different life stages that are at least two stages, or twenty years, apart.[35] The present generations living and ministering together in religious life often span four, five, or even six life stages, such as when a twenty-something temporary professed member lives with a grouping of seventy- or eighty-something finally professed

[34] Susan Dewitt, *We Carry on the Healing: PeaceHealth and the Sisters of St. Joseph of Peace* (Vancouver, WA: PeaceHealth, 2016), 10.

[35] VanderVen, "Intergenerational Theory," 79.

members. If one of the members of this living community was in her mid-fifties, this would add a third life stage, making the community multigenerational and thereby "increasing the complexity of the dynamics of the relationship."[36]

Amy Hereford, CSJ, offers another helpful way of considering this experience. "It is fair to say that there are two age cohorts in religious life today: the dominant cohort between the ages of sixty and one-hundred, and the minority cohort between the ages of twenty and fifty-nine."[37] The dominant cohort is "relatively homogenous in age, culture, and ethnicity." They experienced religious life before the Second Vatican Council, and they engaged in the "excitement and challenging process of renewing their congregations."[38] Their worldviews, theological perspectives, and spiritualties evolved over time in tandem, particularly in their shared response to the spirit of Vatican II and from expanded educational and ministerial experiences.

In contrast, members of the minority cohort generally entered alone or in smaller groups of two or three and make up only 5 to 10 percent, or less, of their own institute. Out of necessity, we have participated in intercommunity religious formation programs and built relationships with other younger religious across congregations from the very beginning of our religious lives. The minority cohort has only experienced religious life, and in most cases church, in the post-Vatican II context. Most of us already have a college education, if not advanced degrees and professional experiences, before we enter. Our worldviews, theological perspective, and spiritualties were formed more by the evolving cultural norms of our generations and social locations than by a response to a common experience over time. Our experience of the structure of

[36] Ibid., 90.

[37] Amy Hereford, *Religious Life at the Crossroads: A School for Mystics and Prophets* (Maryknoll, NY: Orbis, 2013), xii. Also see "An Open Letter to the Greatest Generation" by Teresa Maya (*Global Sisters Report*, January 12, 2015).

[38] Hereford, *Religious Life at the Crossroads*, xii–xiii.

religious life has always been fluid, coinciding with the era of mergers and federations of religious families and letting go of treasured institutions. Perhaps most importantly, the minority cohort is much more diverse in terms of generational culture, formation experience, and ethnic background. For example, while 90 percent of finally professed sisters in the United States are white, 42 percent of sisters presently in formation are women of color.[39]

I have lived in a variety of local communities since I entered, each one unique but also intergenerational. In groupings of three, four, five, and for one memorable year more than twenty sisters, I have shared life with women in their twenties, thirties, forties, fifties, sixties, seventies, and eighties. In all but one of those local communities, I was the only sister in the mix from the minority age cohort. My novitiate classmate was born in Kenya, and the women who entered after me have been from the United States, Korea, the north of Ireland, Nigeria, and India. While we have long had a mix of women of European descent, we are all novices in community when it comes to this kind of intercultural living.

Each of us brings gifts from our experience, or even lack of it, as well as challenges. As a younger member on congregation committees and now in elected leadership, I honestly do not know why it is that we can't do x because of what happened in 1975 (and I usually try hard to hold my tongue and not say that I was three years old when that happened, so can we move on already?). I am often surprised when I step on a landmine of pain and suffering left over from some long ago community struggle. I seek out common experiences in community to build a shared history with women who have already been doing that with each other for more than fifty years. It can be

[39] Johnson, Wittberg, and Gautier, *New Generations*, 19–20. See "Searching for Identity through the Paschal Mystery" by Thuy Tran, pp. 96–109; "The Bridges I Cross and Las Hermanas Who Built Them" by Christa Parra, pp. 128–46; and "Creating a Culture of Encounter: Finding Life in Intergenerational and Intercultural Community" by Madeleine Miller, pp. 110–27.

difficult and painful and frustrating. It can also be beautiful and surprising and life-giving. We are the ones who are here now, brought together for a common purpose beyond ourselves. We cannot be afraid of the places and spaces of tension, because God is there too, calling us into the creative transformative energy that comes from a life lived authentically together in hope.

The God of Surprises

We live our religious lives in common with other human beings. We follow Christ, but we ourselves are human. There is an unavoidable otherness and responsibility that comes from the public witness of our vows and the title Sister (the dreaded pedestal). Please God, however, we live not as holier-than-you-women but as ordinary women, living together in an extraordinary way in service of God and God's people. At their best, our lives in community are incarnational and bring the joy of God's love into being through authentic relationships. We are human, and so we also inevitably cause and experience pain and suffering, but thanks to our crazy decision to live in community, we (hopefully) never do so alone.

These shared and sometimes messy human experiences can also be God moments that carry the surprising seeds of the future, even if it is hard to see the promise in the moment itself. Comedy, tragedy, or even irony can hold a kernel of truth that we need to grapple with together. For example, to borrow an Alanis Morisette[40] song from my early twenties, isn't it ironic that at a time when the need for the witness and presence of authentic, openhearted, committed, and joyful people looms so large, the numbers of women religious available for active ministry is at the smallest number since our founding?

I choose the word ironic carefully and purposefully. The doom and gloom of many conversations in religious life circles

[40] Alanis Morisette, "Ironic" (California: Maverick Records, 1996).

tend more toward tragedy, but I experience my creator God as the God of surprises and laughter. Ironic twists and turns are part of the fun. There are also lessons to be learned and gifts to be born out of our intense experiences of grief and loss, uncertainty, and the other messy bits of this life. The world needs people able to witness to the gift of surprise, to honor the treasure of grief born in love and in lives lived fully together, and to find the willingness to take the next steps, even if it might seem a little bit crazy since we don't really know where we are going or who else might join us along the way.

Imagining the Path Forward

The future of course is now and will forever be a mystery, but it is one to be lived into by faith and hope. Our task is not to figure it all out and single-handedly ensure the future of our charism, mission, community, or religious life itself. That lies in the heart and mind of God. The prophetic task, writes Walter Brueggemann, is "not blueprint or program or even advocacy. It is the elusiveness of possibility out beyond evidence, an act of imagination that authorizes the listening assembly to imagine even beyond the ken of the speaker."[41] We can reflect honestly and hopefully on our reality, learn from our common experience, hear the urgent call of the unmet needs of the world, imagine future possibility and then, in time, see glimmers of light shining on our next steps.

The central question that the present generations of religious life are called to live into together is this: what are we supposed to do now, during this time of fog, for the sake of our present and future as community for mission? I ask myself this question often. It guides how I approach my role in elected leadership and challenges me to discern the unique contribution I am called to bring forward, as a relatively newer and younger member at this time.

[41] Walter Brueggemann, *Reality, Grief, and Hope: Three Urgent Prophetic Tasks* (Grand Rapids, MI: William B. Eerdmans, 2014), 127.

I don't want to wait and figure it all out with my small cohort of younger generation friends who will also be left behind after what Sr. Marcia Allen, CSJ, has named the demographic "collapse."[42] While this time is apocalyptic, it is not in the sci-fi-zombie apocalypse sense. It is apocalyptic because we are in a time of simultaneous breakdown and breakthrough, and God is in the mix inviting new life, imagination, and transformation. We need to crowdsource our next steps on the path to the future. None of us has all the answers, and it will only be by mixing and mingling the diversity of the present generations' hopes, desires, and dreams for the future of this wonderful life that we be able to give shape and form to the call of the Spirit in this time of fog. We need all hands on deck, even if for some it will be a transformed religious life they will only be able to cheer on from heaven. There are too many incredibly smart women, deeply compassionate hearts, and creative thinkers in the present generations to wait.

The Great Commission

One day, I was sitting before Mass in our beautiful but now far-too-large chapel at St. Michael Villa, our regional center in New Jersey, as I contemplated these key questions about the call of the Spirit for religious life at this time. Out of nowhere, the words of an oldie but goodie hymn popped into my mind and heart: "Lord, you give the great commission: 'Heal the sick and preach the word.'"[43] We do not have a mission; the mission of Jesus has us. God is not only in the equation but at its center. "Lest the Church neglect its mission and the Gospel go unheard, help us witness to your purpose with renewed integrity; with the Spirit's gifts empower us for the work of

[42] Marcia Allen, "Transformation—An Experiment in Hope," Presidential Address, 2016 Assembly of the Leadership Conference of Women Religious, 1.

[43] Jeffery Rowthorn, "Lord, You Give the Great Commission" (Carol Stream, IL: Hope Publishing, 1978).

ministry." It's not all up to God either, leaving us simply to hope and pray. We are called to be cocreators. Our priorities and choices impact our ability to participate in mission, now and into the future.

I quickly found myself lamenting that I was not here at the time of our great commissioning, the days when we founded hospitals and schools and opened new missions in far off places. I have never been one in a crowd of joyful young sisters on fire for mission, except in the occasional intercongregational gathering. Truth be told, I complain to God a lot in prayer. God puts up with me, but then usually surprises me when I finally stop complaining and pay attention. This was true that day. Mass was about to begin, and the sisters from our care center drifted in, deftly but slowly navigating with their walkers and wheelchairs the small aisle and pews designed for young novices. "This chapel is a beautiful place to pray," I thought, "but does not fit our current reality."

As it happens, we have been engaged in a congregation-wide planning process for our preferred future. Blueprints and plans may not be prophetic, but they are necessary and important! One of our priorities is to look at our rather large buildings which were commissioned for other purposes—novitiates turned into retirement centers mostly—and repurposing them to meet our current needs and future mission. Most religious communities are at some point in a similar process. We were just about to hire an architectural firm to conduct a feasibility study on future use of St. Michael Villa, including the chapel, when we experienced a major fire. No one was hurt, thank God, but the majority of our sisters were displaced for many weeks while we cleaned and adapted our infirmary building and another building on campus to accommodate living, dining, and prayer spaces for our retired sisters. Now we not only want to repurpose the newly-smoke-damaged main building for our current and future mission, we have to do something. Remember what I said about God having a sense of humor and surprise?

The work of decommissioning is critical, even if at the surface level it does not seem terribly exciting or even focused on mission—but it is! Yes, it involves planning meetings, hard conversations and difficult decisions. It means navigating complicated governance structures of our historic sponsored institutions and freeing them so that the mission can continue in the capable hands of our lay collaborators. It involves letting go, grief, frustration, and a whole lot of uncertainty. It can shake our identity. Who are we if we are not the sisters who run x hospital or y school? And yet, we are called to see through the fog to plant the seeds of transformation for mission through this work.

My chapel experience invites me to engage this incredibly important work of decommissioning itself as part of the great commission of Jesus. We must reverently and attentively decommission the structures of an earlier time to make room for what is needed now and into the future. I am reminded of what happened when the Presidio naval base in San Francisco was decommissioned in the early 1990s. It took a while for its new mission and purpose to take shape, but now it is part of the Golden Gate National Recreation Area and brings joy and delight to millions of visitors each year. More people now enjoy the beauty. Closure led to new life. All it took was a lot of letting go and a little creative imagination.

Buildings and structures are human made. They are meant to serve mission, not dictate or prevent it. This is true not just of our buildings, but how we organize ourselves as human communities. "People who have spent their lives inside congregational structures know those structures are standing in their way, but they seem so solid and unyielding it's hard to see past them. *But* Social 'structures' are just relational processes that have taken physical form."[44] We are called in this place and time both to decommission that which limits mission and authentic relationship—be it governance structures, institutions, buildings, or just the way things have always been

[44] Downey, *Religious Life for a World of Transition*, 616.

done—and recommission ourselves as communities for mission in a weary world.

At least, this seems to be what God is about these days, if we look honestly and hopefully at our reality. "Religious life will never go out of style, but it can't very well continue in the structural sense of today. I think religious life will dwindle down to a nucleus and from that nucleus will emerge leadership for a new type of religious life that will be free to concentrate wherever needed. Global challenges, technological changes are inevitable, and religious life will try to keep pace."[45] Sister Eleanor Quin, CSJP, one of the wisdom sisters I got to know in the novitiate who has since gone to God, wrote those words in her memoir . . . in 1969.

Ellie knew that there is great possibility inherent in the shift from living religious life on a large institutional scale to a smaller and more intimate one. Freedom, connection, relationship, and presence are easier on a small scale. I imagine God at work in this movement. It is not something to resist but embrace as an opportunity and challenge. I cannot help but think of how, in our far-too-large chapel, we struggled to sing together at Mass, but now that we are praying in a smaller temporary chapel space in our infirmary, we sing out loud and clear. Our energy is better able to mingle in the smaller space—so too I suspect in a right-sized religious life.

Critical Yeast for Mission

One way I imagine the potential for small scale religious life is an adaptation of John Paul Lederach's concept of "critical yeast."[46] Our obsession with numbers tempts us to think we

[45] Eleanor Quin, *Last on the Menu* (Englewood Cliffs, NJ: Prentice-Hall, 1969), 141.

[46] John Paul Lederach, *The Moral Imagination: The Art and Soul of Building Peace* (New York: Oxford University Press, 2005), 91–94. I first explored his concept of critical yeast in relationship to religious life in "Critical Yeast for this Crucial Time" (*Global Sisters Report*, September 19, 2014).

will no longer be big enough or will not have enough critical mass to be about mission. Lederach challenges these kinds of assumptions. Instead he looks at the capacity and strength for a small group of people, "if they were mixed and held together, to make things grow, exponentially, beyond their numbers?"[47] We already know that the Spirit draws a crazily wonderful diverse mix of people to our communities. What if we could organize ourselves in ways which make the good stuff of our lives together spread for the sake of mission?

The principle of critical yeast is that a "few strategically connected people have greater potential for creating the social growth of an idea of process than large numbers of people who think alike." Yeast has to move and mingle with others to make an impact. It needs a warm, inviting, safe environment to thrive. We knead and mix yeast into the mass, activating its "capacity to generate growth." Yeast is not static or stationary but "constantly moves across a range of different processes and connections."[48]

I believe that during this time of fog, through the process of decommissioning, God is beckoning us to recommission ourselves as critical yeast for the common good in a weary world yearning for the gifts of our charisms. We do not need critical mass to build big institutions or even start our own new ministries. Rather, we must become critical yeast for mission. In the words of Pope Francis: "Our mission—in accordance with each particular charism—reminds us that we are called to be leaven in this dough."[49]

The Spirit is calling us to recognize the energy and possibility inherent in the small-scaling of religious life. We are being called to collaborate with others, to mix and mingle with other open hearted and imaginative folks. Less bound to this institu-

[47] Lederach, *Moral Imagination*, 91.

[48] Ibid., 91–92.

[49] Francis, "Homily for the Presentation of the Lord and XXI World Day of Consecrated Life," February 2, 2017.

tion or that building, we are called to a freedom of movement and presence wherever the people of God are most hurting. We are called to spread our Gospel perspective and the insights gained from our diverse spiritualities, charisms, and lived experience. Those we meet and touch with our deep story will then spread it even further in ways we cannot even begin to imagine.

The path before us may very well continue to be hidden in fog, but those with eyes to see can discern the outline of the next steps before us. Each generation is presented with its particular challenge. We are called to risk the bigness of smallness. Like our founding and pioneer sisters, we must live into the questions and reshape our lives together accordingly, so that religious life can continue to spread the good stuff of the Gospel for generations to come.

"Traveler, Your Footprints Are the Only Road, Nothing Else":[1] Reflections on the Future of Women's Religious Life

Deborah Warner, CND

"Wait . . . What??"[2]

There is a morbid fascination with the idea that anyone, but most particularly young women, might enter religious life in the twenty-first century. This fascination often shows itself as a supportive yet concerned response to the young hopeful who anxiously broaches the subject with her nearest and dearest. After all, in theory at least, Catholics are supposed to encourage vocations to the religious life and priesthood. Catholics are supposed to (and there are many who do) pray for those who are discerning such calls. Yet, there is a pause. The ques-

[1] Antonio Machado, "Traveler, Your Footprints," in *There Is No Road* (New York: White Pine, 2003).

[2] In the interest of transparency: I only fully read two of my references (Hereford and Arbuckle) before I decided to get down to the business of writing this chapter. All other references were inserted after I had completed the chapter so that I could honestly say that these are my own words. "My own words," however, come from everything I have ever read, heard, or discussed about religious life.

tions which come to mind and which are often spoken are: "Why? Why would you want to do something like that?"

Women entering apostolic communities of religious life in early twenty-first century Canada and the United States are pilgrims in a long line of seekers, responding to an ancient call. Pope Francis notes that "we are invited to be audacious, frontier men and women."[3] In twenty-first century Canada and the United States, where almost anything can be obtained with little more effort than the typing of a few words, where is the frontier and why would we even want to go there? What does it really mean to follow Christ in this world, and what is the future for those of us who make such a commitment in these chaotic days and in the precarious unknown of the days yet to come?

This chapter hopes to respond to both these spoken questions, as well as those questions that are held in silence but seem to hover after the daughter/relative/friend/complete stranger makes the decision to enter. For there is a future for religious life that is unfolding at this very moment in time. Young women of passion, faith, and deep love are responding to the urgent need to manifest the Gospel in a world where Christ's peace is difficult to behold. They are seeking a consecrated life that "is a call to incarnate the Good News, to *follow* Christ, the crucified and risen one, to take on 'Jesus's way of living and acting as the Incarnate Word in relation to the Father and in relation to the brothers and sisters.'"[4]

[3] Congregation for Institutes of Consecrated Life and Societies of Apostolic Life, "Rejoice! A Letter to Consecrated Men and Women: A Message from the teachings of Pope Francis," accessed March 4, 2017, http://www.vatican.va/roman_curia/congregations/ccscrlife/documents/rc_con_ccscrlife_doc_20140202_rallegratevi-lettera-consacrati_en.html.

[4] Ibid., 5, citing John Paul II, *Post-Synodal Apostolic Exhortation Vita Consecrata*.

Context Always Matters

"Generation after generation stands in awe of your work; each one tells stories of your mighty acts." (Ps 145:4)

"Religious life" is a generic and broad term for very individual and, therefore, very different, expressions of living the evangelical counsels (poverty, chastity, and obedience). It is perhaps best to state up front that religious life is a life, not a lifestyle. It is not meant to be a short-term or easily changed way of living. It is meant to be a life-changing experience which requires, if not demands, constant and continual self-reflection and analysis in the crucible of community, knowing that God's promises are real and realizable.

There are, at best guess, thousands of books and written materials which explore the idea, history, and evolution of the attempts at living the call to religious life. The nebulous concept of a call that urges us to "come, follow Jesus" might seem incomprehensible to some. Nonetheless, many of today's more well-known religious communities emerged from one person's insatiable need to respond to an urge to live the Gospel more fully than seemed possible in the religious context of their time. Other religious communities were founded along the lines of these new ways of living religious life because they seemed authentic to those who were seeking God as well as to the needs of the society in which they were established.

None of these evolutions came easily. St. Francis of Assisi's family was seriously unimpressed by his giving away of the family's money to the poor, and they dragged him before the bishop in an effort to force him to stop. The monks who had invited St. Benedict to share his spirituality with them attempted to kill him when he did just that. The founder of my own community, St. Marguerite Bourgeoys, endured almost a half-century of hard-fought battles to ensure her community's survival and the official recognition of the outrageous, newfangled idea of noncloistered and nonhabited religious women. And yet, here we are.

There are modern day hermits whose lives closely resemble those of the first documented religious men and women. There are monastic communities who can plot their histories back to other hermits who came together in community on Mt. Carmel. There are thousands of apostolic religious communities worldwide that can speak to their founding histories as a response to the signs of their times. Religious life exists and is lived in a context which holds both history and a constantly changing contemporary experience.

All people of faith live with the tension between what has been and what still needs to be brought to life. Women who have entered religious life in the last decade find themselves attempting to disentangle and disengage these tensions and contradictions in order to live their individual calls more authentically. Membership in a religious community requires that this "more authentic" living of an individual's vows must be discerned in community, through community, and with community. At the same time, all religious communities are expected to discern the "signs of the times" in the context not only of their communal history but also of their charism and apostolic ministry. We do so with an understanding of what may or may not be possible, even as we remind ourselves and each other that the history of our founding was heavily reliant on Divine Providence and in trust that all things are possible with God.

There Is a Definition for Dead and Religious Life Is Not It

There are many articles, books, and other writings about the "decline" and "diminishment" of women religious in Canada and the United States. The research is clear: the number of sisters is decreasing and the likelihood that there will be enough young women entering religious communities to make up for the deaths and attrition of sisters is nil. What few of these books and articles say is this: having fewer entrants does not mean that religious life is dead. There are new religious communities emerging, even today, alongside those which have centuries of history and service behind them.[5] Young women are still seeking entrance into religious communities.

We can have some empathy for the resistance and reluctance of the parents and families of the earliest Christian martyrs;[6] after all, their daughters (especially) were planning their futures based on the stories of a small band of misfits who were supposedly following an executed itinerant preacher. What future could there possibly be in that life? Of course, the Roman Catholic Church's spectacular rise from that derided and persecuted religious anomaly to an extraordinarily wealthy and incredibly powerful nonstate actor put religious life into a whole new context for a lot of people.

Being a "religious" did not (and does not) necessarily mean that someone was living out a religious vocation. History has proven that residence in a religious community or engagement in a religious ministry does not automatically provide evidence of faithfulness. It has, in the past, been a mask or veneer for much less than the purest of motives for some who have professed religious vows. Certainly, in the Middle Ages, many children were dropped off at monasteries as "oblations."[7] These children were then expected to enter the religious community, and, given the security of the cloister and the strong

[5] "New Religious Communities," *Following the Shepherd's Voice*, accessed March 5, 2017, http://theshepherdsvoiceofmercy.blogspot.com/p/new-religious-communities.html.

[6] The story of St. Agnes of Rome and St. Perpetua illustrate their family's bafflement with such choices. Catholic Online, "St. Agnes," accessed March 5, 2017, http://www.catholic.org/saints/saint.php?saint_id=106, and *Christianity Today*, "Perpetua," accessed March 5, 2017, http://www.christianitytoday.com/history/people/martyrs/perpetua.html.

[7] John Boswell, *The Kindness of Strangers: The Abandonment of Children in Western Europe From Late Antiquity to the Renaissance* (Chicago, IL: The University of Chicago Press, 1988), 231.

likelihood of having regular meals, many of them did enter. Others entered because convents, like the church, offered opportunities if one could sustain the life long enough to earn tenure through perpetual vows.

However, all things are possible with God. An excellent example of God's writing straight with crooked lines is the story of St. Teresa of Ávila, a great Doctor of the Church, who entered religious life at twenty, not necessarily because she felt called but because religious life seemed like her best option. St. Teresa discovered that not only did she have a vocation but also felt a strong, compelling urge to live her vows in a way that was simply not possible in her existing Carmelite community.[8] So began the Discalced Carmelites—the same fundamental spirituality, a very different mode of living.

Religious life wasn't dead then in 1562, though many of us would look askance at what was considered "religious" at that time, and it is not dead today, even though many may not think it visible or viable.

Realities

"We are not called to be successful; we are called to be faithful."[9]

The root of concern regarding the future of religious life may not really be the issue of the numbers that are entering. It is irrelevant whether there are ten sisters or ten thousand, unless you believe that the purpose of sisters is to staff schools and hospitals for next to no pay. Then, yes indeed, wring your hands, for that mode of religious life is almost certainly dead

[8] Catholic Online, "St. Teresa of Avila," accessed January 16, 2017, http://www.catholic.org/saints/saint.php?saint_id=208.

[9] Attributed to Teresa of Calcutta.

and unlikely to be resurrected. The real issue that needs clarification is the role of apostolic religious communities in twenty-first century Canada and the United States.

The image that many of us hold of religious sisters was firmly planted in the 1950s and 1960s when there were hundreds of young women stepping from high schools into the convents. Young, fresh-faced, and eager to engage in clearly set and designated ministries, typically nursing or teaching positions, they exploded onto the scene of 1950s Canada and the United States.[10] Catholic children saw sisters, in a wide array of religious habits, virtually everywhere: at Mass, in Catholic primary schools, in Catholic hospitals, in the neighborhood, and in the parish which, at least in the United States, provided much of the socialization and recreation for the families which lived within its boundaries.

Fast-forward sixty or so years, and we live in a different world. While religious communities may continue to have a presence in the institutions they established, most governments have taken control of education and health care, at least in the overarching social contract. No religious community in Canada or the United States, regardless of its charism, its religious habit, or its apostolic ministry, has hundreds of hopefuls knocking at its doors. Much of the research acknowledges that the surge in religious entrants in the 1950s and 1960s was a blip in the religious life timeline.[11] It was the perfect storm of a population increase in the form of baby boomers who came of age in a peace-seeking, postwar society that was simultaneously receiving an influx of immigrants from impoverished and marginalized populations. Those were ideal conditions for the forms of apostolic religious ministries that flourished,

[10] If you were a Generation X kid and you weren't around to see this for yourself, you still knew it because virtually every book, television show, and movie about sisters seemed to be set in this image of the 1950s.

[11] Kathleen Sprows Cummings, "Understanding U.S. Catholic Sisters Today," (Washington, DC: FADICA, 2015), accessed March 5, 2017, http://www.nationalcatholicsistersweek.org/_resources/FDC_001_Report.pdf.

but they were also the conditions which created a false standard for religious life.

This visual of hundreds of young women, docile and submissive, lined up in an eye-catching variety of habits, became *the* image of women religious in Canada and the United States. The picture of an army of these young women toiling away "for the Church" soon became *the* image of apostolic ministry. As Amy Hereford notes, however, "What is, is passing away."[12] What is passing away, however, is not religious life, but rather an idealization of the "best" mode of living it.

Necessities

"And blessed is she who believed that the promises of God would be fulfilled." (Luke 1:45)

We need to separate institutional ministry from the identity of religious life—a difficult and painful separation for those who have only ever known religious life through institutions. This separation, however, will be a vital exercise if religious communities are to continue responding in dynamic and agile ways to God's call to bring forth the kingdom. The future of religious life in Canada and the United States will not be the continued establishment of schools and hospitals; it simply cannot be so, regardless of the nostalgia with which the secular world holds the memories of those thousands of sisters.

Faithfulness and fidelity to our vows cannot now, or ever, be confused with success as understood by a secular world. To become caught in a numbers game where more becomes the substitute for, and the evaluation of, fidelity to the Word of God and/or to our vows, is a dangerous game, as the true

[12] Amy Hereford, *Religious Life at the Crossroads: A School for Mystics and Prophets* (New York: Orbis, 2013), 87.

faith of a person is known only to God. The betrayal and violation exposed by the Roman Catholic sex abuse scandals, committed by vowed men and women throughout the world, should have opened all our eyes to the danger of such presumptions.

The future cannot be lived in the past, and those young women who are entering religious life today have already come to terms with this reality. The Canadian and American sisters of today and tomorrow are the products of societies whose greatest need is not that of schools or hospitals. They are members of societies that are increasingly wracked by violence and fear and citizens of a globalized world in which rapid advancements in communication have brought instant awareness of the struggles and desperation of other peoples for justice and peace in lands which no longer seem so far away.

It needs to be said that young women are very aware of the many places of discord and conflict within the Church Institutional. Do these influence our discernment? No one entering religious life can be oblivious to those most in need in our world, which seems to be growing smaller, if not closer, each day.[13] Religious communities are posited in a world that is not merely undergoing unprecedented technological and medical advances at breakneck speeds, but one which is simultaneously in social and economic turmoil and crisis.

José Arnaiz notes that we need to move from a Church that has been focused on being a protagonist to one that is concerned with service.[14] Certainly, in the past, young women who entered religious life did so in a Church that was not only powerful but respected, if not feared. There was security in

[13] In a conversation with the collaborators of this book, Ted Dunn noted that "globalization is the trend in everything." It will be interesting to discover what impact this will have on religious life when the young women who have never known another worldview enter religious communities.

[14] José M. Arnaiz, "The Great Challenges of Consecrated Life Today," Capitolo Generale FSP, 2013, accessed January 15, 2017, http://archive.paoline.org/paoline/allegati/15808/Arnaiz_LegrandiSfideVCoggi-eng.pdf.

being a member of a religious community in a society that revered the religious. Those days are past us. We enter during a tarnished time in the institutional Church's history where vowed men and women are being prosecuted by criminal courts on one hand and being martyred around the world, on the other.[15] Any confidence that our status as consecrated religious will somehow protect us is sadly (and dangerously) misplaced.

Religious communities, whatever their charism, cannot fail to note, for instance, that in 2016, the number of displaced people in the world far surpassed the refugees created by World War II[16] and we are not officially engaged in a world war. For apostolic religious communities, the urge to respond to the needs of our world is an imperative. Whatever the sisters who entered religious life in the 1950s understood to be their future, it is clear to those who enter today and tomorrow, that their future is unknown and that the security and stability of religious life is illusory. So we give thanks for the legacies of our communities and remember them with joy, but we cannot allow ourselves to be caught in romanticizing of a world which no longer exists. If we do, we will not be living our call. We are called to go in haste to serve the needs of God's people today, in our own time.

Despite the uncertainty of the future of religious life and the very public brokenness of our church, young women who have eyes to see and ears to hear are still choosing a future that is committed to God, in service of the church—an unknown future it is true, but one which is filled with passion, hope, and joy.

[15] Stephanie Kirchgaessner, "Murder of French Priest Opens a New Frontier for Catholic Church," *The Guardian*, July 26, 2016, accessed January 15, 2017, https://www.theguardian.com/world/2016/jul/26/jacques-hamel-killing-challenge-pope-franciscatholic-church.

[16] UNHCR, "Figures at a Glance," accessed January 15, 2017, http://www.unhcr.org/figures-at-a-glance.html.

What's the Point?

In this new world where religious communities no longer command the education and the health care of societies, where a new sister may or may not go on mission to a country not her own, many ask, "Why bother with all of that when you can do the same thing without being a sister?" So, there can be no speaking of the future of religious life without speaking also of sisters growing into a deeper understanding of the prophetic witness that is their public profession of religious vows. The vows, and the fruit of those vows, are the point. They have always been the point.

In a world that most will acknowledge as being secularized, the profession of religious vows is an anomaly. This was made clear to me when, at the announcement of my perpetual profession someone said: "I'm bringing the kids, because really, when next will they get to see this?" The prophetic witness is this: "At the heart, throughout all the changes, religious life remains a life radically committed to incarnating the Gospel here and now, living the beatitudes, and bringing the love of God to ever new frontiers."[17]

It is prophetic witness that we believe there is a living and loving God; that we believe we are being called to be instruments of that loving God in a world that does not believe that God exists, or does not see a need for God, if God exists. It is prophetic witness that young women are willing to say "yes" to chastity and celibacy; "yes" to being poor (in its myriad forms); "yes" to listening to and with others and to not being the only opinion or voice that matters. The vows are indeed radical. It has always been so, but in twenty-first century Canada and the United States it seems a starkly radical choice. For it makes ever clearer that "religious poverty, chastity, and obedience can speak forcefully and clearly to today's world which is suffering from so much consumerism and discrimi-

[17] Hereford, *Religious Life at the Crossroads*, 37.

nation, eroticism and hatred, violence and oppression."[18] The tension that we hold, and with which we engage, is not so much concerned with the vows themselves, but the ways in which we will live these vows into the future. What does religious life look like in our place and time? How should it look as we move forward?

Religious communities are always founded with an idea as to how its members should engage with the world, and that founding concept has a direct impact on the apostolic ministries in which members invest their energies. Arbuckle outlines these types of communities as "ascetical" communities, where the primary concern is within the religious community (e.g., Cistercians); "relational/mobile" communities, whose concerns are with the world immediately around them (e.g., monasteries); "mission" communities whose primary concerns are with the pastoral needs of the world beyond the community (most apostolic communities).[19]

The Second Vatican Council asked religious communities to go back to their founding articles and to examine and to explore whether the life that was being lived was in keeping with the spirit of their founding.[20] The outcome of renewal clarified, for many, the charism or gift of the religious community as well as identified the wisdom of the community regarding the way forward. The world was changing and congregations engaged the question of how the kingdom of God could be brought forth in our own time and place.

[18] Sacred Congregation for Religious and for Secular Institutes, "Essential Elements in the Church's Teaching on Religious Life as Applied to Institutes Dedicated to Works of the Apostolate" (1983), accessed March 5, 2017, http://www.vatican.va/roman_curia/congregations/ccscrlife/documents/rc_con_ccscrlife_doc_31051983_magisterium-on-religious-life_en.html.

[19] Gerald A. Arbuckle, "Suffocating Religious Life: A New Type Emerges," *The Way* 65 (1989): 34, accessed May 11, 2017, http://www.theway.org.uk/Back/s065Arbuckle.pdf.

[20] *Perfectae Caritatis* (Decree on the Adaptation and Renewal of Religious Life, 1965) urged congregations to seek renewal by examining the original charism of their founders and by subjecting their lives and ministry to prayerful scrutiny.

"How then shall we live?" was the question that religious communities needed to answer in the 1960s and which we continue to ask ourselves today as we assess and evaluate our mission while continuing to bear prophetic witness to the Good News of the salvation of all people given by our living and loving God.

Possibilities

"Oh my Sisters, stand very firm . . .
and see what the Lord can do."[21]

One of the burning questions and much of the anxiety which surrounds any conversation about religious life, especially in Canada and the United States, is: "What will the future be?" Younger women religious have begun to speak of ourselves as the bridge[22] between what is and what is to come in religious life. Our older sisters have been speaking of themselves as the midwives of the future that is to come.[23] Though none of us knows what is to be, we are trying to prepare for and, hopefully, to welcome the new creation that will grow out of this unknown, chaotic present. Perhaps what we really need to do right now is to live the future that we wish to see, for it is already here.

We have a sense of the direction into which religious life is moving as seeds of a rich diversity are budding into a growing internationality and interculturality in religious communities in Canada and the United States. There are newer members in

[21] Cameroonian Litany of the Saints.

[22] I first encountered this at the Giving Voice Conference 2011, "Engage the Emergence" and have since seen it expressed in several articles written by the under-50-year-old sisters.

[23] Leadership Conference of Women Religious, "Annual Report 2008–09: Midwiving New Life," accessed January 15, 2017, https://lcwr.org/publications/annual-report-2008-09-midwiving-new-life.

many religious communities who are from cultures and countries that have been previously underrepresented (or entirely nonexistent) in Eurocentric communities. The effects of this demographic, and potentially cultural, change may not be immediately apparent in their fullness but there is no doubt that the impact will be fundamental for religious life in the future. Such a foundational change is provisional, of course, upon religious communities adjusting to allow for the full growth of the widening and deepening of our sisterhood.

The possibilities of the impact of these changing demographics on the charism and mission of religious communities are almost infinite. How will the discussion and discernment of the mission and ministries of religious communities be affected by the voice and presence of black women, Latina women, and women of color of varying cultures? We remain connected to our countries, cultures, and languages of origin. How will interaction with these countries and cultures flavor or change the theological underpinnings of those Eurocentric communities that have been so immersed in and informed by the experience and theologies of dominant cultures?

Already we know that there is an exchange and collaboration between religious communities that is relatively new, including, for example, intercommunity novitiates, intentional groups like Giving Voice, and virtual communities on Facebook and other social media platforms. The young women religious who have entered within the last decade are the first generation to have had virtual peer groups, to have explored the hopes, dreams, and experience of formation through blogs, connecting their own experiences with those courageous ones who have shared the joys and the challenges that are inherent in initial formation.

As I discerned my own call, I read every blog that I could find,[24] never thinking that I would one day connect with so many of these writers who were in different countries and in

[24] A special shout-out and thank you to Susan Francois, CSJP, Sarah Puls, SGS, and Nicole Trahan, FMI.

different communities. I relished their posts as I too discovered that I was not the only one. Even more importantly, I came to see that these similar experiences were pointing the way toward a deeper understanding of what it meant to be a "religious" beyond what seemed to be the boundaries of location, charism, and spirituality. Through this virtual portal into the initial experience of religious life, I became more confident in my own discernment as I was better able to detect what were cultural and generational differences as distinct from the question of vocation.

Pope Francis notes, "As a global network in which we are all connected, where no local tradition can aspire to a monopoly of the truth, where technologies affect everyone, the world throws down a continuous challenge to the Gospel and to those who shape their lives in accordance with the Gospel."[25] We believe that we, as younger religious women, are already aware of, and attempting to consciously respond to, the challenges of the world, but we are only in the very early stages of these responses. The truth is, we still need to break out and away from the status quo, from the way things have always been done. We recognize ourselves in the position of the servants in the Parable of the Talents (Matt 25:14-30), needing to be careful not to bury our gifts in existing soil, but rather, even though it may seem reckless, to gamble with them in the risky unknown so that there may be a chance for real growth and a new harvest.

We may find ourselves somewhat conflicted because young women religious are often very concerned about respecting the culture of our communities—formation is, after all, concerned with imbuing and enculturating newer members in the history and the ways of their congregations and orders. The question then becomes, how will formation processes and structures be evaluated and reshaped to allow for the sea

[25] Congregation for Institutes of Consecrated Life and Societies of Apostolic Life, "Rejoice! A Letter to Consecrated Men and Women," 57.

change that must happen in the discernment and discussion of mission and ministry and the future of religious life? What are the systemic changes that we need to make to bring this new creation to maturity?

Much has been said of the studies and research that indicate that young women are looking for community and prayer in their potential religious communities. "The new communities they seek are communities of praxis, communities that are dedicated first to living the gospel personally and interpersonally."[26] This has thrown some communities into a tizzy because they have somehow extrapolated from this that if they are primarily communities of older women they will not or cannot receive new entrants. They feel this community life seems to imply a population of younger persons. This is simply untrue. If a religious community is truly open to the challenges that a new voice, a new lens, and a new vision will bring, then the possibilities of creative problem-solving are endless. As Arbuckle said so long ago: "If a congregation or community does not support creativity, then there is no hope that it will welcome refounding persons who are a very special type of apostolically creative people."[27]

The future that is already present challenges all women religious, in whichever stage of formation, to refound not only their community, but also to refound religious life so that the future can grow into its fullness. Ted Dunn calls communal refounding the "paschal mystery" and says it needs "a transformation of consciousness regarding a community's charism and its relevance for today's world."[28] We are all called to be courageous as we step out into the "new world" as our founders and foundresses did, and we are all called to step up to this vocational call.

[26] Hereford, *Religious Life at the Crossroads*, 96.

[27] Gerald A. Arbuckle, "Suffocating Religious Life: A New Type Emerges," *The Way* 65 (1989): 38.

[28] Ted Dunn, "Refounding Religious Life," *Human Development* 30, no. 3 (Fall 2009): 5–13.

The women who are discerning a call to religious life today are making their decisions based on those religious communities which they sense are "walking their talk" and living their vows with passion and joy. If we are serious about a future that is collaborative, based on a shared understanding that the role of religious communities is to provide the space and the encouragement for consecrated persons to fulfill their vows and to be "the humble and simple sign of a star that flickers in the middle of the people's night,"[29] we cannot be wasting our energies on squabbles that can only bear bitter fruit. As we challenge the stereotypes of age (both that of the "young" and the "old"), we also need to challenge the stereotype of religious habit. Those of us younger women who have already entered religious life must remind our sisters that the debate about religious habits is not the debate of our generation. We must also refuse to participate in those conversations as we encounter others who are discerning their call. The vows, and the fruit of those vows, are the point and purpose of religious life. We must not be distracted by the secular world's insistence on trying to define us.

As we pray for our world and for God's people, perhaps we can also very intentionally pray for the success of the work of all religious communities as they seek to speak and witness to the Good News everywhere, for we agree that: "It is a beautiful time for religious life in the Church and we look to all Religious Sisters . . . that together, we may give witness and encouragement to one another as we follow in the footsteps of Jesus, in the pattern of Our Lady, in love and ever increasing holiness."[30]

[29] Arnaiz, "The Great Challenges," 17.

[30] Council of Major Superiors of Women Religious, "A Response to the Final Report of the Apostolic Visitation," accessed March 5, 2017, http://cmswr.org/documents/year-of-consecrated-life/90-cmswr-response-to-final-report-of-the-apostolic-visitation/file.

Young women will continue to enter religious life for the same reasons as Jesus' female contemporaries who walked with him and supported him with their resources (Luke 8:1-3): they wish to follow Jesus Christ and, by their entire lives, to share in his ministry of making manifest the Good News of a living and loving God.

Moving Forward

"Our being proclaims Your greatness, O God;
our spirit finds joy in You." (Luke 1:46)

There really is no way to conclude when speaking about the future of religious life—it is like the kingdom of God, here but not quite yet. We move into a future that clearly challenges us to make manifest God's presence in a world that is unpredictable and unstable, and in which our brothers and sisters in Christ may be deeply afraid. Young women with passion, radical love, commitment to this present and yet unknown future are aware of the many uncertainties. Yet, they continue to enter religious communities and to publically profess their vows. We may not know any more than anyone else what that future holds, but we trust that the good work that was begun by the Holy Spirit in the hundreds of thousands who came before us will continue in us and in those who are yet to come. We know that we will need to engage more fully in the re-founding of religious life and of our respective communities if we are to respond to the challenges and opportunities that are before us. We are ready.

Looking to the Future

More than anything, the thirteen sisters who collaborated on this book want to convey our peace and joy in our lives as consecrated women. We have great hope for the future of religious life. As these essays reflect, individually we have diverse experiences and ideas about the future. However, we converge on at least three central points: we are committed to this life; we center our lives on Christ through prayer; and we rely on community to encourage and support one another.

We have committed our lives to spreading the Gospel, to following Jesus' mission to bring about God's vision for our world. In the centuries-old tradition of religious orders, and in the particular traditions of our communities, we make public vows to God. We believe that our vocation to lives of poverty, celibacy, and obedience helps us to live our commitment to God, the world, and one another. Not only that, our lives witness the meaningfulness of life beyond the secular values that surround us. Our fidelity to religious life means that we are flexible and imaginative as we consider the ever-changing demands of life today.

We could not dedicate ourselves to religious life without centering our hearts and minds in the love of God. From our prayer, we receive the nourishment of God's loving presence, the intimate friendship of Jesus, and the inspiration of the Holy Spirit. In both personal and communal prayer, we are strengthened in courage and confidence to live our call of service to others. It is only with this foundation that we can hear the voice of God in our world and discern the actions we are called to take. God has called all human beings to cocreate with the Creator. As cocreators, we must contemplate in order to dream together with God. Attending to God's voice will lead us to the needs of today and tomorrow, providing a light for our feet amid fog and uncertainty.

Above all, we rely on one another, in communities of all different types. Most young women entering religious life today desire to live in community settings, where we rub elbows every day with one another, negotiating chores, schedules, and shared goods. We desire that daily community life with its intergenerational and multiethnic dimensions, knowing we will be stretched and challenged by sisters who think differently. We know and love our sisters, who awe us with their stories, wisdom, and holiness, and with their ability to recognize wisdom in us. We also form community with sisters of different congregations of all ages, most especially those who go through formation with us. We desire to live out the charism of our individual congregations, while at the same time we understand the global charism of religious life. We form community with the laity and clergy with whom we work and who pass on our charism as fully as we do. All of these communal identities nourish us, and all of them move with us into our future.

We are committed. We are grounded in prayer. We rely on community. In these we find a solid foundation for dreaming into the future together. Within these pages we begin to affirm and claim religious life for ourselves.

These chapters are just the beginning of a conversation we hope will continue among women in religious life and beyond, a conversation in which we have raised some challenging questions. Thirteen voices can never say all that needs to be said about the experiences of younger religious. We hope you will join us and engage others in the discussion. Perhaps our model of collaboration will be helpful for these dialogues. As we met by video conferencing throughout the year and in person in January, we embraced a number of practices that helped us to discern together, and to encourage and gently challenge one another. These practices include:

Set ego aside
Embrace genuine curiosity for the experiences of each other
Avoid judgment
Give priority to lesser-known experiences, so that all voices are heard on equal footing
Engage real differences, even when they are uncomfortable
Raise difficult questions with care for the other person
Share authentically with one another
Trust in the collaborative effort and have faith that we will succeed together
Remain grounded in prayer
Know the Spirit will guide the conversation and our common discernment

In our experience, these conversations became sacred spaces, where we recognized the divine in one another and shared deeply with each other.

As a means to begin conversations, we offer the questions below. They may be applied to each individual chapter or to the book as a whole:

What resonates with your experience of religious life?
What resonates with your experience of younger women religious?
What surprises you about what's here?
What is missing?
What sparks something new in you as you read this book?
What do you want to ask women religious of a different generation after reading this book?
What affirms you in your experience of religious life? What makes you uncomfortable?
What challenges you?

Bibliography

Alandt, Margaret, and Pat McCluskey. "LCWR Assembly Confronts Racism and Religious Life." *Leadership Conference of Women Religious*. Accessed April 27, 2017. https://lcwr.org/publications/lcwr-assembly-confronts-racism-and-religious-life.

Allen, Marcia. "Transformation—An Experiment in Hope: Presidential Address." August 10, 2016. Accessed April 27, 2017. https://lcwr.org/sites/default/files/calendar/attachments/lcwr_presidential_address_-_marcia_allen_csj.pdf.

Ambrosio, Márian. "Weaving Solidarity for Life—Living and Witnessing as Women Religious of Apostolic Life." International Union of Superiors General Plenary 2016, May 2016, Rome, Italy. Accessed May 8, 2017. http://www.internationalunionsuperiorsgeneral.org/wp-content/uploads/2016/04/Pl-2016_Marian-Ambrosio_ENG.pdf.

Anzaldua, Gloria. *Borderlands/La Frontera: The New Mestiza*. 4th ed. San Francisco: Aunt Lute Books, 2012.

Aquinas, Thomas. *Summa Theologiae*. Translated by Fathers of the English Dominican Province. Accessed April 27, 2017. http://dhspriory.org/thomas/summa/.

Araujo-Hawkins, Dawn. "Younger Sisters Preparing to Be the Change in Religious Life." *Global Sisters Report*. August 11, 2015. http://globalsistersreport.org/blog/gsr-today/younger-sisters-preparing-be-change-religious-life-29156.

Arbuckle, Gerald A. "Suffocating Religious Life: A New Type Emerges." *The Way* 65 (1989). http://www.theway.org.uk/Back/s065Arbuckle.pdf.

Arnaiz, José M. "The Great Challenges of Consecrated Life Today." Capitolo Generale FSP, 2013. Accessed January 15, 2017. http://archive.paoline.org/paoline/allegati/15808/Arnaiz_LegrandiSfideVCoggi-eng.pdf.

Arnold, Simón Pedro. *A Dónde Vamos*. Lima: Ediciones Paulinas, 2012.

———. *La era de la mariposa*. Argentina: Editorial Claretiana, 2015.

———. Presentation to the General Assembly of the Canadian Religious Conference, Montreal, May 27, 2016.

Augustine of Hippo. *Sermons*. Translated by Edmund Hill. Works of Saint Augustine 7. Hyde Park: New City, 1993.

———. *Confessions*. Translated by Henry Chadwick. Oxford: Oxford University Press, 1991.

Bauman, Zygmunt. *Vida Líquida*. México: Paidos, 2015.

Bisson, Don. *Intentional Community*. 3 CDs. Workshop Series 49. YesNow Productions, 2015.

Block, Peter. *The Answer to How Is Yes: Acting on What Matters*. San Francisco: Berrett-Koehler, 2003.

Bonaventure. *The Soul's Journey into God, the Tree of Life, and the Life of St. Francis*. Translated by Ewert Cousins. Classics of Western Spirituality. New York: Paulist, 1978.

Boswell, John. *The Kindness of Strangers: The Abandonment of Children in Western Europe from Late Antiquity to the Renaissance*. Chicago: University of Chicago Press, 1988.

Brown, Brené. "Why Dr. Brené Brown Says It Takes Courage to Be Vulnerable." Oprah's Life Class Video, September 22, 2013. Accessed April 27, 2017. http://oprah.com/oprahs-lifeclass/why-dr-brene-brown-says-it-takes-courage-to-be-vulnerable-video.

Brueggemann, Walter. *Reality, Grief, and Hope: Three Urgent Prophetic Tasks*. Grand Rapids, MI: William B. Eerdmans, 2014.

Bruteau, Beatrice. *The Holy Thursday Revolution*. Maryknoll, NY: Orbis, 2005.

Buechner, Frederick. *Wishful Thinking: A Seeker's ABC*. New York: HarperOne, 1993.

Cartledge, Tony W. *Vows in the Hebrew Bible and the Ancient Near East*. Sheffield, England: Sheffield Academic, 1992.

Case, Deana. Interview by Madeleine Miller. Religious Life Book Project Questionnaire. Winnebago, NE, December 2016.

Catholic Online. "St. Agnes." Accessed March 5, 2017. http://www.catholic.org/saints/saint.php?saint_id=106.

———. "St. Teresa of Avila." Accessed January 16, 2017. http://www.catholic.org/saints/saint.php?saint_id=208.

Center for Applied Research in the Apostolate (CARA). Accessed May 5, 2017. http://cara.georgetown.edu/.

"Centro Santa Catalina – The Spiritual, Education and Economic Empowerment of Women." Accessed March 4, 2017. http://centrosantacatalina.org/.

Chittister, Joan. "The Global Sisterhood: Nowhere and Everywhere." *Global Sisters Report*, April 23, 2014. Accessed February 16, 2017. http://globalsistersreport.org/column/where-i-stand/trends/global-sisterhood-nowhere-and-everywhere-381.

Christianity Today. "Perpetua." Accessed March 5, 2017. http://www.christianitytoday.com/history/people/martyrs/perpetua.html.

Cloud, Henry, and John Townsend. *Boundaries: When to Say Yes, How to Say No to Take Control of Your Life*. Grand Rapids, MI: Zondervan, 1992.

Collins, Julie A. "Celibate Love as Contemplation." *Review for Religious* 75, no. 1 (Jan.–Feb. 2000): 79–86. Accessed April 27, 2017. http://cdm.slu.edu/cdm/singleitem/collection/rfr/id/372/rec/1.

Congregation for Institutes of Consecrated Life and Societies of Apostolic Life. "Rejoice! A Letter to Consecrated Men and Women: A Message from the Teachings of Pope Francis," Vatican City, Italy: Libreria Editrice Vaticana, 2014. Accessed March 4, 2017. http://www.vatican.va/roman_curia/congregations/ccscrlife/documents/rc_con_ccscrlife _doc_20140202_rallegratevi-lettera-consacrati_en.pdf.

Corcoran, Nancy. *Secrets of Prayer: A Multifaith Guide to Creating Personal Prayer in Your Life*. Woodstock, VT: SkyLight Paths Publishing, 2007.

Council of Major Superiors of Women Religious: "A Response to the Final Report of the Apostolic Visitation," 2014. Accessed March 5, 2017. http://cmswr.org/documents/year-of-consecrated

-life/90-cmswr-response-to-final-report-of-the-apostolic-visitation/file.

Cummings, Kathleen Sprows. *Understanding U.S. Catholic Sisters Today*. Washington, DC: FADICA, 2015. Accessed March 5, 2017. http://www.nationalcatholicsistersweek.org/_resources/FDC_001_Report.pdf.

Dempsey, Louise. "The Function of Prudence in a Program of Renovation." Master's Thesis, Summer School of Sacred Theology for Sisters, Providence College, 1964.

Dewitt, Susan. *We Carry on the Healing: PeaceHealth and the Sisters of St. Joseph of Peace*. Vancouver, WA: PeaceHealth, 2016.

Downey, Paula. "Religious Life for a World of Transition." *The Furrow* 60, no. 11 (November 2009): 612–20.

Dunn, Ted. "Refounding Religious Life: A Choice for Transformational Change." *Human Development* 30, no. 3 (2009): 5–13.

Dunn, Ted. Interview by Juliet Mousseau, Sarah Kohles, et al. January 4, 2017.

Eliot, T. S. "Preface." In Harry Crosby, *Transit of Venus: Poems*. Paris: The Black Sun Press, 1931.

Esler, Philip F. *Sex, Wives, and Warriors: Reading Biblical Narrative with Its Ancient Audience*. Eugene, OR: Cascade, 2011.

Evans, Elizabeth. "Q&A with Melinda Pellerin, on Having Two Callings." *Global Sisters Report*, May 26, 2016. Accessed October 14, 2016. http://globalsistersreport.org/blog/q/trends/q-sr-melinda-pellerin-having-two-callings-40041.

Farrell, Pat. "Leading from the Allure of Holy Mystery: Contemplation and Transformation." Assembly of the Leadership Conference of Women Religious, Atlanta, Georgia, August 9–13, 2016. Accessed April 27, 2017. https://lcwr.org/sites/default/files/calendar/attachments/lcwr_2016_assembly_keynote_-_pat_farrell_osf.pdf.

Fiand, Barbara. *Refocusing the Vision: Religious Life into the Future*. New York: Crossroads, 2001.

Francis. "Address of the Holy Father." September 27, 2015. Accessed February 16, 2017. http://w2.vatican.va/content/francesco/en/speeches/2015/september/documents/papa-francesco_20150927_usa-detenuti.html.

———. "Address to the Boys of Italian Catholic Action." *Zenit*, December 19, 2016. Accessed December 20, 2016. https://zenit.org/articles/popes-address-to-youth-of-catholic-action/.

———. "Apostolic Letter to All Consecrated People on the Occasion of the Year of Consecrated Life," November 21, 2014. Accessed April 27, 2017. https://w2.vatican.va/content/francesco/en/apost_letters/documents/papa-francesco_lettera-ap_20141121_lettera-consacrati.html.

———. *Evangelii Gaudium*. November 24, 2013. Accessed April 27, 2017. https://w2.vatican.va/content/francesco/en/apost_exhortations/documents/papa-francesco_esortazione-ap_20131124_evangelii-gaudium.html.

———. "Homily for the Presentation of the Lord and XXI World Day of Consecrated Life." February 2, 2017. Accessed April 27, 2017. https://w2.vatican.va/content/francesco/en/homilies/2017/documents/papa-francesco_20170202_omelia-vita-onsacrata.html.

———. "Journey to Poland: Prayer Vigil with the Young People in the Campus Misericordiae." July 30, 2016. Accessed April 27, 2017. https://w2.vatican.va/content/francesco/en/speeches/2016/july/documents/papa-francesco_20160730_polonia-veglia--giovani.html.

———. *Laudato Sí*. May 24, 2015. Accessed February 16, 2017. http://w2.vatican.va/content/francesco/en/encyclicals/documents/papa-francesco_20150524_enciclica-laudato-si.html.

———. "Overcome Indifference, Build a Culture of Encounter." Vatican Radio. September 13, 2016. Accessed April 27, 2017. http://en.radiovaticana.va/news/2016/09/13/pope_overcome_indifference,_build_a_culture_of_encounter/1257732.

———. "To Participants in the International Conference on Pastoral Work in Vocations." October 21, 2016. Accessed April 27, 2017. https://w2.vatican.va/content/francesco/en/speeches/2016/october/documents/papa-francesco_20161021_pastorale-vocazionale.html.

Francois, Susan. "Living, Loving, and Leading in Fog." *Global Sisters Report*, August 26, 2016. Accessed April 27, 2017. http://globalsistersreport.org/column/horizons/living-loving-and-leading-fog-41936.

———. "A Loving Gaze at Religious Life Realities." *Horizon* (Fall 2013).

———. "Shifting Conversations in Religious Life." *Global Sisters Report*, July 9, 2014. Accessed April 27, 2017. http://globalsistersreport.org/column/horizons/trends/shifting-conversations-religious-life-6361.

Gittins, Anthony J. "Mission: What's It Got to Do with Me?" *The Living Light* 34, no. 4 (Spring 1998): 6–13.

Greer, R. Douglas-Adam. "Celibate Chastity: A Sacrifice Because of the Kingdom of Heaven." *Horizon* 29 (2004): 8–12.

Hahnenberg, Edward P. "Theology of Vocation: Attuned to the Voice of God." *Human Development Magazine* 36 (Spring 2016): 54–58.

Hansman, Heather. "College Students Are Living Rent-Free in a Cleveland Retirement Home." *Smithsonian*, October 16, 2015. Accessed April 27, 2017. http://www.smithsonianmag.com/innovation/college-students-are-living-rent-free-in-cleveland-retirement-home-180956930/.

Hereford, Amy. *Religious Life at the Crossroads: A School for Mystics and Prophets.* New York: Orbis Books, 2013.

Hermsen, Kevin. Interview by Madeleine Miller, OSB. Religious Life Book Project Questionnaire. Norfolk, NE, December 2016.

Holy Bible: New International Version (NIV). BibleWorks vol. 9. Colorado Springs, CO: International Bible Society, 1984.

Hyman, Ronald T. "Four Acts of Vowing in the Bible." *Jewish Bible Quarterly* 37, no. 4 (October 2009): 231–38. Accessed March 20, 2016. http://0search.ebscohost.com.grace.gtu.edu/login.aspx?direct=true&db=rfh&AN=ATLA0001743204&site=ehost-live.

Ignatius of Loyola. "Christ Our Life." Suscipe Prayer. Accessed March 24, 2017. http://www.loyolapress.com/our-catholic-faith/prayer/traditional-catholic-prayers/saints-prayers/suscipe-prayer-saint-ignatius-of-loyola.

Jansen, Tiffany R. "To Save on Rent, Some Dutch College Students Are Living in Nursing Homes." *The Atlantic*, October 5, 2015. Accessed April 27, 2017. https://www.theatlantic.com/business/archive/2015/10/dutch-nursing-home-college-students/408976/.

John Paul II. *Vita Consecrata*. March 25, 1996. Accessed March 4, 2017. http://w2.vatican.va/content/john-paul-ii/en/apost_exhortations/documents/hf_jp-ii_exh_25031996_vita-consecrata.html.

Johnson, Mary, Patricia Wittberg, and Mary L. Gautier. *New Generations of Catholic Sisters: The Challenge of Diversity*. New York: Oxford University Press, 2014.

Kirchgaessner, Stephanie. "Murder of French priest opens a new frontier for Catholic church." *The Guardian*, July 26, 2016. Accessed January 15, 2017. https://www.theguardian.com/world/2016/jul/26/jacques-hamel-killing-challenge-pope-francis-catholic-church.

König, Jutta. "Spirituality and Diversity." In *Spirituality and Business: Exploring Possibilities for a New Management Paradigm*, edited by Sharda S. Nandram and Margot Esther Borden, 101–7. New York: Springer, 2010.

LaCugna, Catherine Mowry. *God for Us: The Trinity and Christian Life*. New York: HarperCollins, 1991.

Leadership Conference of Women Religious, "Annual Report 2008–09: Midwiving New Life." Maryland: LCWR, 2009. Accessed January 15, 2017. https://lcwr.org/publications/annual-report-2008-09-midwiving-new-life.

Lederach, John Paul. *The Moral Imagination: The Art and Soul of Building Peace*. New York: Oxford University Press, 2005.

Lee, Bernard. *The Beating of Great Wings: A Worldly Spirituality for Active, Apostolic Communities*. Mystic, CT: Twenty-Third Publications, 2004.

Machado, Antonio. *There Is No Road*. New York: White Pine, 2003.

Maguire, Daniel C. *Ethics: A Complete Method for Moral Choice*. Minneapolis, MN: Fortress, 2010.

Malone, Janet. "A Spirituality of Aging in Religious Congregations." *Human Development* 34, no. 2 (Summer 2013): 8–17.

Maya, Teresa. "An Open Letter to the Great Generation." *Global Sisters Report*, January 12, 2015. Accessed December 4, 2016. http://globalsistersreport.org/column/trends/open-letter-great-generation-16171.

McElwee, Joshua J. "Pope Francis Questions Donald Trump's Christianity, Says Border Wall Not from Gospel." *National Catholic Reporter*, February 18, 2016. Accessed April 27, 2017. https://www.ncronline.org/news/pope-francis-questions-donald-trumps-christianity-says-border-wall-not-gospel.

McLeod, Saul. "Erik Erikson." *Simply Psychology*. October 20, 2016. Accessed May 8, 2017. https://www.simplypsychology.org/Erik-Erikson.html.

McMahon, Sarah. Interview by Madeleine Miller, OSB. Religious Life Book Project Questionnaire. Norfolk, NE, December 2016.

Michalenko, Paul and Dominic Perri. "Authentic Responses to the Future of Religious Life." *Human Development* 33, no. 4 (Winter 2012): 3–9.

Morisette, Alanis. "Ironic." California: Maverick Records, 1996.

Murray, Patricia. "Religious Life: Called to Undertake a Journey of Transformation." Keynote address, Global Call of Religious Life Conference. Catholic Theological Union, Chicago, Illinois, November 3, 2015. Accessed May 8, 2017. http://learn.ctu.edu/category/tags/patricia-murray.

Nanko-Fernandez, Carmen. *Theologizing En Espanglish: Context, Community, and Ministry*. New York: Orbis, 2010.

Nassif, Rosemary. "Supporting the Emergence of Global Sisterhood." Plenary Assembly of International Union Superiors, Rome, Italy, May 9–13, 2016. Accessed March 1, 2017. http://www.internationalunionsuperiorsgeneral.org/wp-content/uploads/2016/01/Rosemary-Nassif-CN-Hilton-Foundation.pdf.

National Religious Retirement Office. "Statistical Report-August 2016." Accessed April 27, 2017. http://www.usccb.org/about/national-religious-retirement-office/upload/Statistical-Report.pdf.

Nava, Gregory. *Selena*. Warner Bros., 1997.

New American Bible Revised Edition (NABRE). Oxford: Oxford University Press, 2010.

"New Religious Communities." *Following the Shepherd's Voice* (blog). Accessed March 5, 2017. http://theshepherdsvoiceofmercy.blogspot.com/p/new-religious-communities.html.

Nouwen, Henri J. M. *Life of the Beloved: Spiritual Living in a Secular World*. New York: The Crossroad Publishing Company, 1992.

NurrieStearns, Mary. "The Presence of Compassion: An Interview with John O'Donohue." *Personal Transformation*. Accessed May 8, 2017. http://www.personaltransformation.com/john_odonohue.html.

O'Murchu, Diarmuid. *Consecrated Religious Life: The Changing Paradigms*. Maryknoll, NY: Orbis, 2005.

———. *Religious Life in the 21st Century: The Prospect of Refounding*. Maryknoll, NY: Orbis, 2016.

Park, Sophia. "A Reflection on Religious Vocation: The Wine Is Ready, But the Wineskin Is Not." *Global Sisters Report*, May 14, 2014. Accessed April 27, 2017. http://globalsistersreport.org/column/speaking-god/trends/reflection-religious-vocation-wine-ready-wineskin-not-371.

Paul, Ann Marie. "Gleanings from My First Ten Years." *Review for Religious* 69, no. 1 (2010): 63–70.

Pellegrino, Mary. "Life on the Margins: Charismatic Principles for Modern Religious." *America Magazine*, October 16, 2013. Accessed January 8, 2017. http://www.americamagazine.org/issue/life-margins.

Perfectae Caritatis. In *Vatican Council II: The Conciliar and Post Conciliar Documents Study Edition*, ed. Austin Flannery, 611–23. Northport, NY: Costello Publishing, 1986.

Phan, Peter. "The Dragon and the Eagle: Towards a Vietnamese-American Theology." *East Asian Pastoral Review* 2–3 (2002). Accessed April 1, 2017. http://www.eapi.org.ph/resources/eapr/east-asian-pastoral-review-2002/2002-2-3/the-dragon-and-the-eagle-towards-a-vietnamese-american-theology/.

Portmann, Pia. Interview by Madeleine Miller, OSB. Religious Life Book Project Questionnaire. Norfolk, NE, December 2016.

Quin, Eleanor. *Last on the Menu*. Englewood Cliffs, NJ: Prentice-Hall, 1969.

Radcliffe, Timothy. "Community Life and Mission: Toward a Future Full of Hope." Presentation at Catholic Theological Union, Chicago, Illinois, February 6, 2016. Accessed April 1, 2017. http://www.ctuconsecratedlife.org/videos/.

Rahner, Karl. "The Consecration of the Layman to the Care of Souls." In *Theological Investigations* 3, translated by Karl-H. Kruger and Boniface Kruger, 263–76. Baltimore: Helicon, 1967.

Ricouer, Paul. *Interpretation Theory: Discourse and the Surplus of Meaning*. Fort Worth: The Texas Christian University Press, 1976.

Rolheiser, Ronald, *The Holy Longing: The Search for Christian Spirituality*. New York: Penguin, 2014.

———. *Sacred Fire: A Vision for a Deeper Humanity and Christian Maturity*. New York: Image, 2014.

Rowthorn, Jeffery. "Lord, You Give the Great Commission." Carol Stream, IL: Hope Publishing, 1978.

Rule of Saint Benedict 1980. Edited by Timothy Fry. Collegeville, MN: Liturgical Press, 1981.

Sacred Congregation for Religious and Secular Institutes. "Essential Elements in the Church's Teaching on Religious Life as Applied to Institutes Dedicated to Works of the Apostolate." May 31, 1983. Accessed March 5, 2017. http://www.vatican.va/roman_curia/congregations/ccscrlife/documents/rc_con_ccscrlife_doc_31051983_magisterium-on-religious-life_en.html.

———. *Religious and Human Promotion*. Boston: Daughters of St. Paul, 1980.

Sammon, Sean D. *Religious Life in America*. New York: Alba House, 2002.

Schneiders, Sandra. *Buying the Field: Religious Life in Mission to the World*. New York: Paulist, 2013.

———. "Call, Response and Task of Prophetic Action." *National Catholic Reporter*, January 4, 2010. Accessed April 27, 2017. https://www.ncronline.org/news/women-religious/call-response-and-task-prophetic-action.

———. *Finding the Treasure: Locating Catholic Religious Life in a New Ecclesial and Cultural Context*. New York: Paulist, 2000.

———. *The Revelatory Text: Interpreting the New Testament as Sacred Scripture*. Collegeville, MN: Liturgical Press, 1999.

———. *Selling All: Commitment, Consecrated Celibacy, and Community in Catholic Religious Life*. New York: Paulist, 2001.

———. "Tasks of Those Who Choose the Prophetic Life Style." *National Catholic Reporter*. January 7, 2010. Accessed April 27, 2017. https://www.ncronline.org/news/women-religious/tasks-those-who-choose-prophetic-life-style.

Schreck, Nancy. Presentation, LCWR New Leader Workshop, March 19–22, 2015.

Shaw, Russell. "Where Have All the Sisters Gone?" *Catholic Answers*, November 29, 2011. Accessed January 15, 2017. https://www.catholic.com/magazine/print-edition/where-have-all-the-sisters-gone.

Simmonds, Gemma. "Vitality in Religious Life." Spring 2016 Assembly Presentation to the Sisters of St. Joseph of Peace.

Sinnot, Anneliese. "Shifting Paradigms: A New Reality." In *Journey in Faith and Fidelity: Women Shaping Religious Life for a Renewed Church*, edited by Nadine Foley, 95–123. New York: Continuum, 1999.

Stockman, Dan. "Forthcoming Book Documents Black Sisters in the U.S." *Global Sisters Report*, May 14, 2015. Accessed May 8, 2017. http://globalsistersreport.org/news/trends/forthcoming-book-documents-history-black-sisters-us-25501.

Teresa of Calcutta. *Where There Is Love, There Is God*. Edited by Timothy Fry. Collegeville, MN: Liturgical Press, 2010.

Tescon, Constance. Interview by Madeleine Miller, OSB. Religious Life Book Project Questionnaire. Manila, Philippines, December 2016.

Treviño, Roberto R. "Facing Jim Crow: Catholic Sisters and the 'Mexican Problem' in Texas." *Western Historical Quarterly* 34, no. 2 (May 1, 2003): 139–64.

United Nations High Commissioner for Refugees. "Figures at a Glance (Global Trends 2015)." Accessed January 15, 2017. http://www.unhcr.org/figures-at-a-glance.html.

Up With People. "What Color Is God's Skin?" Up With People Incorporated, 1964.

VanderVen, Karen. "Intergenerational Theory in Society: Building on the Past, Questions for the Future." In *Intergenerational Relationships: Conversations on Practice and Research Across Cultures*, edited by Elizabeth Larkin and others, 75–94. New York: Haworth, 2004.

Wiederkehr, Macrina. "Prayer Before a Burning Bush." In *Seasons of Your Heart: Prayers and Reflections*. Rev. and exp. ed. New York: HarperCollins, 1991.

Wilson, Robert. "Child, Children." In *HarperCollins Bible Dictionary*, edited by Mark Allan Powell and others. New York: HarperOne, 2011.

Wittberg, Patricia. *Creating a Future for Religious Life*. New York: Paulist, 1991.

———. *Pathways to Re-Creating Religious Communities*. New York: Paulist, 1996.

Ziegler, Yael. *Promises to Keep: The Oath in the Biblical Narrative*. Boston: Brill, 2008.

Zinn, Carol. "Crossing the Threshold: Weaving Global Solidarity for the Life of the World." Presentation, Plenary Assembly of International Union Superiors, Rome, Italy, May 9–13, 2016. Accessed March 1, 2017. http://www.internationalunionsuperiorsgeneral.org/wp-content/uploads/2016/04/Pl-2016_-Carol-Zinn_ENG.pdf, 11-12.

Contributors

Amanda Carrier, RSM, entered the Sisters of Mercy of the Americas in 2010. She made her first vows in 2015. She lives in Connecticut where she minsters as chef at the Thomas Merton Hospitality Center in Bridgeport.

Desiré Anne-Marie Findlay, CSSF, became a member of the Congregation of the Sisters of Saint Felix in 2010. She currently serves as a high school religion, Spanish, and dance teacher in Pomona, California, but is preparing for a new assignment in the fall of 2017. Sister Desiré loves her community and looks forward to making her profession of final vows in 2019.

Susan Rose Francois, CSJP, serves on the Congregation leadership team of the Sisters of St. Joseph of Peace. She professed final vows in 2011 and was previously a member of the Giving Voice leadership core team.

Virginia Herbers, ASCJ, is an Apostle of the Sacred Heart of Jesus. She professed first vows in 1992 and now, after many years as an educator, she currently serves as vice provincial for the United States Province in Hamden, Connecticut.

Tracy Kemme, SC, entered the Sisters of Charity of Cincinnati in 2012. She lives at Visitation House in Cincinnati, Ohio, and serves in social justice and Latino ministry. Tracy is working on an MA in Theology at Xavier University. She also writes for *Global Sisters Report*.

Sarah Kohles, OSF, is a Sister of St. Francis of Dubuque, Iowa. She professed final vows in 2011 and currently is working on her

PhD in Biblical Studies at Graduate Theological Union in Berkeley. She has served in faith formation in parishes in Iowa, Illinois, and Texas, and on the Giving Voice core team.

Teresa Maya, CCVI, is a member of the Congregation of the Sisters of Charity of the Incarnate Word, San Antonio, Texas. Education has been her main ministry. She is currently serving on the leadership team of her congregation and is the president of the Leadership Conference of Women Religious.

Madeleine Miller, OSB, entered the Missionary Benedictine Sisters of Tutzing in 2008. She lives near Sioux City, Iowa, teaches theology, and does campus ministry at Bishop Heelan Catholic High School. She made her final monastic profession in 2015 after spending time in Olinda, Brazil.

Juliet Mousseau, RSCJ, entered the Society of the Sacred Heart in 2009. She lives in St. Louis, Missouri, and serves as associate professor of church history at the Aquinas Institute of Theology. She hopes to make her final profession in 2020.

Christa Parra, IBVM, entered the Institute of the Blessed Virgin Mary in 2008. She lives in Phoenix, Arizona, and serves as a school counselor at St. Francis Xavier, a Jesuit Elementary School. She took her final vows July 31, 2016, at Our Lady of Guadalupe Church in South Chicago.

Mary Therese Perez, OP, entered the Dominican Sisters of Mission San Jose in 2009. She lives in Los Angeles, California, and preaches as a religion teacher at Flintridge Sacred Heart Academy.

Thuy Tran, CSJ, entered the Sisters of St. Joseph in 2007 and pronounced her perpetual vows in 2015. She lives in Orange County, California, and is part of the Mission Integration team with Providence St. Joseph Health. She provides outreach services and partners with others to continue to extend the healing ministry of Jesus.

Deborah Warner, CND, is a Sister of the Congrégation de Notre-Dame de Montréal. She made her perpetual profession in 2012. Raised in Trinidad and currently missioned as a social worker in Toronto, Canada, she went on mission to Sierra Leone in 2017.